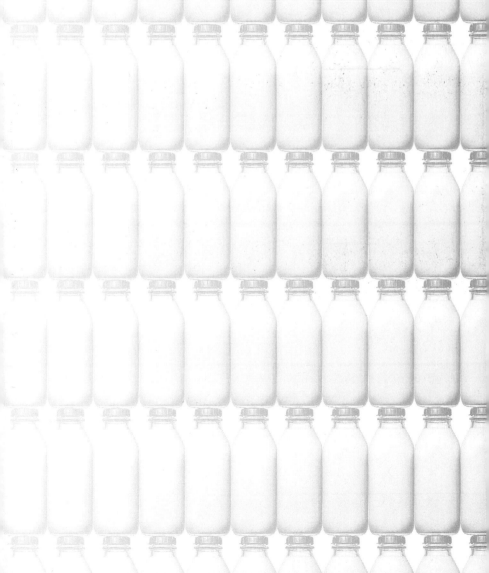

MILK MONEY

KIRK KARDASHIAN

Foreword by Senator Bernie Sanders

CASH, COWS, AND THE

DEATH OF THE

AMERICAN DAIRY FARM

University of New Hampshire Press Durham, New Hampshire

University of New Hampshire Press
An imprint of University Press of New England
www.upne.com
© 2012 Kirk Kardashian

Manufactured in the United States of America
Designed by Mindy Basinger Hill
Typeset in 11./14.5 pt. Arno Pro
Decorative images: Blueee | Dreamstime.com and letterstock | 123rf.com

University Press of New England is a member of the Green Press Initiative.
The paper used in this book meets their minimum requirement for recycled paper.

For permission to reproduce any of the material in
this book, contact Permissions, University Press of
New England, One Court Street, Suite 250,
Lebanon NH 03766; or visit www.upne.com

Library of Congress Cataloging-in-Publication Data

Kardashian, Kirk.
Milk money: cash, cows, and the death of the American dairy farm /
Kirk Kardashian; foreword by Senator Bernie Sanders.—1st ed.
        p.   cm.
Includes bibliographical references and index.
ISBN 978-1-61168-027-0 (cloth: alk. paper)—ISBN 978-1-61168-340-0 (ebook)
1. Dairying—Economic aspects—United States. 2. Dairy farmers—United States.
3. Dairy farming—Economic aspects—United States.
I. Title. II. Title: Cash, cows, and the death of the American dairy farm.
SF232.A1K368 2012
636.2'1420973—dc23   2012012528

5 4 3 2 1

CONTENTS

FOREWORD

Vermont's early agricultural history was dominated by the farming of sheep, for the mills of New England required wool for spinning and weaving. But by the middle of the nineteenth century, sheep and wool production was on the decline, and Vermont's fertile valleys and pasture-rich hills made the state an ideal site for raising cows. By the end of the nineteenth century, there were 35,000 dairy farms in Vermont. The milk that the cows on those farms produced was used for cheese and butter, which were shipped throughout the region. Fluid milk was sold locally.

Vermont's rural communities and its working landscape were formed by dairy farms. Its rural communities, and its working landscape, continue to be shaped by dairy farms today.

Kirk Kardashian looks closely, carefully, lovingly, and at times critically at dairy farming. He has done what a good journalist, a good researcher, needs to do. He has started from his experience, and tried to understand it—fully.

In the preface he recounts the original experience that led him to write this book: the family that provided day care to his daughter worked a dairy farm, and fluctuating milk prices made their lives precarious. He quickly learned that the lives of most family dairy farmers are precarious.

What, he asked himself, is going on in the world of dairy? How can prices shoot up—eras of profitability when farmers can afford to buy new tractors and to fix up their barns—and then suddenly plunge, so that they cannot pay for those tractors or the loans they took out for their barn repairs? For example—and this is a statistic that I did not get from this excellent book but from a report issued by the universities of Wisconsin and Missouri—the U.S. all-milk price in May 2008 was $18.30 a hundredweight; a year later it was $11.60. (Milk at the farmstead is measured and sold by the hundred pounds, not by the gallon.)

Kardashian looks at individual farmers and the difficulties they encounter even as they engage in a pursuit they love, working the land and tending to their cows. But he also takes us back to the origins of dairy farming, to the first men and women who raised cows for milk fifty centuries ago.

Vermonters, and Americans, were good at raising and milking cows, and eventually more milk (a perishable product) was produced than was being consumed. Enter the federal government, which either bought surplus milk or subsidized exports, and helped ease dairy farmers through their crisis. Government intervention has continued, since small increases or decreases in milk production often lead, in a "free market," to wild price swings. And farms, unlike businesses that can slow down or increase production, often face a stark choice: when prices drop, and loans are called in, they all too frequently must be sold. And then, suddenly, there is not enough milk, and the price of cheese and milk to consumers rises rapidly. These huge fluctuations help no one but speculators—not consumers, not dairy-based businesses, not tractor salesmen—and they particularly do not help or sustain farmers.

My own view is that the best dairy policy is to develop a system of supply management, so that dairy farmers never severely overproduce or underproduce, thereby stabilizing prices and ensuring a sufficient amount of high-quality dairy products for our country. It is my hope that we in Washington can produce legislation that will give farmers tools to slow the growth of their herds when milk prices are high—yes, there are profits to be made in the short term, but the slightly longer term result is always an oversupply of milk and milk prices that go into free-fall. Supply management curbs excessive growth of dairy herds when prices are high. And when prices are low, a modest cushion for farmers can provide protection against a hard and destructive landing. Under legislation I proposed, the U.S. Department of Agriculture, working with dairy farmers on a producer board, would set a rate for how much farmers could boost production according to U.S. demand. I think it makes sense that, if we can manage supply so that it is never too high or too low, huge price swings should disappear. And our family famers will live with a security—that hard work and good farming will bring reasonable returns—that eludes them today.

Milk overproduction is caused by too many cows being milked, but it also has to do with dramatic changes that have transformed dairy farms over the past decades. How is it that individual cows today produce much more milk than cows in the past? Kirk Kardashian will tell you, and his recounting of the improvement in milk production is fascinating, a complex story that is nonetheless compelling and remarkably informative reading. You may learn more about artificial insemination than you ever thought you wanted to know, but you will end up understanding how science and breeding have transformed a whole sector of farming. I feel sure that similar techniques in fruit, grain, and vegetable farming, techniques having to do with cross-pollination and grafting and other procedures, mirror the development of our current generation of dairy cows and their great productivity. Similarly, the development of automated milking machines is paralleled by the use of increasingly sophisticated equipment in other types of farming.

Kardashian does not ignore the negative aspects of twenty-first century farming: water and air pollution, the hazards of industrial agriculture (farms in California or Idaho or New Mexico can exceed 10,000 cows), and milk that is perhaps not as healthful as that obtained from pasture-grazed animals. Nor does he ignore the labor situation on dairy farms, which are more and more dependent on immigrant labor from Mexico and Central America. Some of these immigrants are treated as the valuable laborers they are; others, unfortunately and tragically, are not.

And the cows? Some are contented. I have been on many dairy farms in Vermont where the cows were cared for almost as if they were part of the farmer's family. I like what Bovine Practitioner of the Year Joe Klopfenstein of Vergennes, Vermont, says in these pages: "The majority of farmers I work with are farmers because they really love their animals. They treat them well." I think those words ring true for the many Vermont farmers I have met, and I have met a lot. They are wonderful people.

But very large farms, and veal operations, can raise questions about animal cruelty, and this book does not ignore questions about how animals are treated.

What is of greater importance in this fine book is its exploration of the impact of the huge dairy processors, such as Dean Foods and Dairy Farmers of America, which to my mind siphon off most of the money from dairy. When the price of milk drops, prices to consumers don't drop: the middlemen and retailers get wealthy. Farmers, especially modest-size family farms like those we have in Vermont, get little. The price of and demand for milk today is overly controlled by just a few uncompetitive corporate giants, most often through speculation on the Chicago Mercantile Exchange. The Department of Justice, at my request, has investigated Dean Foods for antitrust violations. Dean Foods has paid settlements to farmers to resolve the legal situation, but in my view the virtual monopoly over milk continues. There is something very wrong when large processors reap large profits, and family farmers—and Kirk Kardashian will introduce you to some of them, caught in exactly this terrible predicament—can barely survive, or must sell their farms.

This book ends where it began: it is both the same place, and a very different place. It ends with a family farm, but this is a new version of the family farm that looks toward the future in new ways. Its values—the way in which the farm operates, its concern for its milk quality, the commitment of the farmer to both his cows and the local market—are the traditional values of our nation's family dairy farms. But the way it operates, its "business model," is new and different. So as you go on a wonderful and pleasurable journey—both those who know dairy and those who don't will learn much from this book—you will end up in a place that gives you hope.

Bernie Sanders,
U.S. SENATOR

PREFACE

I wrote this book because of an irksome incongruity. In the spring of 2009 I was driving my daughter eight miles every morning to daycare, and on the way I would listen to *Morning Edition* and the local news on Vermont Public Radio. Almost every day, it seemed, there was one story or another on the so-called dairy crisis and its impact on farms and communities. As an average consumer of milk, cheese, yogurt, and butter, I listened with a somewhat aloof curiosity about the drop in farmers' revenues, the increases in grain prices, the volatility of the global milk market, and the accelerating decline in the number of dairy farms around the country. And then I arrived at my destination, a private daycare in a house on a small dairy farm, and everything I heard on the radio simultaneously angered me and made no sense at all.

Inside that house lived Russell and Mary, their twenty-something son Ryan, and a big, lazy, yellow Labrador retriever named Caleb. Outside, on the pastures, lived seventy black and white cows. On the farm, the men do the milking and the cropping, and Mary cares for the newborn calves. On the side, Russell and Ryan boil sap into maple syrup and plow driveways, while Mary cares for neighborhood kids. They have served on the town select board and school board. They are members of long-standing community organizations that hold annual suppers. In the summer, at the edge of the quiet dirt road that cuts through their farm, they stock a small shed with home-grown corn, cucumbers, and tomatoes. It operates with a price sheet, a metal money box, and the honor system. Arriving in their kitchen on the weekdays at 7:30, I got to know these folks fairly well. By that time, Russell would be in his slippers, eating breakfast and reading the paper, having been up since 4:30. Ryan, tall, skinny, and laconic, would be in the dining room, shoveling cereal into his mouth and watching *Good Morning America*. And Mary would be rinsing the fresh chicken eggs at the sink and putting them in reused cartons to sell. These people struck me, a child of suburban New Jersey, as rugged, rural America incarnate; the best of our national DNA.

Carrying the bitter taste of the radio stories through the squeaky screen door and into the diurnal rhythms of a struggling dairy family proved a potent tonic. Its effect was to make me think Big Thoughts. I wondered how it could be that such honest, hardworking people could produce a nutritious food almost everyone consumes, and do it well, yet lose money. It seemed wrong that, in this greatest of meritocracies, the faithful could deposit their capital, sweat equity, and skill into the market and emerge on the other side with a debit instead of a credit. Surely, I reasoned, there must be a logical explanation.

The newspaper reports did their job, up to a point. They assembled the relevant statistics, plugged in the voices of the analysts and the aggrieved, and hit the refresh button every couple of days. They told of a melamine scare in China that deflated global demand, the rise of ethanol that made food compete against fuel, and a solipsistic milk machine that knew just one setting: more. They counted the thousands of farms that had disappeared in places as diverse as California, Vermont, and Wisconsin. There were heart-wrenching human-interest stories about farmers who killed themselves because of the financial stress, of farm-equipment auctions on sixth-generation farms, of communities left wondering what they really stood for anymore. Without intending it, these dispatches were forming pieces of a mosaic that depicted a country and a culture undergoing revolutionary change.

What was lacking, in my view, was a grand narrative that explored the larger questions few others seemed to be asking. I wanted to know how the dairy industry had arrived at its current location, a place where cows increasingly don't graze on pastures and farms increasingly resemble factories. I wanted to uncover the implications of that journey—from grass to concrete, from farm to factory—on people, animals, and the environment. And I wanted to know how we might navigate to a place more just, prosperous, and sustainable. This book is my attempt at some answers. Though this is a work of nonfiction, some names have been changed to protect the privacy of those who agreed to speak on the record.

Like many other books that have come before it, this is a piece of consciousness-raising journalism. Our world has grown so complex that we no longer appreciate how our food is made, and the impacts our purchases have on our society. The scale of food production today is so large, and our lives so detached from the lives of farmers, that it's easy to assume our individual food choices are meaningless. But that's not true. If consumption is akin to voting, then today we are largely voting for a system that values efficiency over quality, and low, low prices over a healthy environment, fair wages, animal dignity, and robust communities. Changing the system might be as easy as changing your vote.

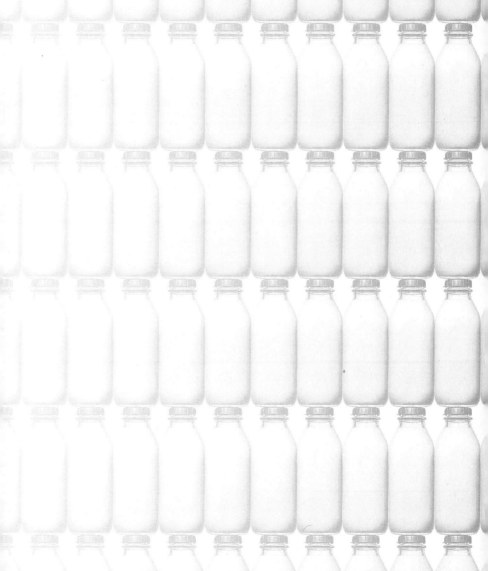

MILK MONEY

DOWN AND OUT

ON THE FARM

HANDCUFFS AND HOPE

He never thought it would come to this.

"Are you Robert Simpson?" asked deputy sheriff Carrie McCool.

"Yes."

"Did you bounce two checks to Feed Commodities, Mr. Simpson?"

"Yes."

"Put your hands behind your back, sir. I need to take you in."

Simpson chuckled, his ruddy face growing a deeper shade of red. "You've got to be kidding me."

"Afraid not," she said.

Simpson, a stocky but gentle fifty-eight-year-old, protested a bit more. But within thirty seconds he knew it was no use. Right or wrong, he was being arrested. So he turned around and McCool fastened handcuffs on his thick wrists. Then she opened the back door to her squad car and helped him in.

As the car bumped down the steep, washboarded driveway, Simpson worried about his herd. He was shorthanded on the farm that day—May 1, 2009—and he needed to move a few dozen of his

Holstein cows from the lower pasture into the feed barn. His wife, Tay, had gone to the store. His son, Andrew, was away for the weekend at a wedding.

"How long's this going to take?" he asked.

"We're going to Randolph," McCool said. "Couple hours, I'd say. Be thankful I'm not taking you to Chelsea."

Chelsea, the county seat, is not many miles away. But in central Vermont, the topography complicates things. Randolph is in the same watershed as Braintree, the town where Simpson's 889-acre farm is situated. Chelsea is on the other side of Hurricane Hill, and to get there you need either to traverse a rugged subrange of the Green Mountains over a frost-heaved, circuitous road, or to go the long way, following the third branch of the White River south to Royalton and then head north, past Tunbridge, to Chelsea. It's a pretty drive in the spring, when the wide river roils with spring runoff, and the trees just start to bud, but Simpson wasn't much in the mood for sightseeing.

At the police station in Randolph, a small, blue-collar town with a cheerful main street of brick storefronts and American flags, Simpson was fingerprinted, photographed, and cited with two felony counts of false pretenses. The charges dated back to an incident in October of 2008, when he had inadvertently written two bad checks, each for roughly $7,300, to pay for a load of grain. This was the first time Simpson had ever been arrested, and if the experience weren't so surreal, so ridiculous, he might have been angrier. But the truth was, Bob Simpson had bigger problems.

His dairy farm, honored as a "Dairy of Distinction" by the Vermont Department of Agriculture, was hemorrhaging dangerous amounts of money every month. Barring some miraculous change in the milk market, the Simpsons would, like fifty-two of their colleagues in Vermont and hundreds more across the country in 2009 alone, be forced out of business and left with a knot of debts that only a bankruptcy judge could untangle.

Times hadn't always been so hard on the Simpson farm, but they were never exactly easy either. Robert Simpson, Bob's father, had bought the place in 1950, about a year before Bob was born. On the February day when Bob's parents tried to move in, the snow was so deep across the road that their pickup truck got stuck. Farming wasn't in Robert's blood: he was born in Boston, and his father was the head of distribution for the *Boston Herald*. He'd gone into the Marines after high school, and when he came back from World War II he attended Amherst College on the G.I. Bill. After working on a dairy farm in Pepperell, Massachusetts, he decided he wanted a place of his own.

Like most dairy farms back then, the Circle Saw Farm was small by today's standards, milking just fifteen cows. But the operation had expanded over the years to forty-two head, and then, in 1966, they built a new barn and grew the herd to seventy-five. There was just one problem: Robert Simpson wasn't a cow person. The creatures constantly frustrated him.

The feeling was mutual. Some cows, like an infamous red and brown Guernsey named Shaky, would stubbornly put their heads down and try to ram him when he approached them in the pasture. And in those days, the milking was done by hand and the stanchions were close together, so the milker had to squeeze himself between the animals and hope they didn't spook. Something about Robert's body language tended to frighten the cows, and he got kicked enough by heifers with names like Dynamite and Thunder to know that he was ready for some other line of work.

At the same time, young Bob was trying to figure out what he wanted to do with his life. He had spent some time at Castleton College, in western Vermont, but its location near the border with New York—a state where the drinking age was eighteen—made the place an unmitigated bacchanal, and Bob, a wholesome farm kid, was shocked by the spectacle. He moved on to Vermont Technical College, and then the University of Vermont, and when his father was preparing to sell the farm, finally decided that he wanted to go into the dairy business. All of twenty years old when he shouldered the responsibilities of the farm in 1971, Bob thought it would be a good way to make some money; that if he scaled up properly, he could afford to hire some help and live a relatively normal middle-class life, perhaps take a vacation every now and then. His dad tried to disabuse him of that idea—"You work and work and never make any money," he advised his son—but young men sometimes need to learn by experience. Shortly after handing the controls to Bob, Robert moved to the Southwest to sell farm equipment.

For the next thirty years, milk prices fluctuated in their usual way, but the farm's balance sheet was good enough to convince a bank to lend Simpson $2 million to build a bigger, state-of-the-art milking parlor, a center-aisle feed barn, and manure and grain storage facilities. Bob and Tay broke ground in 2001 and moved in at the beginning of 2003. Simpson could now milk up to 425 cows, and he calculated that if the price for a hundred pounds of fluid milk stayed above $14, he'd be all right.

And that plan played out nicely for a while. In fact, 2007 proved to be a banner year for American dairy farmers, since global demand for milk surged as developing countries grew more prosperous. Plus, droughts in Australia and New Zealand created a large milk hole that the United States was all too happy to fill. Milk exports rose to more than 12 percent of production, and the all-milk price hit a high in September of nearly $24 per hundredweight. The message to dairy farmers from Maine to Florida to Idaho was loud and clear: the more milk you make, the more money you'll make. "The first thing producers did," USDA economist Don Blayney said, "was buy more cows." Herds swelled, and milk production followed, increasing by 5 percent between 2006 and 2008 to almost 200 billion pounds per year. If there's one thing dairy farmers like to do, after all, it is get milk to market.

The Simpsons were now feeling good about their decision to expand. The gamble seemed to be paying off. Their milk check was robust, allowing them to make the monthly mortgage payment, meet payroll for their milkers, and have some stability. But what they didn't realize, what most dairy farmers didn't realize in the years between 2003 and 2007, was that they were sailing into a perfect storm—the collision of a deep recession with an antiquated, nonsensical milk pricing scheme—that would have ruinous effects on the dairy industry. The farmers who had built their ships to be strong, light, and leak-proof would stand a decent chance of staying afloat. Those with the slightest of leaks would take on debt and more debt, as the rising crest of grain and fuel costs towered over a trough of depressed milk prices—prices nobody had seen in forty years.

The first blow came to the Simpsons in November of 2007. A federal energy bill in 2005 had begun to ramp up the amount of corn-based ethanol in domestic gasoline, moving grain prices a little higher. But when the country got word that another piece of legislation would likely be enacted at the end of 2007, effectively asking for twice the amount of ethanol by 2015, the news set off a bull market in commodity corn. In that one month, Simpson's feed costs rocketed up by $12,000.

And that might have been fine if the price of milk had stayed high. But to see a line-graph of milk prices over 2008 and 2009 is akin to watching a rock bounce down a jagged precipice. Simpson looked on in horror: $22, 19, 19.50, 20, 18, 17, 16. Simultaneously, fuel costs went in the other direction, rising to more than $4.50 per gallon, which made fertilizer more expensive, too. Simpson was getting squeezed on all sides.

Then, in late September of 2008, milk's very image as a healthful and wholesome food came under attack. Over 300,000 people in China, most of them under the age of three, became sick from drinking milk tainted with melamine. Chinese dairy processors had been adding the nitrogen-based industrial chemical to low-quality milk to give it a creamier, more protein-rich mouth feel. It also, incidentally, gave infants kidney stones and caused renal failure. A billion Chinese people suddenly feared milk of any provenance.

The falling milk price reached a terminal velocity in October of 2008 (right about the time when Simpson couldn't cover the checks he had written to Feed Commodities), when the global recession squelched domestic and international demand, causing exports to fall to 5 percent. And yet, all those cows that had been brought on line in the boom times of 2007 were pumping out milk—"That's what Holsteins are for," noted Blayney—and farmers couldn't just shut them off. This created a huge surplus of milk. And when the supply of any commodity exceeds demand, its price will decrease. As complicated as the dairy industry is, that rule holds true, and Simpson understands it all too well.

By the end of 2008, Simpson's milk check was $20,000 less per month than it had been the year before. The year 2009 dawned with milk prices at $15 per hundredweight, only to see the price plummet to $14 in February, and then just over $12 by early spring. Now his milk check, in essence the revenue that would pay for everything related to the farm, was but a stub—"zero dollars and no cents"—because the dairy cooperative he belongs to skims grain bills, co-op dues, milk promotion fees, farm-loan payments, health insurance, workers' compensation, and a host of other charges right off the top. The falling price of milk just made that skim deeper and deeper until, eventually, the skim was everything.

The only way to go on—to feed the three hundred mouths in the barn—was to wring a little more equity out of the farm and get a $150,000 operating loan. It didn't seem suicidal, because "everybody thought that by June the price would go back up," Simpson said. The main reason for that notion was the existence of a whole-herd buyout program, which was being instituted by a collective of dairy farmers called Cooperatives Working Together. The program was a simple supply-management tool. Any participating farmer who wanted to stop milking could sell his herd to the slaughterhouse and get a guaranteed price for each cow. The peaceful euphemism is "herd retirement." It's paid for, in part, by a small deduction from farmers' milk checks, with the hope that a reduced supply of milk will increase the milk price and pay for the deduction. Herds were being culled systematically from the beginning of 2009, and most farmers were looking forward to the July Fourth holiday as the time when the decreased supply would work its way through the system and be reflected in the price of milk on the Chicago Mercantile Exchange.

By mid-August, 187,000 cows had been taken out of the national milk machine through Cooperatives Working Together, and the price of milk hadn't budged—in New England it was pegged at $11.40 per hundredweight. The cost to produce that same amount was hovering at $18: a bright, shining loss with every squeeze of the teat. The situation was getting tense for the Simpsons: their four creditors were calling many times a day, and they began paying close attention to the caller-ID.

===

The Circle Saw Farm rambles from a tree-lined ridge down to a miniature valley with a dirt road, and up and over another ridge, and it's big enough that you can't see the whole place from a single vantage point. On one side of the road are a series of pastures and hay fields abutting forests, forming a sort of green-gold-green pattern against the hillside. On the other side is the bulk of the farming operation: a blue, circular manure tank; the milking parlor; a manure processor that churns out compost for gardens; a feed barn the size of a university field-house; the smaller heifer barn; some corn fields; and, above it all, a modest split-level farmhouse with a silver Ford F-150 out front and a Mini-Cooper stashed in the garage. "There's nothing so much fun as putting that thing through a corner," Bob revealed.

Bob's wife, Tay, is eight years younger than he is. Petite, with blond hair, rosy cheeks, and a runner's build, she grew up in Middlebury, Vermont, where her father was a dean at Middlebury College. She's not from a farm family, yet she never wanted to do anything but run a dairy farm.

Tay and Bob are usually out of the house by 5:00 a.m. to milk the cows and do chores; they then come back to eat breakfast by 9:00. They spend the rest of the day doing office work, moving cows, spreading manure, fixing equipment, haying their fields, or seeing to any number of other tasks vital to a dairy farm's operation. Bob's son from a previous marriage, Andrew, a reserved thirty-three-year-old who drives an ATV at seemingly dangerous velocities, is a late sleeper, so his jobs entail chopping silage and feeding the cows during the day.

You wouldn't know it by looking at the farm, but the noose-tight budget has affected the operation substantially. They've had to cut back on every possible expense, turning the business into something like a V-8 engine running on six cylinders. For example, given a fair milk price, most farms would prefer to milk three times per day: it relieves the pressure on the cows' milk bags and yields 10 percent more milk. But a third milking has its costs, such as the electricity to run the milking pumps, and the payroll expense for another shift. "I don't like milking twice a day," Simpson said, "but right now I've got no choice." Simpson would also like to give himself a paycheck for his toils, but he hasn't done that in months.

The Simpsons have changed the way they feed the cows as well, limiting the budget to $25,000 (down from $40,000) per month by using lower quality grain, and less of it. The result, as you might expect, is less milk. While each cow used to give eighty or a hundred pounds of milk per day, now they can muster only sixty.

These and other measures were recommended by Glenn Rogers, a regional farm management specialist from the University of Vermont Extension Service. He works with farmers on their finances, helping them set up budgets and tweak their operations to squeeze every last dime out of their infrastructure. The year 2009 was tough for him: he scoured operating budgets for excess fat only to see his clients fold a month or two later. In August of 2009, the Simpsons were losing $40,000 to $60,000 per month, just hanging on by the grace of their creditors, who agreed to take interest-only payments on their loans for a limited time.

Waking up every day and working sixteen hours only to lose money is hard enough. But Simpson still had the felony charges to deal with. So he hired a lawyer, scrounged together some money, and paid the grain bill. It turned out that the district attorney had never intended to prosecute anyway; he knew all along what Simpson would do, which was to work it out with Feed Commodities himself and settle his debt. The Orange County sheriff claimed that he had sent the deputy up to arrest Simpson because Simpson had sworn and become combative on the phone with a dispatcher. Simpson is mystified by the allegation. "I don't swear at anybody. I never have," he said.

The intuitive response to the dairy crisis is to keep a steady keel. Bob's instinct, however, tells him to double down, to buy more cows, and to hope to spread the costs—but he realizes that it's a risk. "I don't know if we can produce our way out of it," he said. "We need some financial backers," Tay added, laughing at the thought. They're just hoping the price rebounds to $18 per hundredweight—the break-even point. The bankers are asking Bob when that will happen. "I wish I knew," he told them.

===

The Simpsons have faith that they won't become another statistic in the drawn-out denouement of family dairy farms, but the odds are against them. Between 1970 and 2006, the number of dairy farms in the United States fell by 88 percent from 648,000 to just 75,000. The overwhelming majority of these losses came from farms with 30 to 200 cows—typical small dairies. In a shorter time frame, between 2000 and 2006, the number of farms with more than 2,000 cows has doubled. The force behind this trend is well understood: bigger farms achieve an economy of scale that makes them less expensive to operate. They use their infrastructure more intensively and purchase large amounts of feed at bulk discounts. They contract with breeders to obtain their heifers from off-site, reducing the expense of housing and raising the animals themselves. They confine their milk cows in large barns or in dry-lot feed yards, which cuts down on real estate costs and yields more milk per cow. All of this results in total costs on farms with 500 or more cows that are 18 percent lower than farms with 200 to 499 cows; and costs on farms with fewer than 200 cows are even higher.[1]

If you follow the logic, it's not hard to see where it leads: a stark difference in profitability between large farms and small ones. Nationally, the average net returns for farms with 500 or more cows were positive, while smaller farms reported negative returns. That's probably why a survey in 2000 by the USDA's Economic Research Service found that 25 percent of farmers with fewer than 100 cows expected to close down by 2010. Meanwhile, only 7 percent of the larger operations had the same expectation.

But the trend is not just numerical, it's also geographical. The states with long histories in the dairy industry—New York, Pennsylvania, Vermont, Maine, Michigan, Ohio, Minnesota, and Wisconsin—contain mostly small and medium-size dairy farms. The growth of megafarms is happening predominantly in the Southwest and in California, a state that has operations with upward of 30,000 cows and now produces more milk than any other state or region.

Synthesize these facts and you realize that small farms in the traditional dairy states are disappearing, or are in grave risk of disappearing, and the milk production is shifting—think of a giant sucking sound—to behemoth farms in the West. The global recession has quickened that exodus, presenting a frightening vision for the future of milk. "If we lose the farms in New England," Simpson says, "then people will be drinking milk made from concentrate. They'll pull the water out of it, truck it across the country, and reconstitute it. And if people are fine with that, then the game's over."

NO THANKS

Later on, in August of 2009, Ray Moore was behind his barn, wearing dirt-spattered jeans, muck boots, and a flannel shirt with a hunter-themed camouflage print, loading supplies into the back of a commercial-duty pickup truck. Of medium build, with receding blond hair, pale blue eyes, and a three-day growth of facial hair, he cuts a tough-as-nails figure against the hard-edged backdrop of red tractors, steel silos, and azure skies.

Moorelands Farm is on a hill above the depressed manufacturing town of Springfield, Vermont. On that late August morning, the fog hung thick in the valley along the Connecticut River, shrouding the town and the old machine-tool factories in a gloomy mist. Higher up, the ground escaped the fog and was bathed in cool sunlight. The hills to the east sat above the clouds like islands in a turbid sea.

Across from the barn is the big, mint-green house where Moore and his six older sisters were raised. Moore's parents, in their eighties and now retired, still live there. Moore and his wife, Linda, live in a prefab cape just down the road. Moore's father, Richard, bought the farm—264 acres, one horse, and an old, beat-up tractor—in 1956 for $12,000. Up until that time it had been the town farm, and the seventeen-room house was part community center, part boarding house: in return for their labor, indigent men would get three square meals a day and roof over their heads. Richard had to personally remove the last of them—"old Slim"—before the family could move in.

Ray was his father's son, and from as early as he can recall, he'd wanted to be a farmer. "It used to be punishment for me to stay in the house and not go out into the barn with dad," he said. When he was four he used to stand on a pail and help his father milk the cows. At fourteen he was running the hay baler; at sixteen he was chopping silage. When he graduated from high school he had no desire to go to college. Why bother? Anything he needed to know about dairying he could learn right on the farm. Imagine it: knowing at eighteen years old how you're going to spend the rest of your life, and being content with the prospect.

For most of Ray's youth, Moorelands Farm milked forty to fifty cows. But the father-son team grew the herd internally to ninety head and bought a used milking parlor that fit eight cows, cutting the milking time down to three hours from five. Ray became interested in selective breeding, and liked picking a bull with a certain curve to the leg, or a heifer with a particular shape of teat.

Only one thing satisfied him more than working with cows, spreading manure, planting corn, and getting a good crop: producing a high-quality glass of clean milk. Dairy cooperatives like clean milk, too, which is why they pay a "quality incentive" for milk with low somatic-cell counts. Somatic cells indicate the presence of infection, which is usually caused by mastitis. Mastitis, in turn, is most often caused by bacteria such as *Staphylococcus aureus* in the cows' environment. Moore's milk was so clean that he had cooperatives vying for his business. When he explained how he achieved such cleanliness, Moore morphed from a down-and-dirty farmer with a bit of a temper to a fastidious germ-hawk.

"How?" he asked, as if it were obvious. "Well, you keep them clean to begin with. Clean stalls for them to lay in, clean bedding. Keep them dry. When they come into the milking parlor, you don't want to have to wash mud and dirt off of them, that's a problem right there. And you pre-dip the teats with iodine and let that set for thirty seconds or a minute. I milk four cows at a time. You go down through with 2.5 percent iodine, and you dip all the teats. And then you go back to the first one and you wipe. You wipe them dry and you get them clean. Then you go back to the first one again and you squirt three or four squirts out of each teat to check for mastitis to see if she's got a problem. Those first three or four squirts are the lowest quality milk that cow has in her. You've also got to attach the machine properly and get it off on time, when she's done, so she's not overmilked. And do it the same way every day, twice a day.

"It's a detail thing. You can't just wipe them. The milk comes out of the end, okay? That's the most important part that you want to get clean. You can take a paper towel and wipe them a couple of times and they might look clean, but if you take that teat and you look at the end of it, there's still going to be iodine if you don't make that extra wipe. And they've got to be calm and quiet while they're milking, too. You can't horse them in there. A quiet cow is going to give you more milk. If you're yelling and screaming and they're nervous, the first thing they're going to do is shit all over. If someone comes in while you're milking and yells, 'Hey! How's it going?' ears are up, eyes are up, and tails are up.

"Milking is an important part of that somatic cell count, and quality milk is something that a lot of the large farms don't pay a lot of attention to. I'd rather have a little less milk and better quality, myself."

Moore is also meticulous about keeping sick cows' milk out of the tank that goes to the co-op plant to be processed. If a cow has been given antibiotics, he marks it with blue wound-dressing spray paint and puts orange bands around its legs. He milks them separately, feeds the milk to the calves, and then flushes the system. There's no way penicillin is getting into Moore's milk. "When she walks into the parlor," he said, "you're looking at two bright-orange leg bands, and I've got her marked up like a zebra."

But despite this attention to detail, this good reputation for the cleanest milk in the county, Moore began running into insurmountable obstacles in January of 2009. With the price of milk lower than he'd seen it in twenty years, every milk check that appeared in his mailbox was smaller than the one before. He took steps to stem the losses. He culled his lowest-producing cows and sold them, reducing his herd from ninety to eighty. "The price of grain was going up," he recalled, "so that's one less animal you've got to feed." He shut off his diesel tractors instead of letting them run, even though it's better to keep diesel engines idling.

By May things had gotten desperate. Moore had scrimped everywhere he could, but the milk check was no longer covering the bills. So he looked elsewhere for an explanation. He studied his milk check closely, looking for incorrect charges or deductions that seemed like a waste.

Then he began spending hours every day with his cell phone virtually sewn to his ear, trying to understand why he was losing so much money.

First he called his co-op's field manager, Tim. He wanted to know why his co-op, Dairy Farmers of America (DFA), was charging him a fuel surcharge. The deduction had first appeared on his milk check in the spring of 2008, when the price of diesel fuel approached $5 per gallon and truck drivers were demanding more money. But fuel costs had gone down considerably since then.

"Tim," Moore said, "I don't know where your driver is buying his fuel, but he needs to get it someplace else."

Tim explained that the charge was there because the co-op had to send a separate truck with rBST milk—milk with bovine growth hormone—to a plant in Middlebury for processing. But Moore's milk was rBST-free, and he received a bonus because of it. "Now you're telling me that you're taking that bonus away?" Moore asked, incredulously.

The field manager, Moore soon realized, was just another cog in the machine, like Moore himself.

"If you want answers," Moore said, "you've got to call Syracuse, New York, which is where the big wheels are."

So he called a vice president in Syracuse in April, when the milk price was just over $12 per hundredweight.

"Well, Raymond," the VP said, "I think you've seen the bottom on milk prices."

"Can I quote you on that?"

The voice on the other end of the line snorted a mock laugh. "Well, no."

Next Moore called Senator Bernie Sanders's office and Senator Patrick Leahy's office and Congressman Peter Welch's office, trying to stir something up. The delegation had been very supportive of dairy farmers in the past, and would go on to secure $350 million in extra milk price supports in August of that year, but Moore didn't have time to wait. His comments were noted, and he later received a letter from the legislators laying out the measures they were taking to give dairy farmers some relief.

Then he called the Vermont Department of Agriculture. "Why aren't you doing anything?" he asked.

"We're trying," they told him, but the hard truth, which Moore knew, was that they couldn't do much. Vermont is a small state. If it suddenly stopped making milk, the national market wouldn't even flinch.

Next on his list was the milk promotion office. Every milk check comes with a 15-cent per hundredweight charge that feeds a $300 million marketing campaign with the recognizable milk mustache image, and also the famous *Got Milk?* advertisements. This program, however, has been impotent against the steady downward trend in fluid milk consumption: per capita consumption was roughly twenty-nine gallons in 1975, and today each person drinks about twenty.

Moore was being charged about $200 per month for advertising and milk promotion, and another $200 for marketing. So he called the New England regional office, in Burlington, Vermont, an operation with seventeen employees and an $8.5 million budget.

"OK," he said, "so you've got an $8.5 million budget, seventeen people working. What do you do with this money? I'm curious, because I could really use that $400 per month right about now."

"Well, we do school programs," the representative answered, "teaching kids nutrition and trying to get them to eat more dairy products. We do some of the local fairs. You've probably seen the local dairy booth at your own Windsor County ag fair."

"Yeah," Moore said, "there's always one or two people standing around. But that doesn't impress me. The last time I was at the store and I saw someone picking up a gallon of milk off the shelf, it wasn't a kid, it was his parents. Don't you think we'd be better served to help the parents buy more milk, by lowering the price in the store? The farmers' price is dropping every day, but you don't see it going down in the store. Our price is down 53 percent from what it was a year ago, but it's only down 15 percent in the store."

Moore's efforts were a natural reaction to a situation into which he had little input. They also show what kind of guy he is, that he's not one to take a beating without fighting back. He was hoping that all his calls would have some positive effect, that he could win a series of small victories that would add up to something meaningful. But they didn't. In fact, his telephone campaign solidified a notion that he tried not to believe: that he was just a single farmer on a single farm, and that few people cared whether he stopped milking or not. "You talk all you want," he said, "you make all the calls, and you hang up the phone each time and say, 'I just wasted my breath.'"

Which is why Moore eventually decided to "stop paying for the privilege to produce milk." The farm had lost about $9,000 per month since the spring, and Moore had to take out a loan just to pay some bills. The stress was piling up.

For Linda, a tall woman with long brown hair and a maternal way about her, the decision was a relief. "I was getting pretty depressed," she said, "because I do all the books, and by June we were forking out thousands of dollars every month just to operate the farm." And that didn't include their home mortgage or living expenses.

Moore considered selling his herd for slaughter to the CWT program, but only for an instant before the thought repelled him. "I didn't breed and raise these animals to kill them for beef," he said. "It goes against everything I've done for the last thirty years."

Instead, he found a decent home for them, at a dairy farm fifteen miles away in Chester, owned and operated by a veterinarian. That didn't make the job of sending them there much easier, however. It was a hot, sunny day in a summer marked by cool temperatures and unrelenting rain. Gary Fullam, the owner of Gabby's Livestock Transport, pulled his sand-colored pickup truck and trailer up to Moorelands Farm, and they began loading the seventy-six heifers in, one by one. "That day sucked," Moore said matter of factly. "I was in tears most of the fucking day. It's like putting your kids in foster care because you can't take care of them."

On the same morning, Linda was painting a rental property she owns in Springfield. The most recent tenants had just about destroyed the place, and she needed a thirty-yard dumpster to get rid of all the garbage, which included various dead skunks and rats. She called Ray on his cell phone to see how he was doing. "I could tell he needed someone there," she recalled. So she quit what she was doing and went back to the farm. Neighbors and friends had also showed up to lend their support, some of whom were crying at the sight of the migration, the end of an iconic dairy farm. There was only one cow out of the seventy-six that they needed to put a rope on to get into the trailer. "I guess she didn't want to leave home," Linda said.

Ray has no plans to stop working the land. Milking cows was only one part of the farming life that he loves. Much of the rest of it—growing corn, haying, breeding cows, cutting trees for firewood, and sugaring maple syrup—he will continue to do. And he'll have more time for hunting. To Linda, Ray is a changed man; it's as if a huge weight had been lifted from his shoulders. He doesn't swing from bouts of crazed phone-calling to sullen depression. They're going on their first vacation together in years. But being evicted from his life's work at the age of forty-seven has taken its toll, and not a day goes by when he doesn't contemplate how he can get back into the milking business. He just keeps running into the cold calculus of dairy farm economics.

"You try to figure out why you can't make this business work. You've got to realize, up here"—he points to his head—"that it's not your fault. It's not your fault that you're getting $11 per hundred-weight for your milk.

"You keep thinking, *I've got to make it work. I've got to make it work.* But there ain't no making it work, not when it costs you more to produce it than you can sell it for. There ain't no making it work."

A DEVASTATING YEAR
AMONG TOUGH DECADES

At about the same time that Ray Moore and Bob Simpson and the rest of the dairy farmers in the U.S. were suffering a historic drop in milk prices, the USDA announced a rosy piece of news: according to the latest Agricultural Census, there were 76,000 more farms in 2007 than there had been in 2002. It attributed the increase to the local, organic food movement, and said that the new farms were of the small, diversified flavor. By "small," the report meant farms that have an annual earnings potential of between $1,000 and $10,000. These are the truck farmers you might see on the side of the road in the summer, or at the farmers' market selling eggs from their thirty chickens. The locavores smiled at this report, for it was evidence that the revolution of yeoman agriculture was finally gaining momentum.

But the skeptics weren't so sure. One was Michael Roberts, a former researcher at the USDA Economic Research Service. According to him, the USDA was taking liberties with the statistics—using "weights" to account for nonresponses—and working extra hard to find those $1,000 operations that didn't even self-identify as farms. What's the significance? First, farm numbers impact the allocation of federal funding doled out by the National Institute of Food and Agriculture, so the USDA has an incentive to find more of them. Second, research outcomes are more likely to be skewed, because when you find more microfarms, the percentage of farms depending on off-farm income is artificially inflated.

But whether there really are more small farms, or the USDA is just looking under more rocks to find them, one piece of the USDA's announcement was less equivocal: "The latest census figures show a continuation in the trend towards more small and very large farms and fewer mid-sized operations. Between 2002 and 2007, the number of farms with sales of less than $2,500 increased by 74,000. The number of farms with sales of more than $500,000 grew by 46,000 during the same period."

It's safe to say that those 74,000 new farms were not dairy farms, since you can't run a dairy operation and make less than $2,500 in sales. But the increase on the other end of the spectrum—those farms with half a million dollars in sales—represents in part a shift from medium-size dairies to megafarms. And the data on that particular trend are certain: nationwide, 4,600 dairy farms have closed every year for the past two decades. New England has lost two-thirds of its dairy farms since 1990. Minnesota has lost 10,000 dairy farms in ten years. In New York, 2,500 dairy farms have closed every year since 1999. Yet the U.S. population over the past thirty years has increased by about 30 million. More people, fewer farms. It's a trend we're all familiar with in every other agricultural sector, especially corn, soybeans, wheat, pork, and poultry. What makes the dairy industry special is that there is still a strong contingent of small and medium-size dairy farms existing alongside the huge farms. But with a couple more years like 2009, there won't be many left.

The most obvious force is economic: Ray Moore chose to stop losing money. For others, the choice was made for them by the bank.

But an equally important force is psychological. Farming is one of the most dangerous lines of work you can find, right up there with fishing and forestry. Aside from the physical dangers of working with animals and heavy machinery, farming can take a harsh psychological toll. The suicide rate for farmers is twice that for nonfarmers, and when a crisis comes along, that rate goes skyward. As far as anyone can tell, it has always been this way: during the spread of the railroads in the early 1900s, when farmers' bargaining power was under assault; during the Great Depression; during the farm crisis in the 1980s; the collapse of pork prices in 1998; the foot-and-mouth-disease outbreak in the United Kingdom in 2001; and the dairy crisis of 2009. Agriculture is by nature a mercurial beast, prone to the whims of weather, the spasms of the global economy, and the beautiful terror of chaos.

Of course, everyone lives with a measure of uncertainty. And how do we deal with it? We tell ourselves stories about our place and purpose in the world. We steel ourselves with girders of hope. We push back, as the anthropologist Clifford Geertz wrote, against that "dim, back-of-the-mind suspicion that one may be adrift in an absurd world."[2] Andrew Delbanco, a scholar of American Studies at Columbia University, has pinned an apropos name on that suspicion: melancholy.[3] The word comes from the Greek *melanos chole*, which means black bile. It's a perfect expression for the buildup of something dark and dangerous inside of us, something grotesque that we don't want to consider but that foists itself upon us anyway with its burden of inchoate pain. Herman Melville, in *Moby Dick*, called these ill feelings "hypos" and, by way of Ishmael's narrative, reveals that his own way of "driving off the spleen" is to "get to sea." Today, most of us beat back the bile of melancholy with exercise, with laughter, or with the warm embrace of a loved one. And we endure just a fraction of the uncertainty about our livelihoods that farmers experience. But farmers often operate under such a crushing workload that the idea of exercise or other forms of stress reduction doesn't have time to enter their minds. On top of that, it's been shown that farmers tend not to seek professional psychological services, and that there's a stigma about reaching out for help. When these tendencies conspire, the result can be tragic.

Mike Rosmann has devoted his life to treating the unique psychological challenges of farming. He's a clinical psychologist on the frontier of a new specialty: agricultural behavioral health. Rosmann has bushy gray hair, a frontier mustache, and thin eyebrows; he looks like a modern-day, well-kempt Mark Twain. He grew up on a family farm in Harlan, Iowa, a picture-perfect slice of middle America known as the City of Trees. Like many of their neighbors in the 1950s and 60s, the Rosmanns did a little bit of everything on the farm, growing corn, soybeans, oats, and alfalfa hay, and raising cattle, chickens, and turkeys. Rosmann's father purchased the land for a song in 1942, a time when few people were buying much of anything. And then World War II came along, and the grain shortages in Europe, and corn prices rose to the equivalent of $18 per bushel. Two years later, the Rosmann farm was paid off.

But even during the anodyne days in the middle of the twentieth century, there was a sadness lurking on farms, and the young Mike Rosmann picked up on it. He'd known farmers who had killed themselves, and he wondered why. So he left the farm to find out. Attaining his Ph.D., he spent most of his teaching career at the University of Virginia. Yet his farming roots, his Iowan roots, kept pulling him back. One day in mid-January of 1979, just as UVA's campus was reopening after the Christmas break, Rosmann announced to his graduate students and research assistants that he was leaving the Psychology Department in May and moving his family to Harlan, where they would tend a small farm and where Rosmann would offer psychological counseling to farmers. His audience reflected the spectrum of awkward reactions: some snickered with derision, others laughed as if the announcement were a joke, a few put on puzzled faces. When Rosmann didn't smile with them, everyone became very quiet. Finally, a third-year graduate student asked the obvious question: "Why are you leaving the University of Virginia to work with farmers?"

Rosmann recalls that moment with the clarity that follows the enunciation of a life-changing decision. "Something moved inside of me," he says, "and I felt like I needed to address it. The words that came out were, 'Somebody has to take care of the mental health of farm people.'" When he hung his shingle in Harlan, Rosmann was skeptical of his own plan, because he knew how reluctant farmers were to seek psychological counseling. "To many farmers," Rosmann has written, "mental health and substance abuse problems are a sign of weakness that can be discussed only with a pastor, family doctor or trusted family members." But he proved his doubts wrong. Because he was a farmer himself, he bridged that cultural and linguistic divide that exists between farm people and everyone else. A cattle rancher who was depressed because he had to sell all of his cows to discharge a foreclosed loan said it most succinctly: "You are a farmer like us . . . you understand."

Rosmann had set up shop just in time for the farm crisis of the early 1980s. It had been years in the making. During the early 1970s, when the national economy was strong and farmers were being asked to grow more and more food, they leveraged themselves with low-interest loans to purchase machines, fertilizers, pesticides, and farm services. International demand for American food was robust, and commodity prices rose. But by the late 1970s, that cycle of prosperity was coming to an end. The economy shrank, interest rates shot up, and consumers tightened their belts. To make things worse, Russia invaded Afghanistan in 1980, and in response President Carter issued an embargo on farm products to the aggressor. U.S. economic woes spread across the globe, further restricting international demand for American produce. The result, eerily foreshadowing 2009, was that farmers had high debts from scaling up to meet demand. And then, when that global demand shriveled, American farmers had no way to pay off their loans. Property tax delinquencies increased by 400 percent. Foreclosures mounted. Thousands of farms closed, and rural populations decreased and grayed.

Stress, as you might imagine, was at an all-time high for farmers during the 1980s farm crisis. Feeling trapped, some farmers turned to violence, holding up banks and staging standoffs in their homes when sheriffs tried to evict them. Rosmann, who had recently joined forces with the local mental health center, was one of the first psychologists to think deeply about treating distressed farmers. He knew that clinics had tried offering hotlines as an outlet for farmers wondering how to survive and keep their sanity. But he also knew that they weren't used much. So he tweaked the service just a bit: now, when a farmer called a hotline for advice or someone to talk to, he wouldn't just find a good listener, but another farmer who understood precisely what was going on. Anonymity and confidentiality were guaranteed. The phones rang off the hook.

Rosmann learned another valuable lesson during this time: that losing a family farm is worse than experiencing a death in the family, and that the aftermath of such a heart-wrenching event follows Kübler-Ross's five stages of grief—denial, anger, bargaining, depression, and finally acceptance—but with more acute mental trauma and fewer rituals to ease the suffering.[4] This is a contributing factor to the high suicide rate among farmers, but it doesn't explain the underlying forces at play. Rosmann had known for a long time that modern farmers are a different breed than people in other lines of work, with their willingness to do back-breaking labor for modest remuneration, the tenacity with which they cling to their land, and their pride in a lifestyle suffused with mud, manure, and dramatic uncertainty.

Only recently has Rosmann formulated what, to him, is a plausible explanation for this behavior. He calls it the Agrarian Imperative: a basic human drive to produce life's essentials. According to an article Rosmann published in the *Journal of Agromedicine* in 2010, genetic and anthropological evidence has shown that humans are endowed with an instinct for farming as a survival mechanism. This manifests itself in the urge to acquire land, mark it as our own, and cultivate it for our benefit, raising plants and animals for food, fiber, and energy. We learned these skills thousands of years ago and, as they became essential for our success as a species, passed them on to future generations through our genetic code.

So, regardless of your vocation at this moment, the theory goes, your veins course with farming expertise. Rosmann figures that farm culture recedes from a person after three successive generations of having no connection to the land. But it comes back strong during just one generation of revival. "How quickly our bodies harden and toughen when we leave an urban lifestyle and become immersed in nature," Rosmann wrote. "Our fingers thicken and our hands enlarge; our behavior becomes practical and our manners become brusque, geared toward accomplishing tasks with a minimum of energy and physical wear and tear. We develop an intense attachment to the land we work. We take great pride in our crops and livestock."[5]

The psychological evidence is there, too. In a 2001 study performed on 60 farm people in Queensland, researchers Marilyn Shrapnel and Jim Davie at the University of Queensland found that farmers have a distinct set of personality traits that directly relate to their success in working the land: a capacity for hard work and perseverance; confidence in making their own decisions; great capacity for coping with adversity; comfort with solitude and self-reliance; and diminished need for companionship and a comfort level with a small circle of friends.[6] A similar study was done on 252 farmers in Scotland in the late 1990s, with similar conclusions: successful farmers are conscientious, risk-taking, and self-reliant.[7]

Imagine for a moment, however, what might happen to these people when their genetically encoded lifestyle becomes untenable, or when they fail at the tasks their parents, grandparents, and great-grandparents were able to do with such aplomb. First there is the generational pressure: the feeling that if you lose your land, you're letting down not just your forebears but also the generations to come. And then there are the personality traits. A conscientious person in such a position would feel duty bound to continue farming, for the good of his family and his nation. A person with perseverance in such a predicament would not give in to the forces beyond his control, but persist in the face of adversity. A risk-taking person would try—by borrowing money, for instance—to keep the farm going, despite the odds. And a self-reliant person would do all of this on his own, not seeking help from outsiders. In sum, the very traits that shepherd success for farmers are the ones that, in hard times, militate against their own financial and emotional well-being.

All of that explains the existence of AgriWellness, a nonprofit organization based in Harlan that Rosmann runs. It provides administrative services for a seven-state network of farmer hotlines and helplines in the Midwest called Sowing the Seeds of Hope. The Wisconsin Office of Rural Health and the Wisconsin Primary Health Care Association started it in 1999 with funds from the federal Office of Rural Health Policy. The project partners selected AgriWellness to coordinate services in 2001. Whether you're in Iowa, Kansas, the Dakotas, Minnesota, Nebraska, or Wisconsin, if you're a farmer struggling with financial or psychological issues, you can pick up the phone and talk to someone who can help. It works so well that Congress appropriated funds in the 2008 Farm Bill for the creation of the Farm and Ranch Stress Network, a sort of national version of Sowing the Seeds of Hope. But the money has not been forthcoming: political infighting has stalled the program. Thirty-nine states have expressed an interest in joining the Farm and Ranch Stress Network, yet Rosmann and the rest are waiting for the money to be doled out. "We're kind of just limping along right now," Rosmann says.

It's not a good time to be limping. In 2009, AgriWellness experienced a 20 percent increase in calls. Most of that rise was from dairy farm states—calls from Wisconsin shot up by 40 percent alone. And the intensity of the behavioral health symptoms worsened. More callers were reporting more emotional upheaval, with the main driver being economic turmoil. Scott Hoese, a Minnesota dairy farmer, described the situation to the House Agriculture Subcommittee on Livestock, Dairy and Poultry in July of 2009: "Dairy farmers of all sizes and across all regions of the country are enduring an unprecedented disaster," he said. "Equity is rapidly disappearing, market prices remain at 1970 levels, creditors are cutting off producers—yet there is no relief in sight."

That type of financial pressure is, in a word, stressful. The body gears up for stress by working harder to ignore it—the fight or flight response—or using alcohol to treat it. As the stress continues, we get energized each time we think of the turmoil we're facing, and the body produces adrenaline. Once the body has been keyed up on adrenaline for a while, it needs to rest, so it secretes cortisol, slowing us down and allowing the muscles to deflate. Our breathing slows down and our pupils shrink back to normal size. Cortisol also has a habit of depositing fat around our midsection and making us feel logy and depressed. And when our bodies repeat this cycle over and over again, they become depleted of serotonin, causing us to feel depressed most of the time. "The urge when we're depressed," Rosmann says, "is to shut people out and retreat into our own little hidden world. But we have to do just the opposite. We have to reach out and share our trials and tribulations."

Sowing the Seeds of Hope, and other similar hotlines around the country, serve that very purpose, but they can't reach every troubled farmer. In the first half of 2009, two California dairy farmers committed suicide. Three more took their own lives in Maine that year. "Sometimes, farmers take their lives as a last act of trying to bring insurance proceeds to survivors," Rosmann explains. "Other times, they do things to bring attention to the crisis. Shooting themselves is a way of saying, 'Somebody's got to pay attention to what's happening here.' It becomes an act of martyrdom." Hoese echoed that feeling in his presentation to Congress: "As a producer, it has been frustrating, to say the least, to weather one of the worst economic periods in thirty years, yet it seems as though our society as a whole has not grasped how desperate our situation is."

Hoese was right about that: the public has, in general, failed to understand how hard it is to be a dairy farmer, and how unfair it seems when society doesn't allocate the proper capital to laborers who provide a clean, wholesome food product to the shelves of millions of American refrigerators. It's as if the noise of daily life just drowns out the low-grade crackle of rural dispatches. Every once in a while, however, the dairy alarm will rise above the other noise, drawing us into the barn, or the farmhouse kitchen.

On the morning of January 21, 2010, fifty-two big alarms echoed across America. They were the reports from Dean Pierson's gun as he shot each of his milking cows in the head and then, sitting down in a chair, turned the rifle on himself. He left a short suicide note on a scrap of paper, referring to his depression over personal and financial issues. He said he loved his family, but that he was simply "overwhelmed."

Pierson, fifty-nine, ran the Hi-Low Farm in Copake, New York. He had inherited it from his father, Helmer, a gregarious Swede who had good timing. Dean, an avid hunter and fisherman, wasn't as lucky. For one, he lacked his father's personality. A college friend described him as "taciturn and barely speaking."[8] For another, he was as fiercely self-reliant a farmer as you'll ever find. This Hudson Valley farm, set beneath a low hill of hardwoods and shaded by white pines, was his responsibility. He woke before sunrise for the morning milking, and then milked again twelve hours later. In between he did nearly everything else to keep the farm afloat, running a small sawmill and growing a few summer crops to defray feed expenses. He did it all himself, and perhaps, when milk prices plummeted, he could think of no one else to blame.

And even though he killed his milking cows, he certainly didn't blame them. Mike Rosmann and people in the Copake farming community have guessed that Pierson meticulously picked just the milk cows to shoot because he didn't want them to suffer after he was gone, when there would be no one to milk them. Rosmann asserts, ironically, "What he did says a lot about the bond this man had with his cows." He left fifty heifers and calves alive.

On a cold morning the day after the shooting, Pierson's neighbors came and dug a deep trench in the frozen ground next to the barn. In it they buried Pierson's cows. A few days later, a John Deere tractor pulled Pierson's coffin on a flatbed truck, setting him down to rest in the Copake Cemetery.

THE FIRST

DAIRY FARMERS

A young woman in Bavaria is digging in the dirt. It is a cool, cloudy day in the fall of 2010. Around her stretches the lush, rolling farmland of southeastern Germany: freshly cut hay fields dotted with white plastic hay bales. She takes a break, looks up, and notes the serenity in the air. Big, yellow earth-moving excavators stand dormant and lifeless. On the horizon, a concrete mixing plant is incongruously quiet. It was not supposed to be this way. The earth-movers should be moving earth. The concrete plant should be churning out the material that will form the bed of a new high-speed rail line between Nuremberg and Berlin. It has all stopped because of what archeologist Birgit Srock is looking at: a 7,200-year-old posthole from a Neolithic settlement.

This is not exactly a ground-breaking discovery. Many times, when we push forward as a people, we till up the soil and learn something about where we came from. This right-of-way for a two-hundred-mile-per-hour train was set to tread over a prehistoric village of the Linear Pottery culture, a civilization dating to 5300 BC in central Europe. The name is derived from the incised lines on their fine pottery, found scattered from Slovakia and western Ukraine to Belgium and eastern France. You can thank them for inventing bread. They were also some of the first people on earth to farm and raise livestock. This Bavarian site bears that out: Srock is standing amid forty houses, containing skeletons, a spinning wheel, clay vessels, cows' teeth, and broken sieves for cheese production.

Everyone knows that humans started farming long before 5300 BC, and in the Middle East. What's less clear is how that agrarian revolution—the transition from hunting and gathering to the so-called sedentary lifestyle of farming—spread from the Fertile Crescent to Europe. The latest research, by a working-group of archeologists, chemists, and geneticists spread across the globe, is pointing to a four-letter word as one explanation: milk.

The project's name is LeCHE, which happens to be the Spanish word for "milk," but it's also an acronym that stands for Lactase persistence and the Early Cultural History of Europe. What researchers are finding is not only that milk played an important role in the spread of agriculture, but also that our ability to drink fluid milk had some special significance in the success of the human species.

Archeologists have been debating the origins of agriculture for as long as they've been exhuming our former selves. Coherent theories started sprouting up in the Victorian era with the publishing of Hodder Westropp's *Prehistoric Phases* in 1872. In it, he described a quaint progression, popular in the day, of humans from barbarous savages to genteel pastoralists. The main force behind the progression seemed simply to be that the farming life was better than the alternative. Westropp's descriptions are colorful:

HUNTERS

However humiliating it may be to our pride, we must acknowledge that, in the earliest period of his existence, man was scarcely distinguishable from the brute. The desire to supply his wants absorbed his whole thoughts. . . . He fed on wild fruits or devoured raw fish, or fought with his fellow, or with the brutes for the carcasses killed by them. . . . His life was a continual state of warfare. He fought for everything, for food, for women.[1]

A hunter is a wild man, his food is wild game; he lives as the tiger lives, catching his prey by his superior cunning, strength and pluck. The flesh of that prey is his food, the skin of that pray is his mantle. . . . He may not build a house, he may not till the ground; he may not tarry in one place, for the wild game which he procures is always flying from his poisoned arrow and his plunging knife; and the law of his existence chains him to the buffalo track. He hand is lifted against everything that lives.[2]

FARMERS

A herdsman is a tame man, his food is milk and cheese,
the flesh of goats and calves. He has to provide for his wants by
knowledge, care and kindness. The cow yields him milk, the goat
yields him cloth; yet he wins these requisites from them, not
by murderous cunning but by tender love. . . . When the hunter
sharpens his blade, the herdsman has to sharpen his wits, if he
would thrive in his acts and increase his flocks.[3]

When and where this glorious transformation first happened is fairly certain: some 12,000 years ago in the Mediterranean Levant, an area in the Near East bounded on the west by the Mediterranean Sea, on the north by the Taurus Mountains, on the east by the Zagros Mountains, and on the south by the Syrian-Arabian desert. It includes the coastal mountain range of Lebanon, Palestine and Israel, the Orontes-Jordan rift valley, and the inland hills and plateaus riven with many wadis flowing eastward into the sands.

Where Westropp saw the inexorable evolution of the species from brute to brainy as a triumph of the uniqueness of the human spirit, modern-day archeologists and paleo-climatologists see a strategy for survival in a changing world. During the thousands of years before humans cultivated their food—called the Late Glacial Maximum of the Pleistocene—the climate was slowly getting wetter, broadening the opportunities for foragers to gather fruits, seeds, leaves, and tubers; harvest wild emmer and einkorn wheat; and hunt gazelle, fallow deer, and wild boar, cattle, goat, and sheep. And then came the Younger Dryas period, around 11,000 BC, and things got colder and drier. Wild food wasn't as plentiful, and humans were provoked into intentional cultivation of the cereals and grains they had been accustomed to simply harvesting from nature. In 10,000 BC they were aided by another shift to more moisture and climatic stability, at the beginning of the Holocene. Now getting the hang of this thing, and able to draw calories out of the ground at their whim, the population increased and cultivation spread into neighboring areas and the rest of the Near East. As the population of these early peoples continued to grow, before long they had outstripped the resources of wild game and decided to bring those cloven-footed calories under their dominion as well.

Each form of farming came with its own conundrums. For planting and harvesting, these architects of husbandry engineered the plow and sickle. Such implements weren't too much of a stretch for a Neolithic culture experienced in stone tool-making. The first fauna to be domesticated were the easiest: goats and sheep. They were relatively small and docile, and could be penned in with simple fences. The real challenge was the Middle Eastern cow, which weighed up to 2,200 pounds and had frightening curved horns. Somewhere in the central Euphrates valley, farmers combined ingenuity and courage to approach these beasts and render them cooperative. A Neolithic sculpture tellingly shows a steer with a hole punched through its septum. They also discovered that castrating the cattle improved their temperament and allowed them to be yoked, bringing their massive power under control for other farm chores. Further experimentation revealed that when calves were passed around to different mothers, the cows would consistently produce milk.

We know, from studying lipid deposits on ancient pottery, that the earliest farmers expressed milk from goats (in present-day Iran), and sheep and cattle (in southern Anatolia) in 9000 BC. But they didn't drink it raw, because most of them were not lactose tolerant. So the first dairy products were most likely fermented: kefir, yogurt, and cheese. Farmers kept other animals that made milk—pigs and dogs, for instance—but humans have never made a habit of using dairy foods from those carnivores. As Anne Mendelson writes in *Milk: The Surprising Story of Milk through the Ages*, "[No] society has ever habitually consumed milk from any animal that doesn't live on grass and leaves."[4] This wasn't because of some taboo. These were practical people, after all, who would not have scorned a source of food if it was easy enough to collect. The main reason why they never milked pigs or dogs was that the animals' udders were too small for the human hand to grasp. Goats, sheep, and cows were, in a word, perfect.

Central Europe in 9000 BC was still filled with hunter-gatherers. It would be another few thousand years before the inhabitants there started farming. The conventional explanation for this shift has been provided by, among others, German archeologist Jens Luning, who has written that a small group of immigrants taught the inhabitants of central Europe about sowing and milking with "missionary zeal." The new knowledge was then quickly passed on to others in a spirit of "peaceful cooperation."[5]

But new research by LeCHE scientists, based on excavations in Turkey, Germany, France, Scandinavia, and the Fertile Crescent, and genetic analyses of Neolithic skeletons and domestic animals, is causing archeologists to reconsider Luning's theory. It seems that around seven thousand years ago, large groups of Middle Eastern farmers migrated to Europe, bringing their dairy knowledge with them and intermarrying with a culture that had a specific genetic advantage.

According to Mark Thomas—senior lecturer at the Molecular and Cultural Evolution Lab at the University College of London and, with Joachim Burger, cofounder of LeCHE—the strongest genetic selection in human history is the one that allows us to drink raw milk as adults, otherwise known as lactose tolerance. Burger, a professor of anthropology at the Johannes Gutenberg University Mainz, thought it would be interesting if he used DNA analysis of prehistoric human remains to look for genetic markers of lactose tolerance. Perhaps, between the two of them, they could chart the beginnings of the mutation and understand how and why we became milk drinkers.

That's right: mutation. If you can drink a tall glass of milk and not get sick, you are a mutant. Infants, of course, have no problem drinking their mother's milk; it contains a beneficial sugar called lactose, and infants have a special enzyme—lactase—that allows their stomach to digest it. But normally, after an infant is weaned, the body stops producing lactase because it's thinking, "I'll never see *that* sugar again." If you try to drink milk as an adult without lactase, you'll be in a world of hurt. Since the lactose can't get processed in the stomach, it passes directly into the intestines. In the lower intestine, bacteria have a field-day on the sugar, and, through osmosis, draw water into the area, giving you diarrhea. The bacteria then start digesting the lactose, creating hydrogen and other gasses in the process, producing flatulence. Believe it or not, the majority of the human population, including most Chinese, can't drink milk as adults. A little milk in coffee, sure, but a tumbler of the stuff? No way.

Yet many of us, obviously, can. Why? The genetic mutation that allows lactase to persist into adulthood existed in a small percentage of the first farmers, but since they lived in a hot, arid environment, it wasn't practical for them even to try to drink raw milk. The mutation "began to be selected for very heavily seven thousand years ago, and the level of selection appears to be extraordinarily high," says Matthew Collins, a protein chemist at the University of York who is part of the LeCHE team. "Just this one mutation gives you about a 10 percent higher likelihood of surviving to the breeding age." This is intriguing because it appears that the initial genetic selection for lactase persistence occurred at the same time that farming first began in Europe, and around the time of a large migration of farmers to Europe from the Middle East. Furthermore, this time period marked the beginning of the Linear Pottery people, the first Neolithic cow-centered culture.

If we are to believe the LeCHE researchers, we can begin to tell the story of how milk came to be our favorite drink. It goes like this:

Around about 5500 BC, farmers from the Near East started to migrate north and west into Europe. In their homeland, the conditions had been hot and sunny—perfect for growing grains and using dairy animals to produce yogurt and cheese, but fluid milk would have spoiled quickly. As they moved north, the climate became colder, wetter, and less sunny, making crops less predictable. But there was more grass, and their cows could eat whether it rained or shined. Dairying, therefore, became more central to the culture's survival. While migrating through Europe, the Near Eastern farmers ran into a group of indigenous people around Lake Balaton in modern-day Hungary. A high percentage of these natives had the genetic mutation that allowed them to drink raw milk, according to Mark Thomas's findings. The immigrants intermarried with the natives, exchanging the knowledge of raising dairy animals and the genes for lactase persistence. Since you need only one parent with the lactase mutation to pass it on, lactose tolerance spread quickly.

By the time farming moved into Scandinavia, most of the farmers already had the genetic mutation—think of it as surfing the wave of expansion into Central and Northern Europe. This shows that there was a huge advantage for those people who could drink raw milk. Is it because in Northern Europe raw milk lasts longer before spoiling? Is it because milk is a good source of vitamin D in a less sunny land? Is it because milk is a clean, noncontaminated liquid that could take the place of bacteria-ridden water? No one's really sure.

"What we do know," Collins says, "is that these people became pretty obsessed about cows." Archeologists have frequently found cow iconography at Linear Pottery excavations, as well as at special cow burial sites. "So there's this really interesting link," says Collins, "between the ability to digest raw milk as an adult, and cows becoming a very important part of people's lives." Suddenly the collaboration between Thomas and Burger and the twenty-five others in the LeCHE project makes sense. You need the scientists to give you the data, and the archeologists to explain its significance on the culture. So far, this story has been very Eurocentric. But it doesn't stop there. Thomas and a colleague named Dallas Swallow looked for the genetic marker for lactase persistence in Africa, where there are pastoralist tribes for whom cows are an important source of wealth. They are, not surprisingly, lactose tolerant. But, curiously, right next to these dairy farmers are hunter-gatherer tribes that don't have the mutation. Generally, populations become more lactose tolerant as you move away from North Africa and the Middle East toward Europe. In Ireland, nearly 100 percent of the population can drink buckets of milk without a problem.

As time went on, goats and sheep continued as popular dairy animals, but the star of the show became the cow. Doe-eyed, steadfast, and strong; able to provide food, work, and fuel (in the form of dung); the *Bos taurus* was so vital to pastoral life that some religions—Buddhism, Hinduism, and Jainism—rendered them sacred beings. The Sanskrit word for "cow" is *aghnya*, meaning "that which may not be slaughtered." If you were a farmer in the time of Christ, and you had a cow, you were rich. The Romans' term for money was *pecunia*, which is derived from *pecus*, the word for cattle. The very image of the cow, in Vedic cultures, became a symbol for wealth. For Brahmins, the cow is the "wellspring of life in palpable form, inexhaustibly pouring forth the miracle of milk, a holy substance considered to have been purified by inner fires in the grass-transforming alembic that is the cow's body."[6] And in India, to this day, it is illegal in most states to kill a cow.

While the cow's status grew to mythic proportions during the millennia between the dawn of the first farmers in 10,000 BC and the dark ages, forms of milk consumption didn't change much. People tended dairy animals and turned their milk into yogurt, butter, and cheese for personal use or to trade for meat. There were no "dairy farms," however, because people needed a diversity of animals to survive, and the markets were not efficient enough to satisfy the demands of society, such as it was.

The force that pushed milk, as a stand-alone product, into modernity was the rise of urban land use. Agriculture, the intensive cultivation of land for food production, made dense human settlements possible. Symbiotically, as people moved into cities—a trend that began in earnest around AD 1300—more farmers huddled around the edges to serve them. Some of these farmers decided to keep only cows. They might have taken loads of fresh milk into the cities for immediate sale and consumption as a drink, but more often they pooled their milk in order to make cheese. This pattern would continue for hundreds of years in Europe, and then cross the ocean with the first settlers of the New World.

THE CONTROL OF

AMERICAN MILK

In 1769, Philip Ranney's great, great, great, great, great, great grandfather, Benjamin Ranney, cleared a few rocky acres from a plot of rolling hillside in the southern Vermont hamlet of Westminster West.

This makes Philip, a lanky, loquacious thirty-one-year-old with reddish blond hair, the seventh generation of the Ranney family to raise and milk cows on the same 167 acres. He always assumed that his sons, Garrett and Sawyer, aged seven and four, would continue the tradition, but by the spring of 2009 he wasn't so sure anymore. His debt had been accumulating faster than he could clear it, and he knew that the following six months would dictate his farm's fate. He lay awake at night, thinking about his ancestors and wondering how they'd managed to keep the operation going for so long. The thought of the farm disappearing on his watch was mortifying.

So the question arises: what's different between 1769 and now, between a time when producing milk was a nearly foolproof way to survive, and when a similar job is downright gut-wrenching in its economic and familial calculus? Products come and go, sure, and their stewards often follow a parallel trajectory. The typewriter repairman's purpose has become as obsolete as the typewriters he repaired. Milk, however, is more important to the lives of Americans than it's ever been, not less. And yet, the struggle to provide this staple, while technically easier on the body, is harder in every other way.

The Vermont that Benjamin Ranney found in the late eighteenth century was far more rugged, rural, and inhospitable than it is today. The land was heavily forested—something the settlers considered a nuisance rather than a benefit—and there were only a few improved roads. Vermont had just become part of the United States five years earlier, and it had only recently been opened to British colonists from Connecticut and Massachusetts thanks to a defeat of the French and Abenakis in the 1760s. Ranney, a slight but determined gentleman with a "sterling Christian character," came to Westminster from Haddam, Connecticut, largely by paddling a log canoe up the Connecticut River. The young state was still very much a frontier land, as were Kentucky and Tennessee. Anybody who ventured there had to be prepared for a hard life based at first on subsistence farming and hunting and gathering. This was the tradeoff for vast expanses of inexpensive land and the early opportunities that all frontier areas presented.

Westminster (which the locals pronounce "Westminister") at that time was still claimed by both New York and New Hampshire, but Vermont ignored them and sold lots in eighty-acre tracts to "proprietors" who were supposed to settle the land. Ranney bought two such tracts for £75 and became part of something relatively new in the United States: a uniform agricultural class, made up of freeholders sprinkled among the hills and valleys.

There was no such thing as a dairy farm in 1769. Since markets did not exist, people had to be almost totally self-sufficient, growing all their own crops and tending their own animals. Subsistence farmers urged vegetables out of the rocky, acidic, and nutrient-poor soil left in the wake of Laurentide ice sheet 12,000 years before. They had an easier time raising cattle, pigs, and sheep; making butter and cheese; baking bread from Indian cornmeal and rye; and boiling maple sap into syrup.

Fluid milk was consumed by the farm animals and the farm family. The cattle that provided this milk were the descendants of cows that were first imported into America in 1611 to feed the Jamestown Colony. The word "cattle," in fact, is derived from the Middle English "chattel," which means a personal possession other than real estate. Milk was not yet America's drink, just a by-product of farm beasts that happened also to have nutritional value.

Ranney's wife, Martha Gill, spun their clothes from wool and flax. Their rambling five-bedroom farmhouse, loosely connected to a series of outbuildings, was built with timber from the cleared land. They heated the large structure by burning hardwood in fireplaces and pig-iron cook-stoves. What the Ranneys couldn't make themselves—salt, tea, coffee, molasses, and rum, for example—they acquired through bartering livestock, wool, butter, and cheese. They also sold these things to pay the penny-per-acre property tax that Vermont levied at statehood to reimburse New York for some border land.

Even if there had been commercial markets at this time, fluid milk would have been the last thing available for purchase, because of milk's nature as a "flow commodity." Lactating cows produce milk constantly, and, lacking refrigeration, that milk must be brought to market at least every day. Eggs can be stored; meat can be dried and preserved; vegetables can be shelved for a few days or kept in a root cellar; apples can keep for a few months. But milk "is designed to be drunk at the moment of expression," write Andrew Rimas and Evan D. G. Fraser in *Beef: The Untold Story of How Milk, Meat and Muscle Shaped the World*. Without refrigeration, milk couldn't travel farther than a day's drive before it spoiled. And a day's drive in 1769 didn't get one very far—twenty miles at the most. The only way to store milk in the eighteenth century—just as had been done for millennia before that—was to curdle it for yogurt, cheese, and butter. The Ranneys did produce cheese and butter, but without a decent transportation network, it wasn't destined for far-flung places. (Today's localvores are different from the denizens of the 1700s only in that we have a choice about where our food comes from.)

That all changed with the advent of the railroad. Benjamin Ranney wasn't alive to see it; he died in 1824, passing the fledgling farm on to his son Daniel. But by 1854, railroad cars packed with iced butter were running from Franklin County in northern Vermont to Boston. Vermont produced about 4 percent of the country's butter and 8 percent of the country's cheese—more, per capita, than any other state. That Vermont contained only 2 percent of the nation's cows shows the advantage it enjoyed by its proximity to rapidly urbanizing areas.

At around the same time, the Midwest was seeing a surge of its own dairy industry. The story of a Sauk County, Wisconsin, farmer named N. W. Morley is emblematic of the shift. Morley was a progressive farmer who postulated that he'd never make any money growing wheat. The wheat growers around him were thankful for the 80 cents per bushel they were being paid, but Morley could sense trouble. The yields were shrinking each year, the thin glacial soil growing more barren with every harvest. He tried raising peppermint and turning it into oil, but that, too, proved disappointing. He had already seen farmers in nearby Lake County successfully switch to dairy farming, so he gathered up some cattle and built a fieldstone cheese factory. The Chicago, Milwaukee & St. Paul Railroad Company had just built a rail line that connected Milwaukee, LaCrosse, and Kilborn City, the latter of which was just sixteen miles north of his farm near Baraboo, allowing him to sell his cheese to burgeoning cities with relative ease. He turned a profit immediately, and other farmers caught on. Within a few years, many of them had abandoned wheat and put in their lot with Morley.

H. H. Flint, one of Morley's neighbors, remembers the economic transformation of the area this way: "The farm mortgages were soon lifted. The old log house was replaced by a large and imposing dwelling. The old straw sheds gave place to large frame barns, stables and outbuildings. Now and then, a farmer would stick to grain, but he remained in the same old rut—no enterprise, no improvements." Morley was at the beginning of an agricultural trend that would turn Wisconsin into the number one dairy state—and the state with the largest number of small dairy farms—for the next 150 years. Minnesota clung to its wheat a little longer than Wisconsin, but by the turn of the century dairy had become a pillar of that state's economy, too.

The expanding dairy market in the Northeast didn't make Daniel Ranney rich, but it afforded him the luxury of specialization. His subsistence farm had become a dairy farm because he could count on a regular supply chain for cheese and butter going to southern New England. So he cleared a few more acres of land—using a Morgan horse instead of the ox of his father's generation—exposing additional hump-backed fields littered with glacial till, and added ten cattle to his herd. He sold milk to his neighbors out of forty-gallon tin cans for 40 to 80 cents per quart, seasonal fluctuations in milk production playing a large role in the market rate.

The pattern of demand for butter would continue through the Civil War years, with population growth asking more of dairy farmers, and dairy farmers, in turn, becoming more commercially sophisticated. Creameries sprouted up throughout Vermont, and butter production increased from 5,000 pounds in 1879 to 22 million pounds in 1899.[1] Along the only major road in Westminster West were scattered twenty small dairy farms, many of them sending their milk north to the cheese factory in the village of Saxton's River.

PRICED TO MOOVE

Fluid milk production was slower to expand than that of cheese and butter, due to the limitations of refrigeration technology. And it was still a completely unregulated industry. But before it could be regulated, there had to be a fair and predictable way to measure and price it.

Up until the 1890s, milk was priced, like most any other liquid, by volume. Milk, however, has some characteristics that make it unique. First of all, its color may conceal attempts by less-than-honest farmers to add water to their milk cans. Second, milk is composed of two main components—butterfat and skim milk—both of which can vary by producer, cow, stage of lactation, and season. Under the volume-based system, people and creameries were paying the same amount for all varieties of milk, and getting milk that was sometimes watery or thick with fat. There was no uniformity.

A chemist by the name of Stephen Babcock sought a solution. Babcock, a New Yorker who had been educated at Tufts and Cornell, took a position on the faculty at the University of Wisconsin at Madison. By 1888 the dairy industry had become an integral part of Wisconsin's economy, and many farmers and processing plants were calling for a better way to gauge the value of milk—each, it seemed, was tired of getting screwed by the other. The dean of the College of Agriculture, William Henry, asked Babcock to figure it out.

Babcock was a meticulous scientist who was known for his common sense and attention to detail. He also didn't like being interrupted, so he never put a telephone in his house, and would let his office phone ring endlessly while he performed his tests. After working for a few months, he developed a method that allowed a lay person to measure the butterfat content in milk, and it produced accurate results on every cow in the university's herd except for one—a Jersey named Sylvia. His friends congratulated him, saying "You've done it, Dr. Babcock!" But Babcock wasn't convinced. "No test is going out with my name on it unless it is perfect," he told them. After working a few more weeks on the problem, he burst into the dean's office in a rare fever of excitement. "Well, I have it at last!" he exclaimed.[2]

And he did. The Babcock Test, as it's known today, is an easy and inexpensive way to determine the fat content of milk, and it's used in every dairy plant across the globe. This is how it works: measure 17.6 millimeters of milk in a graduated test tube, and add another 17.6 millimeters of 90-percent sulfuric acid. Put the mixture in a centrifuge at 50 degrees Celsius. When it's done spinning, measure the weight of the fat floating on top. The secret Babcock had uncovered was that sulfuric acid dissolves everything in milk except for fat; the centrifuge merely ensures that the fat floating on top doesn't have any air bubbles in it. Babcock could have patented his invention and made a fortune, but he demurred, choosing to give the knowledge to the dairy industry for free. To this day, milk is priced by weight—hence, dollars per hundredweight—adjusted for milkfat content. The first Babcock testers, looking like giant iron heirloom tomatoes with a crank, still huddle in the corners of a few barns in Vermont, under decades of cobwebs.

The third generation of Ranneys on the Ranney Farm, Henry, witnessed a tumultuous time for the United States and, sometimes in direct proportion, for dairy farmers. By 1900 milk producers had started banding together in cooperative associations in order to bargain with fluid milk dealers or handlers for a flat price for all milk. The efforts were ahead of their time, but they didn't last—nobody had agreed to share the costs of maintaining a milk reserve to cover unanticipated short-run demand requirements, and eventually the scheme disintegrated.

Henry Ranney never had a chance to join a co-op—the first cooperatives in Vermont started in 1919, and they were located in the northern part of the state. He was, however, the first in his family to abandon animal power for a tractor. Tractors were ornery, crude implements in the early twentieth century, but they were much faster at plowing than horses, and Henry could now break up his fields in the spring in just two weeks, a job that used to take him four.

The expense was justified because Vermont still enjoyed a competitive advantage for fluid milk, as refrigerated milk trains connected the state to the thirsty Boston market in 1920. Some western

Vermont farmers had even become part of the New York City milk-shed, which, in 1841, had been the first to be connected to a railroad. By 1930, 85 percent of the milk made in Vermont was being shipped out of state.

It didn't take long, however, for the Midwest to erode Vermont's competitive advantage in the fluid milk market—all it needed was a reliable, efficient transportation link to the Northeast, and the Mid-west would be able to undercut Vermont: its production costs were lower, since it has a longer pasture season and the ability to grow its own feed. It finally achieved that in the 1930s, and New England dairy farms have been declining ever since.

A NEW DEAL FOR DAIRY

The Great Depression changed the dairy industry drastically. It was the dividing line between a time of unrestricted milk markets, and federally controlled pricing systems and subsidies. While the De-pression alone was not responsible for all government-run dairy programs, it did give rise to the biggest, most influential one: the federal milk marketing order.

The roots of that program were laid in the "milk wars" of the 1920s—fierce price competition between milk cooperatives serv-ing the same regions. That behavior contributed to the drastic price swings at the time. Another source was the seasonal fluctuation of milk supply: in the spring, when cows give a lot of milk, prices sagged; in the fall, when milk production wanes, prices went up. The result was massive instability and unpredictability in the market.

The Great Depression was the catalyst for change. Within two years after the stock market crashed, the country was so poor that milk became a luxury. Demand for it dropped precipitously, and a classified pricing system that had developed in the 1920s based on the end use of the product broke down as well. The dairy coop-eratives, blessed with an exemption to the Sherman Anti-Trust Act (more on this in Chapter Eight), rallied for government intervention to stabilize prices. "The attitude of the milk-shed representatives, Agriculture Secretary Henry Wallace recalled, was, 'For God's sake do something and do it quick!'"[3] Roosevelt's nascent New Deal stepped in with the Agricultural Adjustment Act of 1933. This law authorized Wallace to enter into marketing agreements with handlers and processors to raise the price of agricultural commodities, including milk. Its central goal was crop control and bringing supply in line with demand. Though the Supreme Court would later strike down the law as unconstitutional, it was reshaped two years later and went unchallenged. The act laid the foundation for the Agricultural Marketing Agreement Act of 1937, which is the basis of the federal milk marketing order today.

The marketing order, regulated by the Agricultural Marketing Service at the USDA, was designed to "ensure consumers an adequate supply of wholesome milk for drinking, and an adequate price for producers—a little stability," says Robert Cropp, an emeritus professor of agricultural economics at the University of Wisconsin. Aside from some technical provisions about the components of price formulas, the marketing order remains largely unchanged more than seventy-four years after it was first conceived.

The most important thing to know about the order is that it sets minimum prices for fluid-grade milk—prices that processors or handlers must pay to dairy farmers and cooperatives. They can pay more, of course, but rarely do. The prices are differentiated by region, the number of which has consolidated steadily from thirty-four to ten, reflecting the greater distances milk regularly travels today.

One major problem is that the federal milk marketing order price has nothing to do with the cost of production in the different regions; it's all based on supply and demand, and, strangely, how far from Eau Claire, Wisconsin, the milk is produced. In recent years, the Southeast region has had the highest floor price in the country, and that's because Florida has a huge and unmet demand for milk. The Northeast has one of the lowest marketing order prices, because there's a glut of milk. The effect is that the floor price in the Northeast, where the cost of producing milk is the highest, is usually just a few cents more than it is in Western and Southern states. Dairy farmers in the Northeast, who are receiving a few dollars less per hundredweight than their Southern colleagues, would like to ship their milk to Florida, but the hauling costs are prohibitive.

The regulation has created a sort of perverse incentive: the higher price in the Southeast encourages Southern farmers to produce more and meet that demand. The low price in the Northeast encourages farmers to produce more and make up the price losses with volume gains. As will be shown later on, all roads lead to increased supply and, therefore, lower prices.

===

Rollin Ranney was the farm's steward during the Great Depression. In Vermont at the time, one-third of the population lived on farms, and though many of them didn't lose money in the stock market crash, their livelihoods depended on fair prices for their products. And since Vermont shipped most of its milk to the Boston market, the state could not insulate itself from the nation's financial calamity. Vermont farmers, preternaturally tough people, had their farm machines repossessed only to dust off the scythes hanging in their barns. They had little choice. Ranney was well positioned because he farmed in one of the most efficient ways possible, using rotational grazing. He didn't need to plant much corn and barely used grain to feed his cows. The house had been in the family for generations, so mortgage debt was not a concern. Rollin also had three strong boys, who provided all the free farm labor he could want. By the time one of them, Arthur, took over the farm, the dairy industry had again changed dramatically

During World War Two there was a huge demand for milk and dairy products: wartime employment led to higher incomes and increased consumption, and the military purchased millions of pounds of cheese, butter, canned milk, and dried milk. Dairy farmers were glad to make more milk, but they needed some help to do it. The government guaranteed higher wages to farmers, and wartime price controls kept prices down for consumers, with processors receiving subsidies to make up the difference. Out of this era came the Agricultural Act of 1949, which established the second government-regulated influence on the dairy industry: a permanent milk price support program.

As opposed to the federal marketing order, which you can think of as a concrete floor, the price support is akin to a giant vacuum, sucking up all the surplus milk, paying farmers a guaranteed price for it, and then selling it on the market when the price rises. In that way, it's a plain and simple subsidy whereby the USDA's Commodity Credit Corporation says to the dairy farmer: "Make as much milk as you want, and we'll buy enough butter, nonfat dry milk, and cheddar cheese to remove the surplus from the market, all in an effort to keep the price of milk up."

The support price is calculated annually according to provisions in whatever farm bill is most recent. In effect, it has discouraged farmers from limiting their production, because the risk of oversupply is hedged by the government's willingness to be a huge buyer. Wallace's valiant efforts to control farm commodity supplies in the 1930s were, basically, reversed. The floodgates of production opened, and that set off a chain of events.

Farm credit was now easy to come by, as the loans were, in essence, guaranteed by the government price support. The easy money begat more expensive farm equipment, which allowed farmers to manage larger herds. Bulk tanks were installed in most farms by the early 1960s, which meant that milkers no longer had to fill up 40-gallon tin cans. They could now attach their cows to vacuum-powered milk pumps that deposited the milk into giant refrigerated tanks, where it could stay for more than a day before a truck came to pick it up. Innovations in fertilizer and genetically modified corn, plus government subsidies to plant the corn, flooded the market with cheap grain and enabled Midwestern and Western farms to metastasize into 1,000- and 2,000-cow operations, all the while gaining a competitive advantage over small farms in non-corn-intensive states. The changes in the industry could be summed up with one word: consolidation. In 1940, there were roughly 4.5 million dairy farms in the United States. By 1974, that number had fallen to just over 400,000.[4]

In the midst of these changes, Studs Terkel happened to be interviewing a few hundred people around the United States for his book *Working*. Terkel sat down with laborers and asked them to talk freely about their jobs. In all cases, they spoke their minds and described the daily deprivations and violence of work and how what they did defined who they were—or not.

The book was published in 1972, and reading it now, some of the subjects come off as anachronistic, relics from another time: the pharmacist at the corner drugstore, say, or the airline "stewardess" (now they have the PC title of "flight attendant"). At the same time, many of the profiles end up being prophetic, such as Terkel's interview with a Midwestern farmer.

The farmer was Pierce Walker, an older gentleman who grew corn and soybeans on a five-hundred-acre piece of land outside Evansville, Indiana, the same plot his daddy had worked, and his daddy's daddy. He was caught in the undertow of the Green Revolution, a time of unprecedented agricultural expansion, when bigger became better and when Secretary of Agriculture Earl L. Butz told every farmer to plant fence-row to fence-row.

"For a farmer," Walker said, "the return on your investment is so small now that it isn't really worthwhile. A younger person cannot start farming unless they have help from a father or somebody. 'Cause you have to be able to retire a rich man to start out. The only way the farmers are making it today is the ones in business keep getting bigger, to kinda offset the acreage, the margin income. I don't know what's going to happen in the future. I'm afraid it's gonna get rough in time to come."

Walker was stuck between a rock and a hard place, just as so many dairy farmers are today: "The big complaint you hear is that when you take your product to the market, you take what they give you. When you go buy on the other end, you pay what they say. So you're at their mercy on both ends, more or less."

Arthur Ranney, like many Vermonters, was skeptical of the easy credit and the allure of bigger machines to feed more cows that would pump out more milk. On some points, however, he had no choice but to modernize. Bulk tanks, while a major expense, were worth it because they saved so much time. Many New England farmers, already injured by the competition from larger farms, elected not to invest in the tanks, and they simply went on to do other things. Some became builders, mechanics, or snack-bar owners. Ranney was committed to the farm, but he had no desire to grow it. For as long as he could recall, the Ranney farm milked no more than seventy cows, and that was enough for him.

By the time Arthur Ranney retired in 1980 he had witnessed almost a wholesale transformation of the dairy business. Farms where cows were fed mostly grass, once the rule, were now the exception. Corn had become king, and the Holstein its queen. Many cows were now denied even the basic natural function of sex, as artificial insemination was more of a sure bet. By those measures, the Ranney farm was an anachronism. But it was still alive and appeared to have the force of history on its side.

Arthur Ranney's nephew, Harold, took over the farm next. He witnessed another set of supply-side innovations: antibiotics and artificial growth hormones, such as recombinant bovine somatotropin—rBST. The antibiotics seemed like a good idea to Harold—his cows, like anyone else's, occasionally got sick, and it just made sense to treat them with something effective. The growth hormones, on the other hand, contradicted his philosophy about dairy farming, as they were designed purely to put more milk into the system. The Jerseys on his farm were never bred for maximum production; it wasn't in their genes, and it wasn't in his, either.

All of these ever-growing cogs in the milk machine, combined with the dairy price support system, proved one thing: when Americans want to make milk, they can get damn good at it. Too good, in fact, because during most of the 1970s up through the early 1980s, we were drowning in milk, and that meant prices were low. In turn, the price support system kicked into high gear to buy up the supply, and the government spent billions on nonfat dry milk and cheese. The federal government had so much of it that it had to think of new ways to store the stuff. For a time, Armageddon-like, the USDA stockpiled cheese in caves in Utah and Kansas; when room ran out we offered cheese to people on food stamps, and shipped nonfat milk to hungry people in Third World countries.

Our default setting in this country when it comes to milk is "make more." That's because, at first, it's just easier to scale up than it is to scale down. The former can be as simple as adding a few cows to the herd, or adjusting the feed ration, or milking three times a day instead of two. But to downsize, apart from going against some innate American taboo, means "culling cows" by removing them from the herd and selling them for slaughter. This is made especially difficult when there are farm loans to pay—fixed costs that factor in a given income level, which is based on selling a given quantity of milk. So, while the problem of too much milk could be solved by just making less, that's often a last resort. Which is why, in the mid-1980s, the government came up with an interesting idea: if Americans don't want to drink and eat all this milk and cheese, let's find someone who does. In a word: export.

There was just one problem: the rest of the world also had too much milk. The European countries had responded in much the same way that the United States did: by paying subsidies to farmers. They also subsidized their exports, which depressed the world dairy market. Into this situation the United States came with typical muscle, creating the Dairy Export Incentive Program (DEIP). Since the world market price was lower than the U.S. domestic price, exporters had no economic incentive to sell milk and cheese abroad. DEIP fixed that by providing two types of special deals to exporters. The first option was the old buy-two-get-one-free offer, where the exporter says to the foreign importer, "If you buy five thousand pounds of cheese, we'll throw in three thousand pounds of nonfat dry milk at no extra cost." When that failed there was the hard currency solution, which involved paying direct cash bonuses to exporters, allowing the exporters to sell dairy products at a lower price than they had paid to acquire them. The program was never a huge beast—the government spent, at most, a few million dollars a year on it. The DEIP is still in effect today, but it's been largely inactive since 2005, because world prices are now high enough that exporters don't need a boost from the government.

Dairy exports rose steadily after the DEIP was installed, which was good for farmers. But, simultaneously, the government's commitment to the price support system began to wane. Starting in the early 1990s, the Commodity Credit Corporation scaled back its purchases of everything except for nonfat dry milk. At a cost of nearly $1 billion in 1991, it was just getting too expensive. Furthermore, support prices were set well below market rates, rendering the program nearly useless.

To make things worse, the federal milk marketing order began tracking the commodity prices on the Chicago Mercantile Exchange. This had the effect of tying the stabilizing force of the federal order to the volatile tendencies of the commodities exchange. To understand why this is bad for farmers requires a short lesson in how the federal order price is set. Beware: this is almost comically complicated. But to follow it is to understand one of the key causes of depressed milk prices, farm closures, and all the strife attendant upon that.

From the beginning, the federal order was designed to set a minimum price for Grade B milk—the stuff used in manufacturing cheese, butter, and nonfat dry milk. Grade B is inferior to Grade A because the standards are lower for bacteria, somatic cell count, and on-farm cooling facilities. The price of Grade A milk, what we drink, was based on the Grade B price plus a "differential"—a value dictated by the region where the milk was produced. The USDA would

set the price for Grade B milk by sending a weekly survey to the butter, cheese, and powdered milk plants in Minnesota and Wisconsin,
asking how much those plants paid the farmers or cooperatives for
Grade B milk. The USDA picked Minnesota and Wisconsin as the
basis for the national price, because those areas reflected the average
price of milk in the United States. Why? Because those states had
such a bounty of milk that when other areas—the Southeast, for
example—ran short on milk, they would get shipments from the
upper Midwest. So it was, in effect, a national market. Eau Claire,
Wisconsin, was the center of the Minnesota/Wisconsin market,
which is why the price of milk went up as one got farther from that
city—it was designed to reflect the increased cost of shipping.

This was the way milk was priced for decades. Then something
changed. Farmers, for the most part, stopped making Grade B
milk—their milking methods had become so clean and efficient
that it was extra work to set aside a lower grade of milk. Everyone
was going to Grade A. That threw the USDA's system out of whack,
so it was revised to be based on a "product price formula." The new
formula has four classes of milk: Class I is fluid milk for drinking;
Class II is for cottage cheese, yogurt, and ice cream; Class III is for
cheese; and Class IV is for nonfat dry milk and butter. In addition,
instead of asking the cheese and butter plants how much they paid
for Grade B milk, the new USDA survey, which goes out every Friday
through the National Agricultural Statistical Service (NASS), asks
the plants a slightly different question: "How much do wholesalers and/or retailers pay you for your cheese, butter and nonfat dry
milk?" Which means the price of the ingredient—milk—is based
on the price of the final product. But in order to reverse engineer
the price of an ingredient from the value of, say, cheese, you have to
do some math involving the end price, the "make allowance" (how
much it costs the plant to manufacture the cheese), and the "yield"
(how much milk it takes to make cheese). The equation is as follows:
Milk Price = (price of cheese) − (make allowance) / yield.

The equation is the same, whether the product is cheese, butter, or nonfat dry milk (just substitute the end product where appropriate). This results in a national price for these products. Then the price of milk in the various marketing regions is achieved by adding a differential to the higher of the cheese or butter/powder price, according to the prevailing supply and demand situation in that particular region. In the Southeast, where supply is short, the differential added to cheese is about $5. In the Northeast, the differential is about $3.

The catch is this: when the cheese and butter plants answer the NASS survey, they are free to use the commodity prices from the Chicago Mercantile Exchange (CME), instead of the price for which they sell their products to wholesalers. Since it's much easier to report the commodity price, that's what they do. Which would be fine, except for one thing: the CME is where producers go to sell their cheese and butter when they have too much of it. In essence, then, the CME price is the lowest possible price the market will bear.

Here's an example. Say the Associated Milk Producers Cooperative (AMPC), out in the Midwest, has some extra cheese it wants to sell. If it can't strike a private deal with Kraft or some other company, it offers the cheese for sale on the CME. Let's say the cheese price is currently $1.40. AMPC will offer its cheese for $1.40, but doesn't get any takers. Then along comes a buyer who says, "I'll give you $1.30 for your cheese." AMPC says, "Deal," and the new national price of cheese becomes $1.30.

Thus, this little transaction for a tractor-trailer's worth of cheese has a huge power over the dairy market. Even though the commodity price indicates only what some desperate milk cooperative will sell its surplus cheese for, that price becomes the baseline indicator for the entire milk industry.

When this system took effect, farmers became subject to a hand more invisible and less benevolent than that of the government, and they were further disconnected from the people who actually consumed the product they so lovingly brought to market. A new, inverse relationship took shape: as the price support became more vestigial, the commodity market for dairy products grew in its capacity for volatility. This has continued to the present day, and it's a major reason why so many dairy farmers feel helpless against the deflated market.

A COMPACT SOLUTION

"We had things fixed," Tom Debevoise says, sitting in a white Adirondack chair in front of his yellow farmhouse in South Woodstock, Vermont. He is referring to the Northeast Dairy Compact, a program created in the 1996 Farm Bill that allowed the six New England states to regulate the price of milk produced and sold within their borders.

The hills around Debevoise's house used to be alive with farms, but now the place is firmly in horse country. It's the home of the Green Mountain Horse Association, and on most summer weekends passersby can see stiff-backed equestrians leading their steeds through a gauntlet of maneuvers in perfectly manicured rings. Others drag their horses in trailers and meet for fox hunts—or an approximation of the old practice, since they don't hunt fox so much as gambol through the woods in period dress with a bunch of hounds.

Debevoise, fifty-four, barefoot, and dressed in a blue polo shirt and blue-jeans, is tall and thin, with a basso profundo voice, glasses, and sprawling rough hands that call to mind Jefferson's ideal agrarian citizen. Across the road his sixty-five Holsteins graze on a green hillside, climbing ever higher as the sun declines.

The "average dairy farmer" is a mythical creature, as each has a unique story. But Debevoise is probably less average than the rest. His father, Thomas Debevoise, Sr., was a prominent attorney in Washington, DC, then the attorney general of Vermont, the first dean of the Vermont Law School, and a personal legal counselor to Laurence Rockefeller. Tom Debevoise spent the school year in Washington and summers in Woodstock, where his parents had a hobby farm on the west side of town. He became interested in agriculture at a young age, and though he was accepted into Cornell University's College of Agriculture and Life Sciences, he was also given the green light at Yale, and his father prevailed on him to choose the latter. After graduating with a degree in history, he returned to Woodstock to manage the farmland of the recently defunct Woodstock Country Day School. He got some beef cows going there, and then he and his wife rented a dairy farm in the nearby town of Pomfret. When he told the owner of the Woodstock Country Day property that he was leaving to find his own dairy farm, the owner worked out a lease-purchase agreement with the Debevoises, and they've been there ever since.

Debevoise is a friendly, patient, even upbeat fellow. He exhibits none of the financial stress and worry that emanated from the Simpsons or the Moores or Ranney. And that's because, generally, he has none of it. When he saw the cash-flow crunch coming in 2008, he sold his less productive cows and refinanced his farm loans. His feed costs are low because the farm has rich soil and thus rich grass. When he needed some money, he sold some of the hardwood timber on his property—essentially taking assets out of savings. His wife is a veterinarian in Springfield, so there's a diversity of income. They have three sons, two of whom work on the farm all summer for next to no pay. He has postponed repairs.

"We've been conservative," Debevoise says. And that's true. But other factors are at play, too. Milking just sixty-five head, his overhead is low and his debt is manageable. Furthermore, a smaller farm with dual incomes allows a family to spread the risk of low milk prices. When times are good, they're flush. When prices fall, the income from the nonfarmer in the family kicks in to cover losses. By avoiding the trap of specialization, the Debevoises seemed to have taken a page from the 1700s. Compared to the anguished faces of Bob Simpson and Ray Moore, Debevoise's was bizarrely serene.

That a dairy crisis raging seems tragic to Debevoise, because a good solution had been in place for a few years in the form of the

Northeast Dairy Compact. The creation of the compact was perhaps the most strident rebuke to the milk marketing order, which, in the absence of an effective price support program, had become more important to milk pricing than it had been since 1949.

Farmers in the six New England states had long known that it's more expensive to make milk in the Northeast than it is almost anywhere else in the United States. Farmers there have to face a short growing season, long winters, and grain that must be trucked in from Canada or the Midwest. The marketing order wasn't accounting for these facts, and farmers struggled to make ends meet. The states, as a group, wanted to set their own price for milk, but because of the Compact Clause of the Constitution, they couldn't form such a group absent the consent of Congress.

Dairy farmers in New England successfully lobbied Congress in the mid-90s, and they got their compact. For milk produced in New England, the compact paid a guaranteed rate to farmers based on the local cost of production. If the federal marketing order didn't pay a certain threshold price, the compact would collect premiums from milk processors, deposit it in a pool of funds, and then distribute it monthly to farmers.

Congress also granted the compact the authority to regulate the price of milk that was shipped into New England from anywhere else in the United States, by requiring processors to pay an "over-order" premium into the compact's pool. This was a crucial component of the compact's power; without it, retailers in New England would be free to obtain their milk from states outside the compact's area, where the prices weren't as regulated and the costs of production were lower.

Debevoise's cooperative, Cabot, pushed hard for the legislation, and it seemed to be working. The price of milk to consumers was stabilizing, and fewer farms were going out of business. Connecticut, which had been losing twenty farms per year before 1996, lost just a quarter that many during the year after the compact was enacted. New York, which had hurled unsuccessful legal challenges at the compact in its first years, decided to become a member itself. (Congress also stated that six additional states—Delaware, New Jersey, New York, Pennsylvania, Maryland, and Virginia—could join the compact, if upon entry the state is contiguous to a participating state and if Congress consents.) Farmers weren't making a mint, but they were at least covering their costs.

The compact, however, had some powerful enemies, most notably Republican legislators from the Midwest. Their constituents, they argued, were being undercut by a milk cartel, which also had the effect of increasing milk prices to consumers. The compact needed congressional reauthorization in the fall of 2001. A few months prior to that, Vermont's senator James Jeffords, who had done the most work to push the bill through Congress, abandoned the Republican Party to become an Independent. The defection appeared to be another insult to red states in the heartland, and it made the compact's political future even more uncertain. "Milk is a regional blood sport inside the dynamics of Congress," New York representative Thomas M. Reynolds told a reporter. "It's always a tough fight."[5]

But that fight never ensued. Instead, 9/11 happened, preoccupying Congress and the rest of the nation. The compact quietly ran out of time and disappeared into history.

MILC MONEY

The USDA has long known of the cyclical nature of the dairy industry. It seems that every three years, milk prices ride the rollercoaster from highs in the $20 per hundredweight range, to lows in the $12s. Indeed, the federal programs mentioned thus far have attempted to smooth those swings, but they seem powerless against the larger, stochastic forces of the global economy, weather, and political action. The factors at play boggle the brain. Is there a shortage of replacement heifers? Is the Western alfalfa crop weak? Was there a flood in Pakistan? A drought in Australia? Does new research declare that consuming dairy causes acne? What about a hurricane? Is ethanol hot? Is a case of salmonella poisoning on the front page of *USA Today*?

Yet the federal government, to its credit, hasn't given up on dairy farmers. On the contrary, it redoubles its efforts every few years with programs attacking the problem from different angles. They betray the belief that the solution to any of the supply and demand issues is simply to throw money at various people. It seems that each successive federal program attempts to remedy the unintended consequences of the previous one. The price support program flooded the country with milk, and the Dairy Export Incentive Program came in to fix it. Never mind that it didn't work. When the USDA changed the formula for the federal order, tying it more closely to the Chicago Mercantile Exchange, the market prices dropped, necessitating yet another government subsidy: the Milk Income Loss Contract (MILC).

This program with the quaint acronym can be thought of as a national version of the defunct Northeast Dairy Compact. When the compact was allowed to expire, politicians in states with a lot of small and medium-size farms fought for some consolation. In 2002, they got MILC, which gives farmers a direct payment from the government when the price of Class I milk falls below $16.94 in the Boston market. Giving farmers 100 percent of the difference between $16.94 and the actual price would have been entirely too expensive, so the law ratchets it down to between 34 and 45 percent. The program sends farmers money only when their production is at or below 2.4 million pounds of milk—about the amount that a 130-cow operation produces in one year. Once a farm goes above that number during a calendar year, it's not eligible for MILC payments. There's also a feed-cost bonus added to the payment if the National Average Dairy Feed Ration Adjustment—basically, a ration between inputs and outputs—is greater than $7.35.

Fashioning these complex support structures is a fraught adventure. In one corner, you have the small-government advocates who call MILC unfair ("How many other nonfarming entrepreneurs in America receive government insurance against the risk of running their own business?"),[6] expensive (hundreds of millions of dollars per year), and counterproductive ("It creates incentives for farmers to be less careful about production decisions").[7] In another corner, you have the small farms for which the program has been a saving grace. And in yet another corner are the megafarms, those that can make 2.4 million pounds of milk in a few days, who say that MILC doesn't help them at all, and, in fact, keeps too many small farms in business and the price of milk low. In a sense, they're all right.

THE SEVENTH GENERATION

Philip Ranney had never intended to be a dairy farmer. Though he liked being out in the fields during the summer, and he had a good relationship with the animals, there were a few things about dairy-ing that didn't appeal to him. For one, he hated milking cows. And for another, he disliked being cooped up in a barn all day, throwing hay bales into the loft.

So after high school, he went off to work for Pepsi and held a series of clerical jobs in the Northeast. "But I always found myself in the same situation: working somewhere else but being more concerned about what was going on here at the farm," he said. He started to think, *Do I really want to work off the farm, or is my heart here on the land?* The other jobs just seemed generic; anybody could do them. Running a family dairy farm had a personal connection. It was dif-ficult to ignore his heritage.

His first year of full-time work on the farm was in 1999, and he worked with his dad to overcome his dislike of milking. For the next few years he was the farm's only other employee besides Harold, and he gradually learned the business and the science of raising dairy cows. He took charge of the herd's health, the cropping, and the breeding. Harold, who was happy to see his son join the family business, tapered down his own involvement until he was just doing the afternoon milking.

In February of 2007, Philip and his wife, Teah, took the plunge. They purchased the herd from Harold and Joyce, his wife, and got a farm loan for the equipment. It was an auspicious time for the young couple to enter the dairy industry, as milk prices were at healthy levels.

Philip got up every morning excited to be alive. He'd walk from the modest Cape he'd built a few years earlier along an old town road to the night paddocks and see his fifty-five Jerseys, lounging on the grass like bleached mounds of granite. When they saw him coming they would get up and congregate by the electric fence, lowing and gently jockeying for space. He led them into the barn for the morning milking and, three hours later, they would follow him single-file across the paved road. On a calm day, all he could hear as he walked were hoof beats and the breathing of the cows. Sometimes his pet pigeon, Bridget — which a neighbor had rescued from under a bridge along Interstate 91 — would fly over and land on his head. He'd take the cows in a long line up the cowpath that traversed a hillside and then disappeared over a ridge to the upper paddocks. He did it in all kinds of weather; if it rained, he got wet. But on clear days, the view of the 3,100-foot Mt. Monadnock, across the river in New Hampshire, made it all worthwhile.

There were enough paddocks so that the cows had a fresh field to munch every day for two weeks, dining on rich timothy, fescue, and clover washed clean by periodic rains. They would also search out nettles, buckthorn, and other weeds along the line of the forest, choosing whichever plant had the vitamins and minerals they needed. Philip, for exercise, jogged back to the farm. At 2:30 the cows knew it was time for the second milking, and they would line up again at the gate by the road, like school children waiting for the crossing guard. Philip would lead them back into the barn for the evening milking and then put them out into a different paddock for the night.

From November to April the cycle slowed down. He would still milk the cows twice a day, but lacking any grass to eat outside, he kept them in the barn for all but two hours a day, during which time they could stretch their legs and remember what it was like to see the sky. Cows are naturally warm creatures—their normal resting body temperature is 101.5 degrees Fahrenheit—so keeping them inside most of the day allowed him to avoid paying to heat the barn. They ate a mixture of dry square hay bales, pickled hay, corn silage, and a little grain. The hay Philip cut and baled himself; the corn silage he either grew or purchased from a nearby farm; the grain he had trucked from Quebec. The proportions in the feed were calculated to keep the cows as healthy as possible. His vet had told him to think of the cows' stomachs as a system of connected barrels, and if he fed them too much short-length hay and high-protein grain, the feed would go right through them. Such a diet could also increase their chances of getting a displaced abdomen, a dangerous condition in which the stomachs get tangled around each other, requiring expensive surgery to remedy. So Philip made sure to keep the hay long, and to go easy on the grain. It was less expensive that way, too. Given his druthers, Philip would graze the cows all year long; but there was just no getting around the six months of freezing cold, snow, and mud.

This honeymoon period, when he needed to worry about nothing except his cows' health and milk production, didn't last. Within a year, fuel and grain costs had risen by almost 50 percent, and the milk price was dropping steadily. The Ranney farm was now a member of the Cabot cooperative—his father had finally joined in 2000—but that began to seem like more of a hindrance than a benefit. Philip, relatively new to the milking business, was fresh enough to question the utility of the co-op. When prices went south, those thoughts just increased. "Having to pay Agrimark [Cabot's parent company] to come pick up the milk was like rubbing salt into an open wound," he said. That cost alone was $10,000 per year. Moreover, the milk truck would plug its pump into Ranney's electric supply. He never added up the cost of having a 220-volt motor pump five thousand gallons of milk every other day, but he was sure it was expensive. "It just seems totally unfair," he said.

Philip resolved to give the farm another year. He hoped and prayed that the milk price would go up. The longer time went on, the more depressed he got. The situation was beginning to affect his home life, too. Without the means to pay a part-time employee, Ranney was doing everything himself. It was sixteen hours per day, seven days a week. He missed spending time with Teah, Garrett, and Sawyer. He missed being able to go for a mountain bike ride and clear his head.

It was February of 2009 when he first entertained the thought of selling the herd, but he kept it to himself for a few months. The possibility felt like such a betrayal that he was scared to utter it out loud. In the meantime, the reality of his finances had come into stark relief. He owed his parents a monthly payment for the cows, and he owed the bank a monthly payment for the farm loan. His father had sold most of the land to a state senator (then governor) named Peter Shumlin, who leased the farmland to the Ranneys for the cost of the property taxes — just $5,000 per year. While that was good, it also meant that Philip had no equity and no collateral for a short-term loan. When May arrived and the milk price hadn't improved, Ranney had no choice but to put the herd up for sale. "I just couldn't continue on any longer," he said. "The debt was rising too fast and there wasn't enough money coming in."

This decision, the hardest one he's ever made, forced him to begin separating himself psychologically from the cows, many of which he had calved and raised when he was in high school. This wasn't easy, since he spent most of his day with them. He tried to dial down his affection, his pet naming, his tender-voiced calls. He tried to think of them the way most of the dairy industry does: as milk machines. "I told myself every day, it's just a matter of time before they're gone," he said. One consolation was that he was so preoccupied with avoiding bankruptcy that he had little mental energy left to be playful with the animals. They had become something like unloved kids. "To tell you the truth," he said, "I don't know how I did it some days."

Selling cows is a difficult thing to do when they represent an immediate liability for the purchaser. He had paid his parents $900 per cow, so he had to clear at least that much on the other side. But few people in the dairy industry had any money, never mind the extra cash to buy a herd of rotationally grazed Jerseys. He finally found a buyer in June, but she canceled the deal at the closing table. While he had hoped to sell them to a small farm like his own, where the cows could eat grass and live mostly in the pasture, time was running out; he had to prepare himself for selling his girls to anyone who would buy them. "I had to put my own life ahead of theirs," he lamented.

In July, the local newspaper ran a story about the farm, and within a few days Ranney received a call from a farmer in New York who wanted the cows. The buyer agreed to pay Ranney $1,400 per cow, as long as he could pay it in installments over two years. Ranney agreed and was relieved to see the cows go to a good home. By late September, the farmer had been foreclosed upon and was forced to move the cows yet again, this time to a farm outside Schenectady. As of this writing, the cows are in good health, giving fifty pounds per day, and have joined the other herd without a problem.

In the early fall, the trees next to the interstate highway in southern Vermont blush red and yellow, and those higher in the hills turn a deeper orange, like shaggy upside-down pumpkins. Westminster West is a ridgeline enclave about four miles from the center of Putney, a lively town of cultured hippies, artists, and tenacious back-to-the-landers. Local food is as important to these people as the open space and maple trees around them. Within a ten-mile radius are numerous cheese-makers who have won best-in-show awards at the American Cheese Society's annual conference. You can get artisan-quality sheep cheese, goat cheese, and raw milk of any variety by simply finding a dirt road and following it uphill. In the summer, it all flows downhill to the farmers' markets, where pop-up tents burst with every imaginable perishable that can take root in Vermont's soil. In short, it's probably the most hospitable context for a farm of sustainably milked Jersey cows. That the Ranneys couldn't make it there, after more than two hundred years of persistence, is a testament to the severity of the dairy crisis and the dysfunctional nature of the milk pricing scheme.

Within two months of selling his cows, Ranney had come up with the beginnings of a business plan for the farm. It involved selling turkeys, some beef, raw milk by the side of the road, and milk in small batches to the Consider Bardwell cheese company, which has a cave a half-mile away. He kept ten cows for that purpose, hand-picking the best ones from the herd in order to have a good genetic base upon which to build. The bad luck continued, however: a lightning bolt came down in the middle of his turkey paddock and must have scored a direct hit on a group of birds huddling together. The bolt startled him out of a deep sleep. The next morning, he went out and witnessed the carnage. Eight turkeys had perished from the strike. Some were decapitated. Others had their limbs blown off or were splayed in half. "It was like a horror show out there," he said. He took pictures on his cell phone just in case people didn't believe him.

With the benefit of hindsight, Ranney had formed a clear picture of the dairy industry's primary ailment. "I've thought about this a lot over the past year," he said. "Honestly, what's killing the dairy industry and killing small farms are the big farms." He cited the economy of scale of large operations, and how they have an incentive to put more milk into the system, which does nothing but drive prices down in the long run. "The problem is that every couple of years it crashes, and boy did it crash this time. I have a good feeling that this is it," he explained. "In the next eight months, I'd be very surprised if there isn't a major implosion of the dairy industry."

The economic forecasts implicitly agreed with Ranney's predictions. The cooperatives' monthly outlooks were telling dairy farmers not to expect a price increase for at least a year. The most optimistic economists predicted the milk price to rise to $15 per hundredweight by the spring of 2010, but that would still be $3 below the cost of production. Either way, the conditions that forced so many farmers out of business would persist. "There's no way all these farms can continue on for another eight months," he said. "Nobody's savings accounts are that big. And when it's been two years since you got paid even what it costs you to make it, it's just going to be one farm going down after another."

In an odd way, that news gives Ranney some comfort: at least he didn't sell his herd one month just to see the price of milk rebound the next. "For me, a young guy who took over a farm two years ago," he said, "it makes me feel good about the decision I had to make."

He came up with another counterintuitive observation: the dairy crisis, though painful for many farmers, will be good for the local food movement, which he plans to be a part of. "As long as we can make a product that's not outrageously expensive, but still make a living, people will be able to make a choice about whether they want milk from a 500-cow herd or a 20-cow herd."

It's an optimistic viewpoint, when you consider the disfigurement wrought on the dairy industry. For it to come to pass, there must be a reversal of sorts, a turning back of the clock. There were sixteen dairy farms on the Westminster West Road when Arthur Ranney was farming. Today there are two. Both are wisps of their former selves, with herds a fraction of the size they'd been for a hundred years or more. Philip Ranney might be young enough to see his vision through. But it's too late for the Ray Moores and the thousands of others who, after thirty or forty years of hard, honest work, have little to show for it but a stack of bills and some empty barns.

MILK GONE WILD

The American dairy industry is a sprawling, $150 billion per year business, with reams of statistics, charts, and graphs plotting every data point imaginable. Out of that noise, two signals rise to the surface: milk price and supply. They are closely related, of course, but treated very differently. Think of the two numbers as digital readouts on a wall in a control room, like one you'd find at a nuclear power plant. Under the digits showing the current milk price are an amalgam of dials, knobs, and switches. These are the various federal laws and subsidies, either exerting pressure on the price itself, or mitigating the price's effects on farmers further down the line. But the readout showing milk supply is much more bare-bones. In fact, there are no external controls, no dials to turn or buttons to press. The amount of milk on the market is left to the whim of farmers and the innovations that corporations and land grant colleges can put into their hands. What that means, oftentimes, is that we just have too much milk.

More numbers can tell part of the story. In 1944, the United States had 25.6 million dairy cows. Today, there are about 9 million. Those midcentury cows made a total of 120 billion pounds of milk per year. The modern population pumps out 190 billion pounds. Since 1900, we've increased annual per-cow milk yield from roughly 3,000 pounds to 20,000 pounds—a nearly sevenfold rise. At the same time, even though the U.S. population has doubled in the past sixty years, per capita milk consumption has declined. And that is despite the vigorous efforts by the *Got Milk?* campaign. One effect of this overabundance of milk is that farmers' margins are razor thin, leaving them increasingly vulnerable to the price swings that define the industry. Another effect is less obvious, but more weird. People are drinking less whole milk, and, at the behest of their doctor and the USDA, they're drinking more skim and low-fat milk. This, in turn, has left a lot of excess milk fat on the market—the raw ingredient in cheese. Instead of going through the front door, with a *Got Cheese?* promotion, the USDA formed a subagency called Dairy Management Inc. (DMI) in the mid-1990s to covertly push more cheese into the foods we eat.

As the *New York Times* reported in November 2010, DMI more closely resembles a private corporation than a governmental entity. The chief executive of DMI, Thomas P. Gallagher, earned a salary of $633,475 in 2008, and two other officials made more than $300,000 each. In total, DMI has 162 employees. The budget for this marketing organ, whose goal is to put more saturated fat into American stomachs, tops $135 million per year, paid for largely by a mandatory charge to dairy farmers. Meanwhile, the budget for the USDA's Center for Nutrition Policy and Promotion, an advocate of healthful eating, is $6.5 million.

With these resources, DMI has developed some specific goals and helped many fast food chains launch new cheesier foods. According to internal documents obtained by the *Times* in a Freedom of Information Act request, DMI wants to see more "cheese snacking fanatics" and to increase cheese use in sandwiches and elsewhere. One way it achieves this is to make Americans think that eating cheese can help them lose weight. In a 2005 advertisement in *People* magazine, DMI declared that there's "great news for dieters. Clinical studies show that people on a reduced-calorie diet who consume three servings of milk, cheese or yogurt each day can lose significantly more weight and more body fat than those who just cut calories." How is it that eating a food high in fat can cause a person to lose weight? Ask Michael B. Zemel, a nutritionist at the University of Tennessee who in 2004 wrote *The Calcium Key: The Revolutionary Diet Discovery That Will Help You Lose Weight Faster.* DMI paid Zemel for his research and promoted his book, since it was exactly the message they had been trying to send. DMI just didn't want to look too deeply. Zemel told the *Times* that "precisely how dairy facilitates weight loss is unclear . . . but in part it involves counteracting a hormone that fosters fat deposits when the body is low on calcium."

Zemel, indeed, must have the only key, because other researchers working around the same time weren't able to access his wondrous land of cheese-based weight loss. One of them was Jean Harvey-Berino, chairwoman of the Department of Nutrition and Food Sciences at the University of Vermont. Her research, which was also supported by DMI, found no evidence to corroborate Zemel's claim. Another person who couldn't find the key: Dr. Jack A. Yanovski, an obesity unit chief at the National Institutes of Health. Still, since 2006 DMI has stated that "the available data provide strong support for a beneficial effect of increased dairy foods on body weight and body composition." Scientific fact, it seems, all depends on whom you believe.

While aiming at Americans' heads, DMI also targets their stomachs. Since the late 1990s, DMI has been working with restaurants such as Pizza Hut, Domino's, Wendy's, and Taco Bell to devise new menu items topped, stuffed, coated, and baked with cheese. In a 1999 letter to DMI from Pizza Hut representatives Derek "Lord of the Cheese" Correia and Lisken "Lady of the Cheese" Lawler, the authors excitedly proclaim: "Let's sell more pizza and more cheese!" The first campaign in this effort was Pizza Hut's declaring the summer of 2002 as the "Summer of Cheese." During the twelve-week period, Pizza Hut reintroduced the Stuffed Crust and Insider pizzas, increasing cheese use by 102 million pounds by the fall. In October of 2010, with $12 million worth of DMI's marketing funds, Domino's rolled out a new pizza for its Legends line of cheesier pies. Dubbed the Wisconsin, this pizza featured six types of cheese on top and two more in the crust. It even came in a box that said: "One Good

Cheese Deserves Another Five." Undoubtedly, cheeses play nicely with each other. The same can't be said about cheese in a healthful diet; there, it acts more like a bully than a playmate. One quarter of a medium Wisconsin thin-crust pie had twelve grams of saturated fat, more than three-quarters of the recommended daily maximum.

Even while Dairy Management helps Domino's brainstorm these cheese-blasted concoctions, its parent organization, the USDA, issues nutritional brochures such as "Your Personal Path to Health: Steps to a Healthier You," which provides quick hints on good eating habits. Some of the tips suggest portioning snacks on a plate, "not from the bag, to stay aware of how much you're eating"; and ordering appetizers instead of entrees.

Under "When You 'Order Out,'" it offers the strangest advice: "Make your pizza a veggie with toppings like mushrooms, peppers and onions," it says. And "ask for whole-wheat crust and half the cheese."

It's interesting how one agency is telling Americans to eat more cheese, while another is saying to cut down, and it reveals a central dilemma in the dairy industry today: we've made it easier than ever to get milk from cows, but instead of being happy with those efficiency gains, we've gone the route of the overachiever and just worked harder. It's a classic example of the Jevons Paradox.

In 1865, during the height of the English Industrial Revolution, William Stanley Jevons published *The Coal Question*, a book that probed the connection between England's wealth and its supply of coal. The country was eating through coal at a frightening pace, causing some to wonder if achieving greater efficiencies could prolong the supply. Jevons argued the negative. "It is wholly a confusion of ideas to suppose that the economical use of fuel is equivalent to a diminished consumption," he wrote. "The very contrary is the truth."

In many areas, these words have proven prescient. We design more fuel efficient cars, but end up driving more miles. We enlist the help of computers at work, and they follow us home and on vacation, causing us to work more than ever before. The same has held true in the dairy industry, where efficiency has encouraged farmers to make more milk than people want to buy. But in the dairy business, there's the added twist of a feedback loop: farmers make more milk, prices go down, and then farmers need to make even more to cover their costs. They work smarter, sure, but they can't slow down.

THE BEAST OF BURDEN

Imagine is a big Holstein cow, eating the mix of hay, silage, and grain on the floor in front of her. On a snowy day in Burlington, she's content to be inside the University of Vermont's Miller Research barn, a clean, well-lighted place in the shape of a typical college field house. She is a fine specimen of the modern dairy cow: broad sides, bony hips, good legs, well-shaped udders. The man in charge of her is John Barlow, an assistant professor of animal science and the director of the CREAM (Cooperative for Real Education in Agricultural Management) program, which teaches UVM students how to be dairy farmers or work in the dairy industry. On this January day, Barlow is wearing a black skullcap, a few layers of fleece jackets, and knee-high rubber boots. He's stocky and soft-spoken and bears a slight resemblance to a younger Bill Murray, circa *Stripes*. Barlow grew up in northeastern Connecticut and milked cows during high school, developing a deep interest in animal physiology. He was fond of James Herriot's books about the life of a country veterinarian in the British Isles, the most famous of which is *All Creatures Great and Small*. "I'd wanted to be a classic mixed-animal practitioner," he says. "They don't exist anymore." Today, most vets work on pets and small animals. Barlow went the other way and got to know cows.

Growing up, he milked cows that might have produced an average of fifty pounds per day. On a white-board in a spartan conference room at the Miller barn is a table showing the latest numbers from the thirty-five cows there, which put out seventy to eighty pounds. The beasts that make this milk evolved about 23 million years ago, during the Miocene epoch. It's no coincidence that they showed up at the same time and place as the various species of grasses that took hold in the temperate climates of the earth. Cows were born to eat grass. Their teeth are hypsodont, meaning that they extend high above the gum-line and wear down slowly over time, and selendont, endowed with sharp ridges that pulverize stringy greens. As they eat, their jaws move in a circular motion, like nature's own food mill. But what makes cows especially distinct is that they are quadrigastric: they have four stomachs. Humans are monogastric, and while we could theoretically chew and swallow grass, we wouldn't get the same nutrients out of it that cows do. Why? "It's all about the rumen," Barlow says.

When a cow crops a mouthful of grass, she chews it around for a while and swallows it. Down the esophagus it travels to the first stomach, the reticulum. This is a kidney-shaped appendage to the main workhorse of the digestion system, the rumen. Since a cow's natural gut enzymes aren't strong enough to break down the cellulose and lignin in grass, microbes in the rumen ferment the particles first. Informally known as "bugs" among farmers, these microbes are the key to a cow's ability to turn grass into milk, and the most important of them reside in the rumen.

Imagine isn't a totally normal dairy cow. She has something special: a fistula, or a surgically created hole about the size of a dinner plate, on her left side, with a rubber cap on it. Under the cap is the rumen, which is like a big, thirty-gallon vat. Fluid rolls around in there, and the muscle walls perform regular peristalsis, slowly contracting and expanding and mixing the contents. Barlow dons rubber gloves and works the cap from the hole. Imagine seems not even to notice. All of a sudden, there's the inside of her rumen. It smells like a cross between fermented silage and manure; not horrible, but strong enough to alert you to the inner workings of animal organs. He reaches his hand in and scoops out a bit of the rumen contents. It's greenish and wet, with pieces of hay and grass in the process of breaking down. The rumen contains zones with particles of different size. On top are gases; in the middle is a fibrous mat of long particles; and in the basement is the finer stuff. Barlow's sample comes from the middle, and if you looked at it under a microscope, you would see protozoa and bacteria forming on the feed to digest it.

The contents of the middle zone, in fact, have not seen their last rays of light. The longer particles are regurgitated back through the esophagus and up to the mouth for further grinding. During their six to eight hours of chewing per day, cows produce 160 liters of saliva. This process—which functions to reduce the particle size of fiber, expose its sugar to microbial fermentation, and buffer (through the saliva) the acids produced by fermentation—is called rumination. Hence the name of the mammalian order "ruminant," which comes from the Latin *ruminare*, meaning "to chew over again." Once ground into smaller chunks, these pieces then go back down into the rumen, settle toward the bottom, and continue their journey to the third stomach, the omasum, a circular organ that's small in comparison to the trash-can-size rumen. The omasum is responsible for the recycling of some nutrients and the absorption of water, sodium, phosphorus, and residual volatile fatty acids. From there, the rest of the digestive tract resembles that of a human, with the abomasum performing the jobs of the human stomach, secreting strong acids and digestive enzymes. In a cow, the strongest of these enzymes is rennet, the active ingredient in cheesemaking. Next follow the small intestine, the cecum (one last shot of fermentation), and the large intestine. The end of the road is the cliff of the cow's anus, extruding feces rich in organic matter, in the form of undigested microbial debris and elements such as nitrogen, phosphorus, and potassium.

Other parts of the cow are also perfectly formed for a life of grazing. Their eyes are widely set, to give them a wider angle of vision, allowing them to better see predators and other threats. A cow's only blind-spots are directly behind her and a narrow patch in front. And while cows aren't especially sensitive to colors—they can see only shades—their senses are ably augmented by delicate hearing and smell. However, these attuned senses contribute to their tendency to spook. Loud noises scare them, and it's this fact that led Frank Bryan, a historian at the University of Vermont, to speculate that Vermonters are soft-spoken because many of them traditionally were dairy farmers. When your livelihood depends on happy, calm cows, the logic goes, you learn to talk low and not make any sudden moves. When in herds, cows combine their strong senses with a status-based fortification. They like to move as a cohesive unit, with the natural leaders in the center (for protection) and, ironically, the lowly castes on the outside, leading the herd around.

These are the qualities the first farmers had at their disposal when they decided to raise and milk ruminants. Since then, we've managed to reshape dairy cattle in the image that suits us—cash cows—mostly through advances in breeding, feeding, and milking.

A BREED APART

====

"I'll check your semen inventory, Ben?"

"Huh?"

"I said I'll check your semen inventory."

"Oh, yeah. Sure."

It's a winter afternoon in Fairfield, Vermont, population 1,950. The downtown consists of a blinking yellow light at the intersection of two state roads, the town hall, and a homey bakery called Chester's, named after President Chester A. Arthur, who grew up not far from here. The menu at his eponymous eatery features such country delights as "beans w/franks, sloppy joe w/chips, mac and cheese w/ham, hot chicken sandwich w/mashed potatoes, and teriyaki chicken dinner," all priced between $4.75 and $5.99. On top of the case at the front is a glass dome enclosing a carrot cake a good eight inches thick and with the girth of a mature maple. Two large, grandmotherly ladies stand ready to sling any of these items your way with a warm smile. The rest of this small town is given over to dairy farms and vast open fields with corn stubble sticking up out of snow.

Lake Champlain sits like a large estuary to the west. With the sun weakly shining behind a scrim of clouds low on the horizon, and wind whipping across the plains, the landscape here is part peaceful, part brutally bleak. On a rise above the center of town is Moo Acres, the dairy farm owned by Ben Williams and his father, David. Inside their barn resides a mixed herd of seventy-two Holsteins and Jerseys, and today is the day for their biannual breeding consultation with Jerry Emerich, an employee of the semen and fertility cooperative Select Sire Power.

But first, Landis Beyor, from Select Sire Power's competition, Genex, is here to inseminate cow #32, who's been having trouble getting pregnant. Beyor, a twenty-year veteran of the artificial insemination (AI) industry, puts on a long blue rubber glove that reaches up to his armpit. With little ado, he reaches his arm into the cow's rectum and feels around for the cervix, at the same time scooping out manure and letting it fall to the floor, which is feathered with wood-shavings to absorb the mess. Finding the cervix, Beyor uses the other hand to insert the "French gun," a slender metal plunger with a straw of semen attached to the end. The straw is the size and color of a coffee stirrer. When he presses the plunger, it pushes two tiny cotton plugs through the straw, moving the semen into the cervix and the uterus. Throughout these proceedings, cow #32, a typical Holstein, pays Beyor no mind. She's in heat, and thus expecting some activity in her hind region, so this is no shock. Because #32 has been a hard case, the semen Beyor is inserting in her is not specifically targeted to produce offspring with desired characteristics; it is from a bull with a high conception rate and just intended to get her pregnant. A cow that can't get pregnant is a cow that doesn't lactate. Such a cow is a money loser, because you feed her and she gives nothing in return. "My uncle said it best," says Ben, a husky young man with short beard and an earnest demeanor. "You breed with the absolute best semen three times, and if that doesn't work, just get the cow pregnant."

His work done for the moment, Beyor leans against a post in the barn and sticks the semen straw behind his ear nonchalantly. He covers just two small towns in Vermont, and last month he performed 2,300 inseminations. About 70 percent of dairy cows in the United States are bred using AI; for heifers (a female cow that hasn't yet calved) the number is 55 percent. The difference arises from the fact that heifers are more likely to be out on pasture or otherwise not observed as often, since they don't have to be milked every day. That can make it a challenge to get heifers bred in a timely manner, so people rely on bulls to get the job done for them. However, bulls are dangerous to work with, says Beyor. Just the other day, a farmer he knows broke a few ribs in a tussle with a bull he was trying to breed with a cow.

Aside from wanting to avoid a run-in with a horny bull, Ben Williams enlists the services of Select Sire Power to take the guesswork out of breeding. Twice per year, Emerich comes to Moo Acres to evaluate the cows and heifers that are ready to be bred; he studies their pedigree and their traits and then selects a bull that will, he hopes, meet the farm's goals. Some farmers are interested in raising show-quality cattle—big, brawny beauties that represent the Platonic ideal of cows today. Ben and David Williams are more pragmatic—they want healthy cows that will produce a lot of milk for a long time.

Depending on whom you ask, AI companies like Genex and Select Sire Power are responsible for up to two-thirds of the increase in per-cow milk production over the last forty years. Nevertheless, humans have been refining and selectively breeding cows almost since they had the bright idea to domesticate them. The modern-day dairy cow is of the genus *Bos taurus*, and it's a result of a hodgepodge of cross-breeding between the great ox of the olden days—*Aurochs bos primigenius*—and *Bos longifrons*, the Celtic shorthorn. The aurochs occurred naturally across Asia, North Africa, and Europe and was described by Caesar as "approaching an elephant in size but presenting the figure of a bull." They had huge horns and stood 6.6 feet at the shoulder. The bulls sported black coats, a pale stripe on their backs, a topknot of curly white hair, and a white ring around the muzzle; the cows were smaller and mostly reddish. The last of these outsized beasts was killed in a Polish forest in 1627.

F. E. Zeuner, in *A History of Domesticated Animals*, theorized that animal breeding followed five stages into modernity: loose contact between humans and animals that put breeding totally outside of human control; confined animals that bred in captivity but in an unregulated fashion; selective breeding to perpetuate specific characteristics; economic forces that led to the planned development of breeds with desirable properties; and the final stage, in which the wild ancestor was exterminated once an acceptable domestic form was created. Some scholars have referred to the first stages as "animal keeping" and the latter stages as "animal breeding." According to this dichotomy, animal keepers were passive wards, letting ecological and evolutionary forces run wild, while animals breeders were control freaks, picking and choosing the size and shape of the cow they wanted to produce, like an automobile buyer deciding between a minivan and an SUV. Charles Darwin suggested something in between: that human selection accounted for only a portion of the changes seen in domesticated animals, with natural selection, as impacted by the environment and feeding, accounting for the rest.

Long before Darwin, the Romans and the Greeks had some colorful theories about the nuts and bolts of heredity. Leucippus in *The Seed* and Democritus in *The Nature of the Child* put forth the idea that both male and female contributed semen in the process of reproduction. Male semen, they said, derived from the most potent parts of the four humors of the body, as demonstrated by the feeling of exhaustion that resulted from its release. The act of copulation warmed these fluid humors and dispersed them throughout the body, starting in the brain and using the veins near the skin surface as the major routes of transport. In males, the route traced from the brain to the spinal cord to the kidneys, testicles, and penis. The route of the humors in females, mysterious creatures that they are, were noticeably absent from their hypothesis.

The earliest references to animal breeding in Greece appeared in

Xenophon's *On Hunting*, where he advised resting brood hunting bitches before mating them, and letting the puppies nurse from their mother as opposed to a foster bitch, since "nursing by a foster mother does not promote growth, whereas mother's milk and breath do them good and they like her caresses." Xenophon gave little guidance on parental selection, merely suggesting the use of a "good dog." In *The Republic*, Plato wrote that a sportsman would only breed from those animals he judged the best, with criteria being prime age (not too young or too old) and alacrity in hunting. In *Historia Animalium*, Aristotle waxed romantic about the quantities of milk produced by cattle of the Greek island Epirus, a place with rich pastureland where the cows were so large that milkers had to stand to reach their teats. The cattle there ran in loose herds, but Aristotle's writing implies that they were at least closely watched by the Greek farmers, since he instructs that if a cow is mounted and doesn't become pregnant, twenty days should pass before letting the bull try again. The writer Varro observed that the Epiran farmers managed their cattle for optimum fertility; they kept the cows short of food for a month before mating, while the bulls were isolated from the females and fed well for two months prior to their stud service. The thought was that thin females would be more fertile than fat ones, and that the males should be fortified because sex was so draining.

Believe it or not, these fanciful theories of heredity held fast until the seventeenth century, when anatomical research by William Harvey revealed the truth of the blood circulation system. He didn't get it completely right, however, as he asserted that the embryo in a female is infused by the spirit of the male semen, not the semen itself. His answer to embryonic development was a process he called epigenesis, or the steady buildup of organs and body parts in a preordained sequence. In the 1660s and 1670s, microscopic investigation uncovered the presence of follicles in mammalian ovaries, leading to an accurate description of the development of a hen's egg. It was known that females carry the embryo, but the male's role was still a mystery. Anatomists posited that the ovum was the sole origin of the embryo and that the male contribution was just the spark that sets the epigenesis in motion.

All of that changed with a guy named Anton van Leeuwenhoek, a Dutch tradesman and microscope tinkerer. In 1677, he interrupted an intimate moment with his wife, Cornelia, to, within "six beats of the pulse," collect his semen in a tube and put it under his home-made pieces of ground glass. He peered into the fluid and, much to his surprise, could see something moving. Focusing further, he spied "a vast number of living animalcules," all wriggling around like bulbous-headed eels. In those days it was thought that movement was the best evidence that something was alive. Because the "animalcules" that Leeuwenhoek discovered moved with such rapidity and tenacity, his contemporaries believed, rightly, that they held the key to the formation of life. Of course, it would be many years before we understood the exact mechanism by which a sperm fertilizes an egg, but Leeuwenhoek's research advanced the notion that sperm exist and play a key role in embryo development.

This knowledge came at the perfect time for the nascent agricultural revolution in Europe and, especially, Great Britain. From 1500 to the end of the 1800s, agricultural production increased dramatically with the improvement of tools, livestock, and crop management systems. Whole new crops—such as clover, ryegrass, sainfoin, and turnips—were developed to feed the legions of animals grazing on the fields. And where those fields used to be open to any farmer for livestock foraging, they were becoming enclosed and controlled by individual landowners. This encouraged investment in livestock quality, because now your animals couldn't wander off and take up with a farmer a few miles away. Thus, while grain prices held steady, livestock prices increased dramatically, spawning a whole new industry of animal breeding. Breeders came in two basic forms: those who bred animals for sale to other farmers, and those who bred animals for their own use on the farm. Either way, expertise in the traits of different breeds became valuable, and nowhere was this more important than the fledgling dairy sector.

The dominant variety of cattle in the seventeenth century was the black longhorn, described in the parlance of the day as "stately of shape, bigge, round, and well buckled together in every member, short jointed and most comely to the eye, so that they are esteemed excellent in the market." Despite this favorable appraisal, these cows produced, at best, four gallons of milk per day; even a gallon or a gallon and a half was deemed acceptable. At Over, in Cambridgeshire, cows cropping the first flush of April grass would give three gallons per day. Annual milk yields were around three hundred gallons, and the cows lived to be fifteen to twenty years old. The key differences between cows were thought to be based on the regions from which they came. Black longhorns were found in Lincolnshire, while Gloucestershire was known for its red cattle.

The larger dairies acted as both breeders of cows for the market, and makers of milk. They sought out young bulls and let them run wild with the herd, so as to impregnate as many heifers and cows as possible. It wasn't until the eighteenth century in England that breeders began to figure out that the characteristics of animals were influenced by both heredity and the environment. With the work of Robert Bakewell, the idea that animals could be selected for traits and then bred with other animals to produce offspring with specific qualities came to the fore. Bakewell collected longhorn cows from different areas in Northern England and then in-bred them to obtain the traits he wanted. He noticed that a phenotypic indication of a good dairy cow was the size of its milk bag and the presence of large veins leading to the udders. Another breeding pioneer named Thomas Hale noted that "above all things, see that she have a large, good, white and clean looking udder with four well grown teats."

The English breeds—Jerseys, Devons, Ayrshires—of the seventeenth and eighteenth centuries came to America with the Pilgrims and prevailed here until the mid-1850s, when, to keep up with the growing milk demand, New England farmers imported a Dutch breed called the Holstein. All along, the Dutch had been perfecting their own dairy cows by crossing numerous breeds, and the

Holstein, with its distinctive black and white checkered pattern, was their piece de resistance. Weighing in at 1,500 pounds or more, Holsteins, without the benefit of modern technology, could put out ten times as much milk per year as the "comely" English cattle of the 1700s.

Surprisingly enough, although breeders in the United States knew they were improving milk production, they didn't start collecting data in an organized way until 1908, when the USDA Bureau of Animal Industry started its first regimen of cow testing at Michigan's State Dairy and Food Department. In breeding systems and technology, it was Denmark that led the way—Danish breeders had been testing cows since at least the mid-1800s. In the U.S., this effort led to the first dairy herd improvement associations, which spread across the states. In 1914, federal extension workers took over responsibility for cow testing, and a national database—recording the health, size, and milk production of offspring—grew to encompass more than 40 percent of dairy cows by 2008.

Simultaneously with the rise of data gathering, the first bull associations were formed in Michigan, following examples of cooperatives organized in Denmark. The bull associations shared bulls and, by virtue of the Capper-Volstead Act, coalesced into official cooperatives. In these organizations, which would end up having enormous control in the dairy industry, a group of farmers would get together and say, "Let's buy some bulls, breed the best ones, and then share them with each other." Out of such a system came the breakthrough of artificial insemination, also pioneered in Denmark. In 1937, a researcher at Rutgers University, Enos J. Perry, observed his first artificial insemination on a trip to that country. Enthusiastic about the technology, he returned to the United States, formed the first U.S. Cooperative Breeding Association, in New Jersey, and unleashed AI on the dairy industry here. That's why Perry is known as the "Father of Artificial Insemination in the United States." The New Jersey Extension went on to form Select Sires, the umbrella organization that includes Select Sire Power, the cooperative that provides genetic counseling and material to Ben and David Williams on Moo Acres in Fairfield, Vermont.

In the mid-twentieth century there were upward of a hundred AI cooperatives; today there's just a handful of really big ones. Select Sires is one of the biggest. It posts the most sales in the U.S., delivering about 11 million units of sperm per year to dairy farms. A "unit" of sperm consists of a couple of cc's and a milk-based "extender," which helps keep the 10–20 million sperm cells alive longer. Most of this sperm comes from SS's headquarters in Plain City, Ohio. Visitors aren't allowed to see the bulls—they're quarantined to prevent disease outbreaks—but if you were to gain access to the many barns at the facility you'd see about three thousand bulls ranging from a few months to fifteen or twenty years old. The big bulls can top two thousand pounds. Mature bulls are on a twice-per-day "collection" schedule.

How does one "collect" semen from a two thousand pound bull? Thankfully, the bull wants to help out, so it goes something like this: an employee attaches an "artificial cow vagina"—basically a cozy sheath—to the bull, and tries to get him to have a few false mounts, which ups the sperm count. Then, after the vagina is warmed up with water and reaches the right temperature, the bull lets loose. At the end of the sheath is a test tube that holds the semen. The test tube is then removed and the semen is tested and processed. That can be a dangerous job, says Kirk Sattazahn, the marketing director at Select Sire Power, "but generally, the bull knows the routine and doesn't fight too much." These bulls aren't allowed to roam outside, because of health concerns, but their life inside the barn doesn't sound too bad: air conditioning, mattresses, a balanced diet placed in front of them, a vet on staff, and sheath-sex twice per day. "They're well taken care of," Sattazahn says. "I can't speak for the bulls, but that's probably the way they'd want to live." Leslie Hansen, a professor of dairy genetics at the University of Minnesota, who's been a fair critic of the AI industry, concurs that there's no animal welfare issue at most semen collection facilities.

Once the semen is collected and tested, it can go one of two ways: straight to the packaging department, where it's prepared for shipment, or to a flow cytometer to produce the marvel of "sexed semen." It used to be that no matter how much you played with selective breeding, you still had to abide the casino of gender. You could spend hundreds of dollars on the best semen, thousands on the services of a genetic consultant, and still have only a 50/50 chance of reaping a cow. In 2006, sexed semen changed all that. Born out of an increased global demand for milk, and to give virgin heifers an easier time in their first calving experience, scientists devised a way to separate the male sperm cells from the female cells. The glib perspective of hindsight makes it sound easy: just dye the sperm cells and then run them under a laser. The female cells, it turns out, are actually a little bigger and brighter than their male counterparts. ("The ladies like hearing this when I talk about it," Sattazahn says.) The flow cytometer sorts the bright cells from the dim, and voila—for about $20 more per straw, the farmer is basically guaranteed a cash cow.

Lots of producers combined the breakthrough of sexed semen with the practice of embryonic transfer—putting fertilized eggs into surrogate cows. Some cows were able to give birth to a hundred calves in a year this way, but the average was closer to ten. Still, that's a lot of pregnancy! The plan worked, bringing hundreds of thousands of dairy cows into existence. But by the time they were old enough to make milk—2009—the market tanked and the cows became a liability. Many of them ended up being culled and slaughtered through the organization Cooperatives Working Together, in an effort to bring down the quantity of milk going to market (and thus raise the price).

Back at Moo Acres, Jerry Emerich is ready to size up the cows and determine which bull might provide the genetic material to produce the best offspring. All the cows and heifers are in the barn now, because snow covers the fields. They're lined up in tie-stalls, which means that each cow's neck is tied to a metal post, with enough length to let the animals lie down and get up to eat. There's no extra heat source in the barn, but because of the animals' high body temperature, the air in the barn hovers around 35 to 40 degrees, depending on how cold it is outside. The first cow Emerich studies is a two-year-old Holstein. He's holding a handheld computer, like the one you'd see a person using to take inventory at a supermarket. Into this unit Emerich punches scores for a variety of "linear traits"—the things that best indicate the utility of a cow. They include such categories as "stature," which is the height and overall size of the cow, and "dairyness," the quality of being bony, angular, and wide-ribbed—the theory being that a lean cow puts more energy into making milk than putting on muscle, and that an open rib pattern means there's lots of room for a big rumen and thus more processing power. Also important are the feet and legs, which should be straight and strong for good mobility and longevity. He looks at "rump width" and "rump angle," where an abundance of each means a good likelihood of fertility and no problems in calving. Most crucial of all is the udder. Here, Emerich judges a host of qualities: height, width, support, depth, and the teats thereon. You want the udder to attach as close to the "pins"—the hip bones—as possible, because an udder that starts high stays higher throughout the cow's life. Why is a high udder sought after? Because gravity takes its toll, and over time the udder will want to sag, which opens it up to injury and restricts the cow's movement. Udder "support" is the ligament that forms a cleft between the left and right sides; a strong cleft means a healthy udder. Teats should be close to each other and facing in, the better to attach to the milk machine.

"This cow is slightly below average in size," Emerich explains, "has an acceptable foot and leg, but a very nice udder."

Over the last forty years, selective breeding has resulted in more cows with high udders. But some low-hangers are still out there, and Ben points one out to Emerich. It's an older cow with high milk production, and her udder sags almost to her feet, making it difficult to get the milking machine on her. It also gets dirty more easily and is thus more prone to mastitis infections. "We're going to want to use a bull that sires increased production but very shallow udders,"

Emerich says, "because we don't want to make another cow like her, but she has some characteristics, such as high production, that we want to continue."

When Emerich says he wants a bull that sires high udders, that means the bull is transmitting high udders to his offspring because, somewhere in his lineage, are the genes that express for that trait. But related cows don't necessarily get the same genes from their parents—nature's not that predictable. Take, as an example, a bull with strong legs. There are many, many genes working together to create his strong leg conformation. Yet even the strongest legged bull is going to have a few lousy genes. He may pass on mostly favorable genes to one daughter, but by random chance pass on a sampling of his lousy genes to her less fortunate sister. Additionally, some traits are heavily influenced by the environment. The daughter with favorable leg genes could still end up with legs that are visually unappealing due to poor environmental circumstances.

Aside from the computer unit, Emerich is also clutching a list of the cows and their milk production and component numbers. The Vermont Dairy Herd Improvement Association compiles these lists during its monthly testing of herds, and Emerich uses the data to guide him in his breeding analysis. Once Emerich scores all the cows he's here to see, he goes home and uploads the data into a proprietary computer program. It analyzes the linear trait scores, sorts Holstein cows to Holstein bulls and Jersey cows to Jersey bulls, and reviews Ben Williams's preferences to come up with a roster of potential studs. Emerich will glance over the recommendations, but he doesn't have time to second-guess the computer: last year, he mated 68,000 head. "For the most part," he says, "I always agree with how it mates."

If you want to talk milk production per cow, Emerich and the AI industry to which he's attached have, on the whole, done good work. They have weeded out the cows with poor traits and selected for the superstars—the sturdy, steady milk makers. Cows today are models of efficiency, pumping out milk with fewer inputs than ever before.

But there is a shadier side to the story. To shed light on it, you have to go to Minnesota—in 1964.

That was when Charles Young, a professor of animal science at the University of Minnesota, had the bright idea to create a control line of Holstein cows. He was prophetic in his belief that AI would change the dairy industry in major ways, and he wanted to maintain a baseline so we wouldn't lose sight of how we'd altered nature. Through retrospective genetic studies, he knew that no genetic improvement for milk production had been made until the 1960s. So he gathered twenty average bulls, collected five hundred units of semen from each, and mated them to randomly culled, non-genetically improved cows with the intention of perpetuating the genes into the future. Their production average in 1964 was 12,000 pounds per year—about half of what a good Holstein will give today. And they looked rather different, more like Angus beef cattle, thick throughout the body, with substandard udder conformation. They milked about 100 days per year, and then their lactation was done. And all of this holds true today at the U of M dairy barn, where Leslie Hansen, Young's successor, keeps close watch over the antique bovines.

For a while, the control herd seemed an extravagance. The Holstein cows were selectively bred for "type traits"—good udders, legs, feet, and bodies—but not for functional traits, such as fertility, health, or longevity. Yet the cows hung tough. By the mid-1980s, the Holstein was in its golden era: giving lots of milk, with a 50 percent conception rate when artificially inseminated. "She really had it all," Hansen says. "In my opinion, no other cow, purebred or cross-bred, could compete with her."

Things have gone downhill in the last twenty-five years. "The AI companies know what's happening," says Hansen, "but their role is to sell semen and leave the impression that everything is hunky-dory. But it simply is not." As a side note, it's apropos that Hansen used the term "hunky-dory" when talking about Dutch cows—the phrase originates from the Frisian word *hunk*, which means "house" or "safe place." And why aren't Holsteins today in a safe place? Mainly because their fertility and reproductive health have substantially degraded.

What happened is that we began shaping cows in the aesthetic sense and not so much in the practical sense. After the 1980s, breeders continued selecting for milk production, "but we decided to get a little silly," Hansen explains. "We said, 'Oh, let's make her sexy, let's make her tall, thin and glamorous.'" That has proven misguided. We used to think that big, angular cows translated into lots of milk, but that's apparently wrong. The University of Minnesota just completed a forty-year study, selecting for large and small Holsteins, and the results indicate that bigger cows don't produce more milk than smaller ones. "Anybody off the street would think you'd want to select for milk production but make sure the cow maintains enough body condition so she stays healthy and can get pregnant," Hansen says. The dairy industry lost sight of the foundation of milk production: overall cow health and happiness.

But it gets worse. "The real kicker right now," Hansen says, "is that the breed is getting so highly inbred, because we've been breeding the best of the best as fast as we can all of these years." We've come to rely on AI so much that two bulls—Chief and Elevation—make up 30 percent of the gene pool in the Holstein breed today.

In 2010, researchers finished sequencing the entire bovine genome, and AI companies are using that information to speed up the process of selective breeding. The industry has identified the gene expressions of 50,000 single nucleotide polymorphisms (SNPs) and can now pick out the ones that result in good udder shape, overall size, and more. This is great news for Select Sires and others because they can promise quicker gains in milk production through their genetic services. The downside is that identifying the specific genes in bovines encourages even closer relations between animals—more inbreeding. Once again, we're choosing quantity over quality, and it's having negative effects on the animals.

Fertility rates, for example, have been cut in half since the 1980s, and are now just 25 percent. And that's despite the precise tools—such as the French gun—that are being used commonly, and the regular doses of fertility-advancing hormones and hormone synchronization. "It's becoming routine now for multiple injections to assist the cow in reproduction," Hansen says. Furthermore, dairy cows confined to wet concrete free-stalls today are not displaying their estrus cycles as visibly or as long, so it's much more difficult for farmers to tell when cows are ready to be inseminated.

To the rescue, predictably, is the AI industry. After pushing the breed to this state, the industry is capitalizing on the low fertility trends by offering the services of full-time reproductive consultants and selling new technologies that assist farmers in getting their cows pregnant.

The key here is estrus detection. Farmers used to spend enough time with their cows—either milking them or moving them from pasture to pasture—that they could see for themselves when the cows were in heat. When a cow is ready to be mounted she will move around a lot, swing her head, and just generally seem restless. Not only are farmers spending less time with their cows (there are usually too many to keep track of now), but the cows aren't making their estrus cycle obvious anymore. For a while there had been low-tech ways around this. Tail paint is a good example. Farmers who suspect a cow is in heat can spray the rear end of the cow with a type of paint that rubs off if the cow has been mounted.

Recently, however, the marvels of dairy science have made spray paint seem quaint. The European company Dairymaster has devised a cow collar that uses the same accelerometer technology that's in an iPhone or a Nintendo Wii. The units—$158 each, and $8,000 for the computer system—are housed in a little plastic box worn around the cow's neck. Once a baseline is set for the cow's average daily movement, it can detect when that movement increases enough to indicate that the cow is in heat. It sends all the cow's movement data wirelessly via Bluetooth to the farmer's computer, allowing the farmer to keep a virtual eye on his breeding-eligible herd. The system is so sensitive that it can pinpoint a fifteen-hour window when it's optimal for the cow to be inseminated. The farmer can even choose to receive a text message when a cow is ready to go. It brings a whole new meaning to the term "booty call."

Yet the underlying health issues continue. These days, it's much more common to see embryos not survive, and the Holstein breed's notorious difficulties with calving (calves are too big for the moms) are worsening. There's also been a dramatic increase in fatty-liver syndrome, which occurs when cows metabolize too much body-fat after they calve. This is one result of selectively breeding for skinny cows—they become super-model thin and end up frail and diseased. The industry is judging cows by their external appearance; what really matters is their internal health.

Thankfully, there are solutions that don't require us to go back to the cows of the seventeenth century. Much of Hansen's research, in fact, has been on the promise of cross-breeding. Because there are two genes on every locus of a chromosome, there's an opportunity for one gene to mask the effects of a deleterious recessive gene. When you cross-breed, you have a greater chance for this sort of masking. On the other hand, if you inbreed, you can double-up on the recessive gene, rendering it fully expressed. "That's what in-breeding depression is all about," Hansen says, and it's the story behind the negative traits frequently showing up in Holsteins today. "Hybrid vigor" is the counterpoint to in-breeding depression. It's why mutts are usually healthier in the long term than purebred dogs. Cross-breeding, in fact, is a standard practice in many other sectors of agriculture, from hybrid corn to pork, beef, sheep, and poultry. Hansen has been studying red breeds from all over Europe (Swedish, Finnish, Norwegian, Danish, German, and Australian), and the Montbeliarde and Normande cows of France. These breeds have been genetically selected for functional traits as well as milk production. They don't quite match gallon for gallon with a Holstein, but they come close, and they're much healthier. What has taken so long for the dairy industry to come around to cross-breeding? Hansen chalks it up to the hide-bound ways of the industry, and that, twenty-five years ago, there was no problem to solve. The Holstein had it all.

FEEDING FRENZY

The noted nutritionist of the twentieth century, Clive M. McCay, wrote that "as long as men have eaten and animals have been fed, there has been a mixture of science and art in nutrition."

The recorded science arguably began with Robert Boyle, who was alive during the better part of the 1600s. His central contribution to the field of nutrition was the idea that an animal's body can change depending on what kind of feed it is given. Along this line he discovered that the flesh of Irish swine fattened on shellfish had a distinctive flavor.

For dairy cows we haven't been so worried about the effects of feed on the taste of milk—except for the "swill milk" episodes in the rapidly industrializing cities of the late nineteenth century—but on its quantity. From time immemorial, cows have eaten what people in the industry call forage—whatever they can find in the fields of their domain. This usually meant grass or alfalfa or clover or fescue, depending on what the soils would naturally sprout up. By the early twentieth century, farmers were supplementing forage with corn silage, which consists of the entire corn plant, cob and all, chopped up and packed into a silo. It ferments nicely and emits that sweet, pungent aroma you smell when you drive slowly past a dairy farm on a sunny day in the spring. This was laid down in front of cows when they came in to be milked and acted as an extra protein source.

That worked well until the milking machines got more efficient, and didn't allow the cows enough time in the barn to get the supplemental nutrients they needed to maintain high production. So farmers experimented with "slug" feeding—two ten-minute all-you-can-eat sessions with highly soluble protein and carbohydrates. In theory, the cows would get the calories they needed, and it didn't disrupt the strict assembly-line of milking that was becoming the norm. But it didn't work out that way. The thing is, bovine digestion isn't so simple. Human digestion is complicated enough, and we have only one stomach. Imagine an animal with four stomachs, each with a different purpose and chemistry, and you begin to understand that feeding cows, as McCay would have agreed, is indeed a serious science and an art.

The rudiments of ruminant digestion begin with the rumen. The pH in the rumen has to be just right, because it's a sort of ecosystem of microbes, and they're tricky little buggers. One way to guarantee good pH levels is to feed a cow longish pieces of forage. This stimulates saliva production during rumination, and the saliva gets swallowed with the grass bolus and buffers the naturally high pH in the rumen. Give a cow too much short-length forage and it passes through the rumen too quickly, avoiding a second or third trip up the esophagus, and thereby reducing the saliva production. This can result in rumen acidosis and kill the beneficial flora. But give a cow too much long forage and you don't maximize nutrient availability in the particles. It's a delicate balance.

The most successful approach to that balance thus far has been something called the total mixed ration, or TMR, which was developed in the late 1970s. "Cows, they want to eat stew," says Mary Beth de Ondarza, a dairy nutrition consultant based in northern New York. "They want their protein and nitrogen synchronized every minute of the day. Whereas for us, we can have our potatoes at eight o'clock in the morning and our steak at two o'clock in the afternoon and it doesn't make much difference."

The TMR being fed to cows on a standard Northeast farm is composed of corn plant parts chopped up, hay, alfalfa, ground corn, and corn grain. It's all mixed together in a fluffy yet moist mound, and the cows go at it with gusto. Lately the percentage of food and beverage by-products in cow feed has gone up. Examples include barley waste and brewer's yeast from beer manufacturers and alcohol distillers, whole cottonseed, processed soybean meal, heat-treated soybean meal, fish meal, and even pig-blood meal—slaughterhouse offal dried and pulverized into a powder. In Florida farmers can't grow good forage, so they feed cows waste from citrus farms, including mashed up and, yes, whole oranges. In the American West, almond hulls are popular. In England, you might see cows eating turnips.

Since the corn boom of the 1960s, corn grain has been a staple of the dairy diet. It was inexpensive and abundant and an easy energy source to mix in with forage from the farm. In the past five years, however, this practice has become less tenable. When corn started to be diverted to ethanol refineries, it jacked up the price of corn feed. And as fuel prices rise, so too do grain prices. Lastly, too much reliance on off-farm feeds is just not environmentally sustainable: it's grown with fossil-fuel-based fertilizer, then trucked to its final destination. The question, then, is how to make better forage. If farmers can produce their own feed, it both helps their bottom line and contributes to the sustainability holy grail of a closed-loop system. Most farms aren't even close to that yet, especially the huge farms in the West, but progress is being made.

The quest for better forage is actually a chemistry problem, and nutritionists such as de Ondarza are on the front lines of research. What is better forage? It's grass and hay that packs more protein than ever before, and it does this by taking advantage of the cow's own protein factory: the bacteria in the rumen. In other words, if you feed cows the right forage, their bacteria will produce 70 percent or more of the protein they need, and then the farmer doesn't have to buy it. "The more we can make of that bacterial protein," de Ondarza says, "the more efficient it is to make milk, because that protein source is a lot cheaper than others, such as processed soybean meal, heat-treated soybean meal, and fish meal." A key part of improved forage is that it's less fibrous and therefore more easily digestible. The way to reduce the fiber in forage is to cut the hay more often, before the lignin in the plants has time to develop. Twenty years ago, farmers in the Northeast might have started cutting in the first week of June, and then every forty-five to fifty days thereafter. Now they're cutting in mid-May, and repeating it every month (depending on the weather). Yes, more cutting equals more fuel used in tractors, but, environmentally and financially, it's likely to be a net winner.

If "cut more often" sounds simple, that's because it is. But the rest of dairy nutrition is often too complicated and important for farmers to figure out themselves. That's why they enlist the services of a nutrition consultant who's either independent or part of a feed company. De Ondarza, who grew up on a dairy farm in southern New York and earned her Ph.D. in nutrition from Michigan State University, has done both. She used to work for Blue Seal Feeds but is now on her own. And when she works as a consultant to a dairy farm, "usually the goal is to make more milk for less money," she says. To accomplish that, she analyzes the milk production numbers and devises nutritional fixes to squeeze more from each cow. She takes forage samples and analyzes their makeup in a laboratory, then uses computer models and algorithms to increase production and reduce the cost of the diet. She solves nutrition-based health problems such as displaced abomasums (twisted stomach resulting from fiber deficiency), milk fever (not enough calcium after calving), and retained placentas (mineral imbalance). As an independent contractor to feed companies, she runs feed trials at dairy farms, testing new additives and collecting the data. Most larger dairy farms have a full-time nutritionist tweaking the rations of the cows to maximize production and health. They'll feed different rations to fresh cows (just starting to make milk after calving), high producers, low producers, first-lactating heifers, and dry cows. There's a lot to keep track of.

"Most people don't realize we don't just throw a bale of hay in front of them anymore," de Ondarza quips.

PARLOR GAMES

Somewhere in the back of every American's mind is a Norman Rockwell painting. The whimsical yet witty illustrator of classic small-town life, Rockwell serves as a port in the storm of our technocratic society, where new gadget-dependent activities are born like stars and fade even faster. Rockwell is the rock; in his world, doctors made house calls, Boy Scouts carried little girls across puddles, and grandmothers delivered huge Thanksgiving turkeys to tables of smiling families. He didn't ignore the role of milk in American society, either. In a 1935 painting, "Couple with Milkman," he depicted a young man and woman coming home so late from a party it was early—and the milkman met them at the front door. He drew a few milkmaids, too, always with cute little wooden buckets near. The European version of Rockwell might be Johannes Vermeer. He immortalized the female milker in his 1658 painting "The Milkmaid." It shows a young, clear-skinned, Ruebenesque woman pouring milk from a pitcher into a bowl surrounded by breads—the very essence of wholesomeness and comfort. Her burly arms and shoulders hint at the hypertrophy caused by hand-milking cows every day.

Which was how it was done for hundreds of years. Many farms had six to ten cows, because that was all farmers could milk in a day, sitting on a low stool and working their forearms and hands into muscled but supple claws. But how long could such manual labor hold out against the rising tide of mechanization flowing over society?

Until 1889. In that year, the first successful commercial milking machine came to market in England. Called the Murchland Machine after its inventor, William Murchland, a plumber, it used vacuum suction—provided by a hand pump and a water column—to draw milk out of the cow's teats, rather than the pressure it took to squeeze the teat manually. Advertisements for the machine, which could milk up to four cows at a time, boasted that its pump could be operated by a single boy, while the more skilled job of fastening the machine to the teats could be performed by up to three girls. Suddenly, milking cows was mere child's play.

It would be another forty years before milking machines spread out through the United States. Their propagation was made possible by rural electrification programs. When electricity got to dairy farms, one of the first things the farmers did was install a bucket milking machine. "Right after the lights," says Douglas Reinemann, a professor of biological engineering at the University of Wisconsin-Madison. These first milking machines gave farmers' hands and forearms a break but kept everything else the same: they still collected milk in buckets, which then had to be carried to bigger cans. And before refrigeration, those cans were often dunked in a cold spring or kept on ice until ready for use.

This system was improved markedly in the 1950s, with pipeline milkers. They rendered buckets all but obsolete, since vacuum pressure not only drew the milk from the teats but also sent it through overhead pipes into refrigerated bulk tanks. The trip from hand to bucket milking allowed a farm to increase its herd from ten to twenty; pipeline milkers opened the door to fifty- and sixty-cow herds.

The next big jump came in the 1960s and '70s, with a whole new way to manage the milking process. Up until that time, cows were milked in the barns where they ate and slept. The farmer had to bring the suction machine to each cow individually, attach it, remove it, and then go to the next one. This would not do after Earl Butz's "Get big or get out" dictum. With the "milking parlor" system, the workflow was reversed: instead of bringing the machine to the cows, the cows were brought to the machine—inside a separate building specifically designed for milking. The basics of the vacuum system remained the same—albeit faster and more powerful—but now a farmer could bring in a load of twelve cows (six to a side, for instance), attach the suction cups to all of them, and then move 'em out and bring in a new batch. From above, some of these parlors resemble the diagonal fletching on the tail of an old arrow, with the cows lining themselves up in parallel stalls. In the jargon of the industry, this is called a herringbone formation.

Herds jumped in size to one, two, and three hundred through the 1970s and progressed into the thousands during the 1980s, but thanks to bigger and bigger milking parlors, labor costs for milkers could remain reasonable. The pinnacle of the milking parlor today is the rotary milker, a true wonder of industrial design. It's like a giant Gatling gun, only instead of bullets in barrels there are cows in compartments. They step onto a platform that spins slowly, and are delivered to one of the human milkers standing inside the circle, who then attaches the suction machine. A team of three or four milkers on a modern rotary system can milk five hundred cows per hour.

But the automation doesn't stop there. After all, even a rotary machine requires constant oversight and input from a human being. Humans—with their need for pay and health care and time off—cost money, and as margins for milk went lower and lower, farmers searched harder and harder for ways to save cash and still pump out more milk. One answer has been the robotic milking machine. First introduced in Europe in the mid-1990s, these machines came to the United States in the early 2000s. They make perfect sense for European dairies: labor costs there are higher, land isn't inexpensive and available, and there's a milk quota system in place. Here, larger dairies often use undocumented immigrants (more on this later), and land is cheap: it's been more economical to add cows than to add technology.

But there are a few hundred milk robots lurking in various parts of the United States. Even Vermont has two. The newest one is on the Rainville farm in Fairfax, not far from David and Ben Williams's Moo Acres in Fairfield. In April of 2008, an electrical short in a fan caused Pete and Madonne Rainville's barn to burn to the ground. Starting from scratch on a 240-acre farm that used to house sixty-five heifers, they had a couple of options. They could go back to the old-fashioned, tie-stall milking barn, in which Pete would have to attach the milk pumps to his cows manually. But all that bending down, getting up, and lifting was wearing out his joints so much that he was already—at the ripe old age of thirty-eight—on a regular regimen of physical therapy. (Wisconsin led the nation in knee and hip replacements for a while, on account of dairy farmers' repetitive motion injuries.) Or they could build a more efficient and ergonomic milking parlor, with elevated stalls and overhead pump holders. But that would still shackle Pete to a six-hour-per-day milking schedule, and they couldn't imagine any of their four young daughters ever taking up that burden. Then they discovered the Lely Astronaut, a robot with a high-flown name that bears no relation to what it actually does—unless astronauts can milk a barn full of cows twenty-four hours per day, seven days per week.

At a cost of $200,000 for a single unit, plus the new barn, the capital investment of almost $1 million seems steep. But when they considered the labor savings—in cash for a hired milker, or time for Pete—the deal began appealing to the Rainvilles. "It was always just the two of us," says Madonne, a short and stocky woman with close-cropped hair, blue eyes, and work-hardened hands. "He did all the milking, I did all the feeding, plus we started raising our own heifers, which added to the labor."

Native Vermonters are generally skeptical of, if not averse to, new-fangled ways of doing what they've done for generations. The Rainvilles' family wrote off the idea of a robot from the start. "There was a lot of negativity toward it," Madonne recalls. "They assumed that it can't work. But then you ask them how many robot farms they've been to, and the answer is zero." So the Rainvilles went on a road trip, to Wisconsin, Pennsylvania, and New York—just called up farmers out of the blue and said, "Can we come see?" They went, they saw, and then they bought in. Standing in the robot room of their shiny new barn, as a Holstein saunters into the machine's stall and succumbs to the softly tentacled apparatus, Madonne says they were pushed over the edge by the prospect of never needing to hire a stranger to milk their cows. "Neither one of us is a people manager," she says. "My husband can't stand it. Now he hollers at the robot, but the robot can't holler back."

Now, about that cow being milked. She's wearing a collar with a radio-frequency ID. Perhaps she was hungry, or wanted to be milked, so she walked up to the gate of the robot. This is not some anthropomorphic approximation of a dairy farmer; it's basically a metal and plastic bower with hoses and arms sticking out. On the left side is a computer screen, and in front is a big red arm that moves on a track.

But it's still smart. The astronaut identifies her by reading her collar and knows immediately when she was last milked, how much milk she produced today, how much feed she's already eaten, and what stage of lactation she's in. The robot deems her a good candidate for another milking, and it opens the gate. So the cow walks in and starts eating the feed that is rationed out for her in a big bowl. While she eats, the robot weighs her and its laser eyes scan her udder and teats, orienting the machine to her location in the box. Then a set of rotating brushes clean the teats with a germicidal wash. Thirty seconds later, the robot attaches four vacuum tubes to the teats and begins drawing the milk from the udder. A cow's udder has four milk compartments, and they don't always contain the same amount of milk, so the robot knows to monitor the flow of each tube individually and slow down or stop when one quarter is nearly empty. The suctioned milk travels through a quality control device with light and sound sensors. The light sensors are checking for mastitis and blood and any deviations in milk quality. The sound sensor is listening for flow rates and figuring out when she's empty. It's all harvested in one receiver jar, and the milk quality monitor is sending data to the main computer to be graphed. If the milk's clean, it's sent through pipes to the bulk tank; if it's no good, it's diverted to the drain or a bucket, whatever the farmer prefers. Meanwhile, the machine is removing itself from the cow, the bowl of feed is retracted, and a gate in front of the cow is opened. After being taught once or twice, the cow knows it's time to walk back into the barn, or back to the pasture.

In a small room next to the robot is a simple desk with a Dell PC. Paul Godin, the regional sales and service representative for the Lely Group, clicks on a desktop icon and opens Time for Cows, the program the farmer uses to monitor the system and the cows' production and health. On the screen is a virtual dashboard with animated dials showing the Rainvilles' preferred reports: cow lactation, udder health, grain intake, milk visits, failed milkings, total milk produced for the day, and so forth. "My daughter's eleven, and she can zing through this stuff," Godin says. "Their twelve-year-old is already using this." Just as in 1889, milking is child's play once again.

These machines were introduced in Canada in the year 2000, and now there are more than five hundred in that country. Godin says he can cross the border—just thirty miles, as the crow flies, from Fairfax—and visit ten farms with robots within a thirty-minute radius. "It's just a matter of time before they take over here," he predicts. "Any farmer that comes here, they're amazed. It's so quiet. The cows are happy and the farmers are not beat down. What happens is, because they're freed up from the milking monotony, they'll do a better job with their crops, do a better job managing their cows, and that all equates to money.

"You're also eliminating the lower-caliber help," he says. "The ones with the housing issues, the drinking problems, and all the baggage. And you're keeping your quality people; you're keeping your kids because it's more high tech and not such a physical drain."

Indeed, that drain has increased in recent years on farms without robots, despite advances in milking parlors. For many farms trying to hang on to the single-family, owner-operated system, the way to pay the bills has been to add more cows. But it ends up being a trap. When you run a three-thousand-cow dairy farm, work happens around the clock, between feeding, cropping, and milking. With no time for leisure, and little rest, quality of life suffers. Machinery eases the physical workload, but when you increase the work frequency, those strain gains disappear.

If the equation is something like "more milk = more problems," does the reverse hold true? Not necessarily. The opposite of a typical factory dairy farm is a farm that uses rotational grazing and milks a small herd. It's a more relaxed pace, with lower physical demands and stress, but the trick is to make it pay. When you're competing with the rest of the industry—replete with Gatling gun rotary parlors, sexed semen, and robots—the sustainable, rotationally grazed herd doesn't stand much of a chance. Just ask Philip Ranney.

THE ENVIRONMENT

Tom Frantz is surrounded by milk, but you won't find any in his refrigerator. "I've been suing and fighting this industry," he says. "I'm not about to support it."

A retired high school math teacher, Frantz is tall and laid-back, with frizzy gray hair, a mustache, and tinted square glasses. He lives in a single-level ranch with a jungle of ornamental and fruit trees on all sides, and a vegetable garden befitting a green-thumb with time on his hands. His place is an oasis of flora and suburban comfort compared with the tumble-down shacks of farm workers, the dusty alleys of the so-called colonies of poor Latino laborers that form the tattered edge of Shafter, California.

About a half-hour northwest of Bakersfield, in Kern County, this town of 16,000 lies in the heart of the San Joaquin Valley, and like much of the valley it has a growing population of Hispanic farm workers that exist alongside the dwindling remnants of white people who grew up here or are at least a few pegs higher in the farming industry hierarchy. The main drag through town, with its short, boxy storefronts and authentic Mexican restaurants, has a sort of Old West feel, but one that's giving over to globalization and homogenization in the form of fast-food joints and chain retail outlets.

Just up the road from Shafter is the bigger city of Delano, where Cesar Chavez led the National Farmworkers Association in a labor strike against grape growers, and then in an international grape boycott that resulted in the passage of California's landmark Agricultural Labor Relations Act and a cascade of improvements in labor rights and working conditions. In some ways, the agricultural landscape here today is similar to what it was in 1965, when the big strikes began: thousands of acres of vineyards still spread across the pan-flat valley floor, and interspersed are tracts of almond and pistachio trees, pomegranate groves, fields of roses and cotton, and every type of citrus tree imaginable. As you drive by these outfits, with their thousands of identical trees in great rows of geometric precision, you can't help but think that this is a place where man reigns supreme, subduing and harnessing nature for his own benefit. Out on the eastern horizon in early spring, a formidable wall of snowcapped mountains looms like a dark forest, a visible reminder of the earth's ultimate dominion.

Inside Frantz's house, a gas fireplace is going and NPR plays on the stereo. Although he's an astute environmentalist capable of rattling off accurate facts and figures about the dairy industry, he's not a back-to-the-land hippy who moved here to claim a piece of untouched soil, hoping to cordon off his own den of sylvan beauty. On the contrary, his grandparents settled in the Central Valley, and he and his parents were raised just three miles from where he now lives. For a time, he taught in the same school where his grandmother taught.

In 1994, Frantz left for Jamaica on a Catholic church project helping poor farmers become more self-sufficient. While he was gone, in 1995, a dairy farm with about 3,000 animals was built in his neighborhood. "I didn't even know it until 1998, when I got back," he says. It was the first trickle in a gush of dairy farms escaping the rapid suburbanization and stricter environmental regulations in the Chino area, east of Los Angeles. Eight more dairies moved to Shafter between 2000 and 2004: they contain 60,000 cows and all exist in an eight-mile radius of each other and Frantz's house. In Kern County in 1995 there were 35,000 cows being milked. Today there are about 180,000.

It makes sense that they moved to the Central Valley: land is inexpensive, and there is plenty of it. The valley is huge: 450 miles long and forty to sixty miles wide. To get from Redding, in the north, to Bakersfield, in the south, is about an eight-hour drive. It's the source of almost 10 percent of the U.S. agricultural output. It contains eighteen counties and over 5 million people and has an area of 42,000 square miles, which is about four times the size of Vermont. And California, largely because of the San Joaquin Valley, is ranked first in milk production in the United States, accounting for 21 percent of the national supply. The industry contributes $5.9 billion annually to California's economy.

The farms here don't accomplish that the old-fashioned way, with cows dotting green pastures. The average size of a dairy farm in California is 700 head, and many farms contain upward of 5,000, 10,000, or even 20,000 cows. From these cows, California dairy farmers squeeze a total of more than 40 billion pounds of milk per year. For a variety of reasons, the business model here is that of a factory farm—otherwise known as a CAFO, which stands for confined animal feeding operation. The cows don't live in traditional barns so much as underneath metal-framed shade structures, and they spend the bulk of their days standing in mud and manure, eating grain and feed mostly trucked in from other parts of the valley or neighboring states.

With shrinking margins for milk, farmers out here have done the economically shrewd thing—they've created economies of scale, cut costs, and become ruthlessly efficient, just like thousands of other dairy farms across the country. And they are not necessarily to be faulted for that. It is this way of farming that allows us to buy a gallon of milk for $3.50.

In general, food today is less expensive than it's ever been. According to the USDA, Americans in 2010 spent 9.4 percent of their disposable income on food—an all-time low. The current wholesale price of milk is about half of what it was twenty-five years ago, and about one-third of the price fifty years ago. It's easy to argue that inexpensive food is one of the greatest advances in modern history because it increases our freedom. Theoretically, the less we spend on the basic necessities of survival, the more we can spend on improving the quality of our lives: the more we can spend on education, health care, innovation, art, music, and technology. The less we spend on food, the greater our disposable income, which frees us up to buy fun stuff like iPads and sports cars.

The only problem with cheap food, and in this case cheap milk, is that it's a lie. The milk in the dairy aisle is inexpensive, historically speaking, but that's not where the transaction ends.

One of the major awakenings of our time is the idea that everything is connected. The milk you buy in the grocery store is connected to the environment where it's made, which in turn is connected to the people in that environment. Their actions, like yours, spool off their own chain of connections, some of which may include you. It's like playing six-degrees of Kevin Bacon on a global scale, and we're all included. We pay less for food, and have commanded farmers to become factory efficient, but we don't give them enough money to operate in harmony with their communities. Is cheap milk actually cheap if it contributes to an asthma epidemic?

That's the question you must ask when you buy milk from the San Joaquin Valley. Enclosed on three sides by mountains—the Sierras on the east, the Tehachipi on the south, and the San Gabriel on the west—the valley constitutes a single air basin and has some of the worst air quality in the United States. Many of its cities are in the top ten of the American Lung Association's most inauspicious lists: People at Risk in 25 U.S. Cities Most Polluted by Short-term Particle Pollution; People at Risk in 25 U.S. Cities Most Polluted by Year-Round Particle Pollution; and People at Risk in 25 Most Ozone-Polluted U.S. Cities. One-third of the children in Fresno suffer from asthma.

What's the dairy industry's role in this? Dairy farms are a contributor to PM 10, particulate matter less than 10 microns in size that forms when dust particles get kicked up into the air and attach to water vapor. Regular exposure to PM 10 causes a whole range of respiratory diseases. Dairies are also the largest source of volatile organic compounds and ammonia in the valley. The VOCs come from the alcohols off-gassing from silage piles; the ammonia emanates from the giant manure lagoons that most farms use to store animal waste. VOCs mix with nitrogen oxide (NOx) to form ozone during the summer, and they react with diesel soot and wood smoke in the winter to form PM 2.5, a more harmful form of particulate matter pollution that delves deeper into the blood and brain. Ammonia mixes with NOx in the winter and forms ammonium nitrate, another type of PM 2.5.

Of course, dairies are also a large source of greenhouse gases. Three to four hundred pounds of methane are burped or farted from each dairy cow every year, and about the same amount comes from their manure. Methane is twenty-three times more powerful than carbon dioxide as a greenhouse gas. Cow-generated methane accounts for about 5 percent of California's greenhouse gas emissions. When too much manure is spread as fertilizer, the excess that's not absorbed into the ground is off-gassed into the air as nitrogen oxide. As a greenhouse gas, NOx is 296 times as potent as carbon dioxide.

The cost of global warming might be hard to quantify, but that's not true for ozone and particulates—they cost every person in the San Joaquin Valley $1,600 per year in lost life and earnings. The affluent have health insurance to cover the costs of their asthma treatments; many poor people don't. And the San Joaquin Valley, for the most part, is poor. It has high unemployment and child poverty rates, and is said to be worse than Appalachia in the usual metrics of community health. Just ask Linda Mendez, thirty-six, a farm worker from Mexico who now lives next to a coal storage facility in Wasco, the rose capital of the United States. She, her brother, and her husband and three children share a two-room house, and they all suffer from asthma. There are days when she must rush to her daughters' school and bring them their inhalers. When she and her husband suffer bouts of asthma symptoms, they can't afford to go to the doctor. "It's very difficult," she says, "and so what happens is we tough it out for a few weeks until the symptoms end."

If you ask her why her family is stricken with this disease, she's not circumspect about it. "The government is not enforcing the rules," she explains. "Actually, there are very few rules on the dairies themselves, and that has a lot to do with it. So they continue without controls, because of the greed for a few, and they contaminate the rest of us. Here in the valley we're suffering and going through a slow death, because there's so much contamination, and the majority of it is coming from the dairies."

The truth is, no matter who you are, if you live in the lowlands of the San Joaquin Valley, you're likely to have breathing problems. And that's one of the reasons Frantz has taken dairies and governmental agencies to court. "It bothers me that they're messing up our air so bad," he says. "Since I got back in 1998, I've developed asthma. My father developed asthma too in the last ten years, and my brother-in-law. The three of us, all living right here, surrounded by dairies. And all since these dairies came in. I can't prove there's a direct relation."

He doesn't have to. All he has to do to breathe cleaner air in his hometown is get the Environmental Protection Agency to enforce the Clean Air Act on the dairy farms in California. The letter of the law is on his side, but more than ten years after the first brief was filed, there's no resolution.

Similar stories can be found around the country: stories of air pollution, surface water pollution, and groundwater contamination, all largely a result of uncontrolled dairy farms. When dairies were encouraged to get bigger, they unwittingly outgrew the land on which they operated, and an unsustainable system was born. As they got bigger and made more milk, they fueled an oversupply of the product, which further eroded its price and farmers' revenues, making it difficult for any farm—large or small—to afford the pollution control measures necessary to protect natural resources and public health.

Tom Frantz has made it nearly his full-time job fighting dairy farms. Will it do any good? It's an open question.

THE GREEN WATER STATE?

To celebrate Earth Day in 2011, the *Wall Street Journal* produced a ranking of the greenest states—environmentally speaking—in the nation. Vermont was at the top of the list. No shock there—it has the only democratic-socialist U.S. senator (Bernie Sanders) and is home to a town with more organic farms in a 10-mile radius than any other place on earth (Hardwick). Ben & Jerry's, that beacon of corporate social responsibility, is from Vermont; so is Seventh Generation. It was one of the first states to pass a statewide land use law that makes commercial development more difficult (some argue) than elsewhere. Its very name is a French-derived approximation of *green mountains*: Les Monts Verts.

But in the early 1990s, a different sort of green started shading Lake Champlain, the sixth largest freshwater body in the United States, which is shared among Vermont, New York, and Quebec. It was an infestation of green algae. Described by some as "chunky pea soup," this is not the benign stuff you slide your feet across when wading a river, but massive blooms of toxic blue/green slime that poisons the water and destroys the aquatic ecosystem. Even in this greenest of states, with its small collection of small dairy farms, pollution from farms and other sources has turned into an environmental disaster that the state is still trying to clean up.

It's somewhat hard to believe the scale of devastation these algae blooms have caused. After all, there's very little industrial activity on or near the lakeshore, and it's not huddled beneath millions of people. Nonetheless, pet dogs have died from drinking lake water, beach closures are common, and the lake is listed in a book entitled *Don't Go There*. In a state that relies heavily on tourism for revenue, this is an expensive and embarrassing problem. Not to mention that

200,000 people get their drinking water from the lake, and to drill each of them a new well would be unfathomably costly.

If the algae is a beast, then it dines on phosphorus. What is phosphorus? Basically, it's a nutrient that attaches to soil particles and is released into the water column when soils are disturbed. There are two general ways phosphorus gets into water bodies: through point-source pollution (such as a wastewater treatment plant), or non-point-source pollution (for example, storm water runoff from developed lands, soil erosion, and runoff from agricultural fields and unstable stream banks). When the Clean Water Act was passed in 1972, it focused tightly on point source pollution—those direct pipes of effluent draining into water sources. As a result, discharges from point sources have decreased dramatically over the past forty years, and in Lake Champlain today, point source pollution accounts for only 5 percent of the total phosphorus reaching the lake. Because non-point-source pollution can't be traced to a distinct outflow, such as a pipe or a drain, it's much trickier to control and monitor. Still, over the years we've developed reliable ways to quantify non-point-source pollution, and we know that developed lands contribute about 46 percent of the phosphorus runoff to the lake, and agricultural lands (mostly dairy farms) are responsible for 38 percent. And those numbers vary within the lake itself. In Burlington Bay, at the low point of the state's largest city, 99 percent of phosphorus loading comes from developed land. In Missisquoi and St. Albans Bays, north of Burlington and downstream of lots of dairy farms, 64 percent of phosphorus comes from agricultural sources.

One of the biggest challenges with phosphorus is that it's a persistent nutrient. In other words, it doesn't go away naturally, but cycles through its matrix. New phosphorus runoff feeds algae blooms, and when that algae decays, the phosphorus is released into the sediment. It gets churned up on windy, warm days and feeds new algae blooms, and the process begins again. Which raises the question: how do you stop the cycle? Do you dredge the lake bottom? Do you dump clean sediment on top of the nutrient enriched sediment? The conundrum resembles that of PCBs released into the Hudson River by General Electric. GE ultimately worked out a deal with the EPA to dredge the river, squeeze the water and PCBs from the sediment, and then ship it to disposal sites. All told, it will cost GE more than $1 billion.

Cleaning up the existing sediment in the lake won't cost that much, but it won't be inexpensive, either. And if you value the lake based on the services it provides to the natural and human environments, even $1 billion might be reasonable. The lake performs a range of services people often take for granted, or at least don't think about in a dollars-and-cents sort of way. It provides supporting services, hosting interactions between biotic and abiotic components that create soil which, in turn, grows food and fiber. This category also includes the processes that break down waste by-products, create fisheries, and contribute to the food web. More specifically, when these supporting services are degraded by pollution, the result is increased water treatment costs, waterfront property devaluation, and fish kills. Then there are "regulating" services, such as water filtration and flood management; "provisioning" services, which provide agricultural and forest products for local communities and economies; and "cultural" services that fortify us with recreational, spiritual, and educational opportunities. Vermont, more than most states, is especially dependent on this last category, with visitors in 2007 spending $1.6 billion, supporting 37,000 jobs, and contributing more than $200 million in taxes and fees to the state. Of course, not all of those dollars and jobs can be traced back to the lake, but it is a significant player nonetheless.

It's acknowledged that dairy farms are a major source of phosphorus pollution in Lake Champlain—basically, the rain washes manure from fields into ditches, streams, and rivers—so the problem is less about finger-pointing than it is about deriving solutions and installing best practices. The regulating body for non-point-source pollution from farms is the Agency of Agriculture, Food and Markets. This authority has been ceded to them by Vermont's Agency of Natural Resources in a memorandum of understanding. Some consider this arrangement a conflict of interest: since the AAFM's mission is to promote agriculture, charging it with policing farms is like letting the fox guard the henhouse. Implicit in this complaint is the idea that AAFM could do a better job of forcing dairy farms to control their phosphorus runoff. In general, this analysis misses the bigger picture. Vermonters and visitors love dairy farms for the open landscapes they maintain. The farms are a crucial part of Vermont's identity, economy, and food supply system. Reducing non-point-source pollution is costly, and that cost must be borne either by the farmer, or the state, or a combination of the two. Putting the onus solely on the farmer would put this embattled sector in further jeopardy; and the state could never afford to fix every farm without raising the revenue to do so. The remaining option is a public/private partnership in funding greater runoff control, and that's basically what's happening. It's just not working as quickly as Vermonters had hoped.

The partnership works mostly through cost-sharing between the state and federal government, and the farmers, for the installation of various sorts of improvements and practices. The "Best Management Practices" program from the state, for example, focuses on structural improvements, such as clean water diversion ("keeping clean water clean"), manure pits, feed storage runoff collection, and better manure spreading habits (injecting manure beneath the soil with special spreaders; and soil aeration to absorb the manure more quickly). The state aided 104 farmers in 2010, spending about $1.5 million by covering about 80 percent of the cost of improvements.

Vermont also implements the Conservation Reserve Enhancement Program, a project born from the Soil Conservation Service of the Dust Bowl era. It's goal is to, in the simplest terms, conserve the soil and its nutrients so that farms are more efficient and less polluting. This is not cutting-edge stuff: we're talking grass and tree buffers on streams; cover cropping in winter; and no-till planting. Thus far, Vermont has helped farmers create 2,400 acres of buffers, and has spent over $9 million since 2002, most of which came from federal matching funds. With cover cropping, farmers plant such things as winter rye in the fall to keep organic matter in the soil, which has the effect of stabilizing the soil and keeping it from breaking apart and running away when it's pelted by rain. Vermont has pitched in with financial assistance for about 7,000 acres of cover cropping per year. "In my opinion," says Laura DiPietro, the deputy director of the Agricultural Resource Management Program (ARMP), "it's one of the most important things that we do." No-till planting is equally intuitive but important: it involves injecting the seeds beneath the soil surface, and the idea is that by not disturbing the soil too much, farmers allow the microbe populations to grow, which creates healthier, more porous soil. In concert, cover cropping and no-till planting are especially effective and take some of the burden off the buffers.

Another tool is the nutrient management plan, which helps farmers attain the right formula for manure spreading on a given type of soil. Most farmers hire private consultants to create such a plan—they come out and take soil and manure tests and tell farmers how much manure they can safely spread over a certain area. The state provides about $14,000 to each farmer to create a plan; sometimes that covers the cost, sometimes it doesn't. The gripe from farmers is that the funding is a one-time thing, but the costs of keeping the plan current go on forever. Of course, implementing a plan also saves money, since farmers can apply just the right amount of fertilizer, or target their manure spreading more accurately.

The Vermont ARMP has been diligently monitoring water quality in relation to all these programs, but they haven't seen a dramatic reduction in nutrients and pollution. According to DiPietro, that unfortunate news is slightly misleading. She says that the USDA has run algorithms to account for increased rainfall over the past decade (more rain equals more erosion and runoff), and if you control for rain, there have been improvements in nutrient loading and pollution discharges.

The progress is barely noticeable, however, and in early 2011 the EPA decided to commandeer Vermont's water quality plan for Lake Champlain, a stinging rebuke to a state that likes to feel good about its environmental record. DiPietro stands by Vermont's approach to the algae bloom issue, adding that the state does the same thing that other states are doing, and that it has the people and programs in place to make progress. "I think it's just a matter of time," she says. "It didn't get this way quickly, and it will take time to remedy."

It's been said that by allowing farmers to dump phosphorus into the lake at their discretion, the state has basically provided a pollution subsidy to dairy farms, one that the public is being forced to pay as governments figure out how to clean it up. Roger Rainville, a former dairy farmer and the chair of the Farmer's Watershed Alliance, doesn't see it that way. "The average Vermont farmer spends $1,000 to $2,000 per cow, over a career, to implement water quality practices," he says. "For some reason, we're not getting credit for that. We're still the ones being blamed."

Rainville owns Borderview Farm, so named because it's across the dirt road from Canada, way up in Alburg, Vermont. Though Rainville no longer milks cows on his three-hundred-acre spread, "you're a dairy farmer until you die, when you've been at it as long as I have," he says. Now he raises replacement heifers and has turned his land into a giant research laboratory for the University of Vermont Extension Service. Rainville has always enjoyed the brainier side of dairying, and when he began to collaborate with UVM it was on an experiment to grow canola seed for biodiesel. The test started with seven plots; now there are almost three thousand. He's also helping with trials of bread wheat, hops, and various cover crops. "If farmers want it, we'll try to get it researched here so we know what it looks like on the ground," he says. In 2010, he grew oil seed and produced enough biodiesel that they didn't have to buy a drop of fuel. "It's kinda nice not to be beholden to Qaddafis and those types of guys," says Rainville.

Rainville's outside-the-box thinking partially explains why he's a founding member of the Farmer's Watershed Alliance, a group that helps dairy farmers in northern Vermont get on track with runoff mitigation and nutrient management. Another important factor: Rainville's farm is in the watershed that contributes the highest quantities of phosphorus to Lake Champlain, which has resulted in nasty algae blooms in St. Albans and Missisquoi bays. Things came to a head in 2005 when the Tyler Place Family Resort, a vacation destination on Lake Champlain's Goose Bay, started to hold meetings to find a solution to the algae blooms—nobody wants to go to a lakeside resort if you can't swim in the lake. Out of those meetings the Friends of Missisquoi Bay was formed, and when they realized they needed a separate group to focus on dairy farms, the Farmer's Watershed Alliance was born. Foremost, Rainville says, the FWA folks wanted accountability from the state. "They were spending millions of dollars on research," he explains, "and we weren't seeing results. We wanted to know why." So they pressured the Vermont legislature and secured annual funding for water-quality improvement practices on farms. Disillusioned with bloated government bureaucracy, the FWA made it a mission to fix the worst problems with the least amount of money. The projects are all voluntary and confidential, which puts farmers at ease that they won't be singled out as polluters. Over the past few years, FWA has helped farmers exclude cows from streams, divert clean water from barn roofs, and reduce soil loss from steep banks, among other things.

Rainville asserts that there is no single major polluter responsible for phosphorus in Lake Champlain. When asked who's to blame, Rainville says it's an easy question. "It's our fault. It's your fault. If you live here and flush a toilet or spread a load of manure, it's your fault," he says. That isn't entirely accurate, since phosphorus loads from wastewater treatment plants have been reduced by 80 percent since 1990. Still, his point is perhaps deeper: people who drink milk are also to blame, since they contribute to a system that puts farmers in impossible situations. The way Rainville sees it, economics is the main limiting factor for cleaning up Vermont's surface waters. Moving earth and installing storm water collection infrastructure isn't cheap. The FWA's projects run into the tens of thousands of dollars, but it doesn't have the resources to help every farmer who needs to make such improvements. That leaves most farmers with a decision: do you feed the kids or put in a stream buffer?

With the help of the state and federal programs, and the FWA, Vermont farmers are making some progress in reducing the phosphorus that washes from their farms into streams and lakes. The question is, how quickly does society want the total fix to happen? If we decided, somehow, to pay farmers a fairer price for their milk, they would be empowered to take preventative measures and make the water quality investments they know they should.

There's just one hitch, Rainville points out: "We can't ask the consumer to pay more for something that we overproduce."

PUTTING THE "BROWN" IN BROWN COUNTY

For a few weeks in March of 1998, Lake Champlain became the nation's sixth Great Lake. It happened when President Clinton reauthorized the National Sea Grant Program with a bill coauthored by Vermont senator Patrick Leahy, who slipped Champlain in with the rest of the big lakes. This was significant for more than the bragging rights it bestowed: states bordering Great Lakes could apply for $290 million in federal research and education grants. When the traditional Great Lakes states discovered Leahy's sleight of hand, they lobbied vigorously for the bill to be amended. They didn't want the power of their club to be diluted by the skinny lake stuffed between New York and Vermont. Congress worked out a comprise, taking Champlain off the list but still allowing Vermont to compete for the research dollars. "We have agreed to call Lake Champlain a cousin instead of a little brother to those larger lakes in the Midwest

Ray Moore sending the last
of his herd to their new home.
Kirk Kardashian.

Mike Rosmann.
*Steve Kowalski/A Better
Exposure Photography.*

Philip Ranney and
Bridget. *Kirk Kardashian.*

Paul Godin and the Lely
Astronaut robotic milking
machine. *Kirk Kardashian.*

A typical dairy farm in
California's San Joaquin Valley.
Kirk Kardashian.

An advertisement from PETA's
"Unhappy Cow" campaign.
Image courtesy of PETA, www.peta.org.

Sam Simon. *Kirk Kardashian.*

Cows grazing on Sam Simon's
Plankenhorn Farm. *Sam Simon.*

while accomplishing our goal of improving the ecology of our lake," Leahy said. "This is a win-win solution that achieves our purpose and skirts the symbolism."

Champlain might be a little cousin to the Great Lakes, but they have another connection: phosphorus pollution—most acutely, in Lake Michigan's Green Bay. It happens to be at the terminus of the Fox River, which flows north from the dairy country of Brown County. People in the water quality field like to use numbers to describe phosphorus loading, but to the lay person, a picture does a better job. Thankfully, on April 14, 2011, photographer Steve Seilo was taking aerial photos of Green Bay and captured stunning images of underwater plumes of brown muck dumping into Lake Michigan; the sediment billows from the Fox River and penetrates deep into the body of the bay, like an ink stain slowly spreading across a sheet of paper.

The Fox River is the largest contributor of phosphorus to Lake Michigan, and the third largest contributor of sediment. Wisconsin's water quality standard for phosphorus concentrations is 0.075 parts per million (ppm), but in every creek draining into the lower Fox River, recent concentrations have ranged from 0.12 to 0.4 ppm. Some 70 percent of the agricultural fields mapped with more than 0.075 ppm of phosphorus had streams connected to them, and many of these fields are located close to livestock facilities.

But, perhaps worse than polluting Lake Michigan, agriculture in this part of Wisconsin has poisoned the groundwater.

There are a few things you should know about Brown County, Wisconsin. First and foremost, it's the home of the Green Bay Packers. And Packers fans don't call themselves "cheeseheads" for nothing: this part of the state is a dairy powerhouse, with the industry generating $3 billion of economic activity every year. It has eighteen CAFOS, farms with at least a thousand animal units or seven hundred dairy cows, which is more than any other part of Wisconsin. These CAFOS are home to 41,000 cows that produce 260 million gallons of manure each year, equivalent to the annual waste from 250,000 humans. The town of Morrison, where the largest number of wells were rendered unusable, has fewer than 2,000 people.

Oh, and it has a lot of karst. Derived from the German name for a limestone-rich region of Slovenia, karst is a geologic feature that's exemplified by shallow bedrock, sinkholes, fissures, and underground towers of rock. Brown County is bisected by a swath of karst known as the Niagara Escarpment, a ridge of rock that arcs from the southwest to the northeast, shooting through Wisconsin and Ontario and ending at Niagara Falls. By itself, karst is fairly harmless—though a nuisance if you're trying to excavate a foundation. But don't count on karst-addled terrain to clean your groundwater: since there's so little soil between the surface and the aquifer, there's no time for the bacteria or nitrates to be filtered. In the case of sinkholes, a stream flows directly into the groundwater, with no filtering at all.

The first time karst became a very public problem for Brown County was in January of 2006, when rain fell in January onto frozen fields that had been recently treated with manure. Shortly after that, Bill Hafs, the county conservationist and department head for the Land and Water Conservation Department, started getting calls from Morrison town officials saying that residents' wells had a funny smell. But in fact, the problem dated back before 2006. Since at least 2004, various towns in the county had been issuing sporadic "boil water" advisories, when two or three households would report a manure smell coming from their faucets. The complaints piled higher than ever in 2006, so the University of Wisconsin commissioned a groundwater monitoring study, testing five hundred wells over four years for *E. coli*, coliform, and nitrates, the kind of contamination that usually flows from manure runoff. The results of the study were scary: more than a hundred wells were found to be contaminated, and they remain so today, which means that a high percentage of the township—a six-by-six-mile square—is drinking and cooking with bottled water. Unfortunately, they learned the hard way. Scores of people suffered chronic diarrhea, stomach illnesses, and ear infections, all as a result of wells poisoned with coliform bacteria and *E. coli.*

It doesn't take a genius to make the connection between manure-smelling water and the dozens of large dairy farms in the neighborhood. The question was the catalyst: what change precipitated this large-scale groundwater poisoning? The answer lies in the evolution of the dairy industry and the steady march of population growth. Since 1969, milk production per head of cattle in Wisconsin has increased from 9,959 to 22,300 pounds per year (and more milk equals more manure), yet the acreage of farmland has decreased from 300,000 (2,600 farms) in 1954 to 162,000 (1,053 farms) in 2008, mostly thanks to sprawl from the Green Bay metro area. When you factor in setbacks from streams, wells, and wetlands, that acreage decreases to about 106,000. And on that land, the production of oats has stopped, hay has decreased, and corn and soybean crops have gone up. What this means is that there's less ground cover over winter, and a drastically reduced amount of land being asked to soak up a drastically increased amount of manure. Studies from Clemson University and the University of Wisconsin have shown that you need about two to three acres of land per animal to absorb manure effectively; by that standard, Brown County is about 50,000 acres short.

"It's an unsustainable situation," Hafs says. "We don't have enough cropland to absorb the amount of animal waste being generated."

But the power of the purse can't be overestimated. Any industry that brings billions of dollars of economic activity into a rural area is going to be treated delicately, and that's what happened with dairy regulations in Wisconsin. The University of Wisconsin, for example, drafted a karst report, providing recommendations to lawmakers about how to prevent further groundwater contamination, but the legislature didn't act on it. Another effort is underway to map and identify the karst features and put them into GIS systems, so farmers know precisely where the hazards are. That, however, would require farmers to voluntarily check the GIS maps before they spread manure. And if the map says a farmer should be driving another few miles to spread manure on a field without karst, it creates a tough decision, since hauling manure is expensive. "The tendency will be to land-apply manure as close to the buildings as you can," Hafs explains, "because it will be a savings." Now imagine the calculus when diesel prices reach $5 per gallon and milk prices don't budge. You end up with farmers either going out of business or choosing the easier, and more harmful, way to spread manure. "The dairies are here to stay," Hafs concludes. "One answer may be that people will just have to drink bottled water."

CLEARING THE AIR

In 1997, at around the same time that Tom Frantz was discovering his new megadairy neighbors, Brent Newell, a summer intern at the Center for Race, Poverty and the Environment (CRPE), was poring over a proposal by J. G. Boswell Co. to build a 55,000-cow suite of dairies in the Kings County, California, town of Hanford, in the Central Valley. Newell's work basically formed the beginning of CRPE's dairy campaign, a series of lawsuits designed to both raise awareness about the sudden influx of megadairies, and to change the policies and laws that regulate them.

Today, Newell is general counsel at CRPE, a nonprofit organization that provides legal representation and community organizing on things like the siting of hazardous waste dumps and pesticide drift—classic environmental justice and civil rights issues. And the dairy campaign he began in 1997 is still going, it's just tied up in a legal limbo of massive proportions. For Newell, the heart of the issue hasn't changed. The lax regulation of dairy farms in the Central Valley is a bona fide environmental justice issue: the more affluent parts of the country are benefiting from low milk prices, but not bearing the environmental and health costs occasioned by the industrial way of dairy farming.

This brings us back to the 55,000-cow farm complex J. G. Boswell had planned. You may have heard of J. G. Boswell: it's one of the largest cotton producers in the world, and owns about 150,000 acres in the San Joaquin Valley. The story of the company and its namesake was recounted in stunning detail in *The King of California: J.G. Boswell and the Making of a Secret American Empire,* by Mark Arax and Rick Wartzman, a book that paints a picture of a guy unapologetic about the size and influence of his business. "I'm the bad guy because I'm big," Boswell once said to the *Los Angeles Times.* "I'm not going to try to fight it. I can't change an image and say, 'Well, I'm righteous and good and all that.' But I'm telling you . . . I'm not going to apologize for our size."

One example of that size is the story of how in 1949 the company used its clout to encourage the construction of the Pine Flat Dam, which stopped the water from flowing into Tulare Lake. Once the largest freshwater lake west of the Mississippi, Tulare was drained at Boswell's urging and the bed is now farmland, owned by Boswell.

J. G. Boswell Co. tried to use that power to construct five dairies with 11,000 cows each. The plan wasn't actually Boswell's idea, but that of R. Sherman Railsback, the company's chief of operations. Given the expertise in obtaining land use permits J. G. Boswell Co. had gained over the years, Railsback figured that he would market seven thousand acres of Boswell land with all the permissions necessary to run the dairy farms, and try to sell them to the dairy farmers escaping the sprawl of Southern California—the same cohort that was invading Frantz's neighborhood.

The proposal sailed through the local permitting processes, for this was friendly territory. Nearly everyone who had a say in approving the project had either worked for Boswell at some point, or had family who did. CRPE, on the other hand, had no conflict of interest. When its lawyers discovered that Kings County was issuing permits to dairy farms with barely a lick of scrutiny, they dug a little deeper. It turned out that the county believed the dairies represented no possibility of an adverse impact on the environment, so it ruled that the proposals were exempt from the California Environmental Quality Act (CEQA). This law is the state analog to the National Environmental Policy Act (NEPA), and while it doesn't have the power to reject a proposal outright, it has the nearly equal power of requiring applicants to do intense disclosures, conduct environmental reviews, and provide comprehensive reports. Since these laws were passed (NEPA in 1969 and CEQA in 1970), they have been a central tool for countless environmental organizations to slow down projects and make sure the relevant communities and interested parties have a full understanding of what a piece of development might augur for the human and natural environments.

By exempting a megadairy from CEQA, the county lets the applicant through the process without making any statement about the project's possible adverse environmental impacts—in other words, saying that there *won't* be an adverse impact. In the case of the Boswell proposal, CRPE knew this position was untenable. Some 55,000 cows? They're going to have an impact. Initially, CRPE thought the main issue would be water pollution. But then it learned that, given the size of the dairies, air pollution was going to be the major problem, and because the air quality in the valley is already bad, the farms would exacerbate it.

CEQA is a "self-executing" law, which means that it's up to the governmental entity issuing the permit to comply with it. But when that doesn't happen, it's common for environmental organizations to take the entity, such as a county, to court. That's what CRPE did with the Boswell case, and then did it again for a 28,000-cow dairy proposed for nearby Kern County. They argued that these dairies would undoubtedly have a negative effect on the environment, and when that is the case, CEQA requires the applicant to complete an environmental impact report (EIR). Filing a report might not sound like a difficult thing to do, but an EIR is both expensive and time consuming (sometimes running into the thousands of pages). But what's most troubling for applicants is that if the report, in all its truth and glory, shows that the project will have significant environmental impact, the applicant must either offer less impactful alternatives, or come up with a way to mitigate it. Many times, these two requirements have been the death knell of megadairies. CRPE won both lawsuits, with the 28,000-cow proposal being the first time an EIR was done for a dairy farm. J. G. Boswell, on the other hand, decided the EIR was too much trouble and just gave up. The result, however, was that now two counties acknowledged that dairies were not exempt from CEQA, and a third county, Tulare, soon followed suit. All told, by 2004 these lawsuits organized and litigated by CRPE had halted about a hundred proposed dairy farms in the San Joaquin Valley. That same year, Kern County issued a moratorium on new dairy farms, stating that it wouldn't issue a single dairy permit until all the proposed projects completed a group EIR, showing the impact of the farms as a whole. That moratorium is still in effect, and no dairies have been built in Kern County in more than eight years.

In Tulare County, the specter of an EIR slowed dairy permitting down substantially, and it seems that every time a dairy is proposed, somebody starts a campaign against it. The last big one was proposed in the tiny hamlet of Allensworth, a settlement of five hundred souls in the middle of a prairie. Its main street is no more than a jug-handle off "dairy alley," California Highway 43. Nettie Morrison, a seventy-six-year-old African American with a grandmotherly kindness, is the de facto mayor of the town, though modesty makes her loathe the term.

"So many people don't know where Allensworth is," she said, on a bright spring day in the dining room of her tidy ranch house. Next door is the elementary school; across the street is the community center. If you count the water district building, those are the three public buildings in town. "Allensworth has a beautiful history," she continues. "That's why I moved here thirty-two years ago."

Long before that, in 1908, Colonel Allen Allensworth, an escaped slave from Kentucky, founded the Allensworth colony under Booker T. Washington's tenets of self-reliance. It was the westernmost settle-

ment among the many that were created by blacks fleeing segrega-
tion laws, sharecropping, and lynch mobs. Allensworth, who was
once the highest-ranking black Army officer, selected this spot in
Tulare County for the same reason that dairy farmers do: land was
inexpensive, the soil is fertile, and there is plenty of water. The community thrived for a while, putting up those things that define a
town—church, library, school house, hotel, and general store—and
grew to a population of two hundred. Things started to go downhill
in 1914, when the railroad bypassed the town and cut it off from most
of the California economy. Then more towns sprouted up between
Allensworth and the mountains, making claim on the water that
flowed into Allensworth. Then came the Great Depression, and in
rapid succession the post office closed, public services dried up,
and people moved away. By the mid-1970s, Allensworth was pretty
much a ghost town.

Yet, some people never forgot Allensworth and what it symbol-
ized for African Americans—freedom, self-determination, and opportunity. In the early 1970s, they made an effort to save the town,
and by 1976 it had become a state historic park. Today, many of the
original Allensworth buildings stand restored, in vibrant colors of
mint green, blue, and red, and people can tour them on the weekends. Out on the main drag of Allensworth, where people actually
live, the town seems like a sleepy outpost in the wide-open country,
immensely vulnerable but making a go of it just the same.

"We want to see Allensworth grow in a positive way," says Morrison. "We've been offered a sewer sludge treatment plant, an industrial food grease dump, a chemical plant, and then a megadairy.
Just because we're poverty stricken doesn't mean we're going to let
you dump anything on us."

The megadairy, proposed in 2006 by a wealthy rancher named
Samuel Etchegaray, was the most recent attempt at "economic development" for Allensworth. It would have contained 16,000 cows
and a couple of waste lagoons, all within a few hundred yards of the

town and state historic park—the only one in California devoted to African American history. Since Allensworth—officially a hamlet of the town of Earlimart—lacked a spokesperson, the town supervisor asked Morrison to be it. She was one of the longest-tenured residents, and she seemed to have the guts and passion to execute the job. "It wasn't something I wanted to do," she says, "but it was something that needed to be done." For the next eight months, Morrison traveled up and down the San Joaquin Valley, speaking out against the proposal—and the manure smell, swarms of flies, and groundwater pollution it threatened—and gaining support in the fight. Luke Cole, a founder of CRPE, put his organization's team on the case, calling the proposed dairy "about as close to intentional discrimination as you can see."

The popular outcry was powerful, linking this massive dairy with a brand of racism that California couldn't tolerate. Jerry Brown, then the attorney general, sued the Tulare County board of supervisors to stop the construction of the farm, and then the California Assembly passed a bill to block any type of CAFO from moving in next to Allensworth. In exchange, the state paid Etchegaray $3.5 million for the development rights, and Etchegaray has turned the land into a pomegranate orchard. The land, right across the highway from Allensworth, is peaceful now, encumbered only by a vast grid of pomegranate saplings, and when the wind kicks up across the valley, the most it deposits in Allensworth is a little dust. Colonel Allensworth moved out there to escape discrimination, and the last place he must have envisioned it coming from was a dairy farm. Nettie Morrison, who is happy to stay at home these days with a small dog named Gizmo, feels good knowing that if Colonel Allensworth came by today he would see his work carrying on.

====

CRPE helped Allensworth escape the fate of having a megadairy next door, but its most important work still continues, and has a much larger scope. While general counsel Brent Newell was waging the CEQA battle, he learned something shocking: that California's version of the Clean Air Act had a giant exemption for agriculture. With the CEQA victories in hand, and the dairy farm EIRs being made public, Newell had a trove of evidence showing that agricultural operations were a real source of air pollution. As such, the next move was to tell the Environmental Protection Agency that it was approving California's state implementation plan (SIP) of the Clean Air Act, even though the SIP was vastly more lenient than the federal law. Under the Supremacy Clause, anytime there's both a federal and a state law on the same subject—in this case, air pollution—the state law must be at least as strict as the federal. California's Clean Air Act didn't pass that test.

That message became the general thrust of *Association of Irritated Residents (AIR) and Communities for Land, Air & Water v. EPA,* a 2002 lawsuit, partially organized by Tom Frantz, that succeeded in forcing the EPA to withhold California's federal highway funding until the legislature removed the agricultural exemption from the state's Clean Air Act. Senate Bill 700, the new law that obliterated the exemption, took effect on New Year's Day of 2004 and had the effect of requiring new and expanding dairy operations to comply with the pollution control rules of the Clean Air Act. The most onerous of those rules requires any major air polluter, such as a large dairy farm, to install what the industry calls "BACT"—best available control technology—and buy offsets for its emissions of particulate matter, volatile organic compounds, and NOx. Even though this law now applied to dairy farms, it was fairly obvious that the industry was ignoring it. So CRPE returned to court, filing two lawsuits against dairies and one against a chicken farm. In the 2007 case of *AIR v. C.R. Vanderham Dairy,* the defense argued that there were further exemptions in state law that relieved the dairy of its duty to comply with Senate Bill 700. The judge wasn't buying it; as before, the Supremacy Clause reigned supreme, and the dairy industry was facing the most disadvantageous ruling it had ever seen. "That sent shockwaves through the industry," Newell says, "because it was the first time we successfully enforced the state implementation plan."

The ruling came down in 2008, during the waning days of the big-ag-friendly Bush administration, so naturally, the dairy lobby pushed hard for a bailout. The EPA came back, predictably enough, with a shameless proposal: a rule that would retroactively exempt dairies from buying offsets—the most financially painful part of the opinion. The federal judge considered the proposal and, as if caught in no-man's-land, paused the battle and asked the California attorney general to submit an opinion on the effect of one provision of state law. As it stands the attorney general hasn't penned the opinion, so the EPA has an excuse to do nothing on its proposal. In short, "We're sitting on our ass," Newell says.

By CRPE's account, if the EPA does the right thing, it will refuse to amend the state implementation plan retroactively, the *Vanderham* ruling will become official, and hundreds of large dairy farms will be forced to buy offsets for their emission of various air pollutants. The way Paul Martin sees it, dairy farmers have come a long way in reducing their harmful impact on the environment, and if you force them to move too quickly on offsets it will have a devastating effect on the industry. Martin is the director of environmental services at the Western United Dairymen, a group that represents dairy farmers making more than 60 percent of the milk in California. Since Senate Bill 700 went into effect, he points out, every dairy farm with 175 cows or more has "stepped up to the plate" and followed the rules. For PM 10, that means putting a conservation management plan into effect that reduces emissions caused by disturbances of soil. Diaries have done this in myriad ways, including paving dirt paths, following speed limits, installing wind barriers, and applying water to dry areas. The San Joaquin Valley, he notes, is now in "attainment" for PM 10.

But that still leaves ozone—that nasty brew of VOCs and NOx. The valley is an "extreme nonattainment" area for ozone (believe it or not, the San Joaquin Unified Air Pollution Control District, which is charged with implementing the Clean Air Act in this part of California, voluntarily downgraded itself to "extreme nonattainment" so it would have more time to concoct a solution), and the most stubborn contributor to that problem, apart from the cars everyone drives, is the off-gassing from feed piles on dairy farms. New rules for controlling VOCs from silage are coming out soon, but critics contend that they pay lip service to the issue, since they consist of practices that are already in the farmers' best interests: covering feed piles, for example, which allows the feed to ferment more fully and passes more microbes to the cows. Research on best management practices for silage is ongoing.

In the meantime, Martin reports, "milk prices have increased, but feed costs have accelerated faster. Farmers are still in a negative situation, and I don't know how a lot of them are hanging on." As a former dairy farmer, Martin says he'd experienced plenty of tough times, but there had always been a light at the end of the tunnel. "Our farmers are not seeing the light," says Martin. "There's some pretty scared people out there." They have good reason: 225 dairies have gone out of business in the past three years in the valley, and operating as a factory farm will likely get more expensive as air pollution standards get ratcheted up. Some dairies already must buy offsets for PM 10, which is a substantial amount of money, but the real fear is that farms will be forced to offset VOC emissions—that could destroy the business model completely.

Newell is well aware of the consequences of CRPE winning the *Vanderham* case. In broad terms, it would mean that factory-style milk producers would internalize their costs instead of pushing them out onto society. "Dairymen will have a choice of absorbing that cost, going out of business, or choosing a different model for milk production," Newell says. "The alternative model for milk production is pasture-based dairying. And when you do it that way, you're not subject to the permitting requirements of the Clean Air Act." New research from Pennsylvania State University shows why: pasture-grazed cows produce 30 percent less ammonia than cows kept in barns, and 8 percent less methane, NOx, and carbon dioxide.

"I wouldn't say my clients are on a mission to make the dairy industry change its economic model," Newell adds. "Their objective is much more simple. They live in the most polluted air basin in the United States, and they want to breathe clean air."

THE WORKERS

Early one morning in the spring of 2009, Jose Obeth Santiz Cruz awoke and dressed for the biggest adventure of his life. A fresh-faced nineteen-year-old with boyish Mayan features, he was born in San Isidro, a small town of lush hills in southwestern Mexico in the state of Chiapas, just a few miles from the Pacific coast. For a long time, the people of San Isidro grew and sold coffee to earn money, but when the price of that commodity plummeted they decided to switch to another: corn. To grow corn in the soil of Chiapas, however, you need a lot of fertilizer, and the added cost makes farming close to a break-even proposition. From the air, San Isidro looks poverty stricken in a rustic, bucolic sort of way, with narrow dirt lanes lined by telephone poles and wooden fences. On the ground, where the floors of most homes are muddy and shaded by corrugated metal roofs, where the cooking is done on open hearths and there's little indoor plumbing, the economic reality takes on a more desperate hue.

Santiz Cruz was frustrated with being poor, so he decided to leave for the United States. "Mom, I need to go make a living," he said.

His mother, Zoyla, a short, weathered woman with grayish black hair and expressive brown eyes, asked him not to go. Three of her sons had already died, and she didn't want to lose another. But Santiz Cruz was committed to the journey. He considered it his duty to make some money and send it back to his family.

"Well, it's your decision," Zoyla told him. "We will be here. As poor as we were born, poor we will die."

Santiz Cruz shouldered his bag and set off on the nearly two-thousand-mile journey north to the desert on the border of Arizona. He waited on the Mexican side for twenty days, subsisting mostly on bread and water, and then crossed illegally and made his way to Vermont. It took him six months to find a job on David and Peg Howrigan's farm in Fairfield, and then a few more months to pay off his debts to those who had helped him cross the border and obtain a fake social security card and I.D. But by late fall, Santiz Cruz appeared to be in good spirits: finally able to send money to his family, a picture shows him wearing jeans and a flannel shirt, giving the thumbs-up to the camera as he experiences his first snowstorm.

Not long after that, on a cold afternoon in late December, Santiz Cruz was raking manure into the automatic gutter-cleaner on the Howrigan barn. The mechanism, which uses a giant chain to drag scrapers across the floor, is powered by an electric motor that turns a series of flywheels and pulleys. While Santiz Cruz was working close to the machine, his shirt was pulled into a flywheel. Before he could get it off, the shirt was pulled deeper and deeper into the machine and strangled him to death. When he was discovered by a coworker, a compatriot from San Isidro, his body was propped up by his arm, which had also been tangled in the mechanism. He was barely twenty years old.

Vermont is a small state, so when someone dies in a farming accident, word gets around. This time, in addition to the widespread sadness about a young life snuffed out too soon, there was the mystery of who the boy really was and where he had come from. The idea that a person could live, work on a dairy farm, and die in Vermont without anyone knowing his identity was upsetting to a lot of Vermonters, but perhaps to none more than Brendan O'Neill, who teaches English to migrant farm workers in the western part of the state. After the authorities figured out Santiz Cruz's real name, there arose the question of how to afford the young man a proper burial. That's when O'Neill founded the Vermont Migrant Farmworker Solidarity Project, which organized a candlelight vigil in Burlington and raised money to return Santiz Cruz's body to San Isidro. O'Neill, along with filmmaker Sam Mayfield and activist Gustavo Teran, accompanied the body to Chiapas and filmed the documentary "Silenced Voices," which uncovers the deep connection between this distant corner of Mexico and the villages of Vermont. They discovered that about eighty people from San Isidro, a community of indigenous Tojolabal Mayans, work on dairy farms in Vermont, and it is their regular shipments of money from north to south that keep the town from descending further into oblivion.

On January 13, 2010, as women wailed in despair, six men dressed variously in leather jackets, jeans, and baseball caps lifted Santiz Cruz's simple coffin into the back of a white pickup truck loaded with pink and white flowers. The truck crept down a dusty road and much of the community followed, saying good-bye to the boy who so bravely had left his home so that he could make it better.

Troubling as this story is, it isn't a random anomaly in an otherwise anodyne narrative of the dairy industry. A 2009 survey of five thousand dairy farms by the National Milk Producers Federation (NMPF) found that 50 percent of the farms used immigrant labor, and that those workers are helping to supply 62 percent of the U.S. milk supply.[1] Without these approximately 57,000 milkers and farmhands, says the NMPF, retail milk prices would increase by 61 percent, U.S. economic output would decrease by $22 billion, and 133,000 people would lose their jobs.

This puts dairy farmers in a tough situation. In order to keep their farms running, they must hire workers who are most likely illegal aliens and then take pains to make sure they don't get deported. It also creates a class of unrepresented workers who are an easy target for exploitation and abuse. Consumers, too, don't like knowing that, in all probability, the milk in their refrigerator was expressed by the hands of an illicit labor force suffering the indignities attendant to the underground economy. The best solution, according to everyone from farmers to politicians to workers, is some form of immigration reform. But reform has been a long time coming, and proposed bills seem to keep getting pushed to the bottom of a pile of other congressional business deemed more urgent. However, for the farmer who wakes up one morning to find all of his workers arrested, and 1,200 cows waiting to be milked, urgency is an understatement.

=====

Young Mexicans like Santiz Cruz have crossed the border to work in the United States at least since the mid-1800s. Generally speaking workers follow the money, and by 1869 in the United States, where a transcontinental railroad was connecting the coasts, there was suddenly a lot of money to be made in shipping produce from the warmer environs to the Northeast. The money, of course, wasn't in the picking—those jobs have always paid a pittance—but in owning the means of production. That was what U.S. citizens wanted to do, not stoop down all day in the hot sun and pluck fruit off the vine. So there was a void to be filled, and Mexicans filled it. There were few border stations in those days, so when the Mexican revolution hit in 1910, refugees streamed into the United States and became the backbone of American farms. These refugees had traits that would define border-hopping Mexicans for years to come: desperation and a willingness to work for paltry sums just to survive. The first time Mexicans began to be deported was in 1931, during the Dust Bowl, when white workers migrated to California looking for jobs. The border cinched up during the Depression and stayed fairly tight through the early 1940s. Then World War II began and, with it, a new labor shortage. The Chinese who had helped build the railroads had moved into the cities; many Japanese farm workers were forced into internment camps; and the mainstream whites who weren't fighting were manning assembly lines to feed wartime production. That left a farm worker vacuum yet again, and again we turned to our neighbors to the south. This time, the recruitment was active and explicit, and it took the form of the bracero program, which started in September of 1942 for the Californian sugar beet harvest. The program proved extremely popular among farmers, for it gave them a nearly unlimited supply of hard workers whom they could pay pennies on the dollar. The program was phased out in 1964—mostly in response to stories in the press about exploited workers—but in those twenty-two years approximately 4.5 million Mexicans immigrated to the United States to work on farms.[2]

In about the middle of the bracero period, another immigration law was passed for migrant workers: the H2 temporary visa. It allowed people to enter the United States to perform temporary work as long as the farmers could prove two things: that U.S. workers were not available, and that wages and working conditions of the guest workers would not adversely affect those of U.S. workers. Predictably, while the bracero program was in effect the H2 program wasn't popular—why would farmers choose the paperwork and headaches of H2 when they had plenty of willing workers? But once the bracero spigot was shut off, H2 was the only way farmers could get legitimate foreign workers.

During all of the bracero days, and many of the H2 days, farm workers were readily abused, underpaid, and completely vulnerable to the whims of farm bosses. A wave of awakening swept over the country in the mid-1960s, as the Chavez-led United Farm Workers staged strikes and boycotts to improve working conditions for farm laborers. A series of events opened a brief golden period for farm workers until the late 1970s: Chavez appeared on the cover of *Time*, California passed the Agricultural Labor Relations Act, and, as a result, farm wages rose to twice the minimum wage under UFW contracts. But the improvements were short-lived. In response to the rising cost of labor, farmers invested heavily in mechanization wherever possible. Then, in the early 1980s, Mexico devalued the peso, which exerted downward pressure on wages. Also, because there was no penalty for farmers who unknowingly hired illegal immigrants, farmers turned to "farm-labor contractors" to recruit undocumented workers, resulting in hundreds of thousands of Mexicans entering the U.S. workforce. By 1984, it was estimated that 20 percent of the 2.5 million people employed on farms were undocumented.[3]

It's understandable, then, that talk of immigration reform worried growers across the United States, since they had come to rely upon undocumented workers. In 1986 their fears were largely allayed by the Immigration Control and Reform Act (IRCA), which ushered in the Special Agricultural Worker (SAW) program and the H2-A visa, the successor to H2. SAW gave permanent legal residency status to undocumented workers who could prove they had performed agricultural work during a two-year period. The changes in H2-A required farmers to give preference to U.S. workers and make an effort to recruit them; only once those efforts had failed would the Department of Labor issue the farmer a certificate to import workers to cover his farm labor needs. As a form of amnesty, SAW was great for immigrants and farmers, even though critics say amnesty encourages people to enter the country illegally in the hope they will be granted permission to stay later on. The H2-A program, on the other hand, has been more of a failure. It's decried as cumbersome and unfair, and is thus unpopular—only 2 percent of the total agricultural worker population are in the United States on H2-A visas.[4]

All told, the IRCA legalized about 1.2 million farm workers, and 90 percent of those were Mexican.[5] The law mandated enhanced border control but failed to appropriate the funds necessary for that control, so illegal immigrants, answering the call of American businesses, continued to migrate north. As a result, in the twenty-five years since the IRCA was passed, the proportion of undocumented laborers has tripled to about 60 percent of all farm workers (on dairy farms, the percentage is closer to 40).[6] Now more than ever, farmers are in a tenuous relationship with their key employees.

Factors influencing people to migrate for work usually fall into two categories: push and pull. When wages in one's home country are very low, or if employment opportunities are sparse, the bad conditions there "push" people to leave to find work elsewhere. When a favorable employment market exists in another country, those conditions "pull" people into its economy. In either case, the power dynamics between employers and workers can be toxic for communities, as a vicious circle of increased farm employment, immigration, and poverty takes hold in rural towns. It's a common juxtaposition that plays out: neat rows of crops in the fields, shabby tenements in the farm worker neighborhoods. Fresno County, California, for example, is the nation's largest farm county, and it has six of the ten poorest towns in the state.[7]

It wasn't until the mid-1990s that the dairy industry contributed to this cycle of immigration and poverty. Before then, most farms were small enough that they could be operated by the family or families that owned them. Yet, as margins shrank and farms had to expand to achieve economies of scale, they soon outgrew their internal capacity for labor and had to start recruiting workers from wherever they could. According to Tom Maloney, a senior extension associate at Cornell University who specializes in human resources on farms, families reach their breaking point when herds start rising past two hundred. As he's watched farms grow he's seen farmers evolve into human resource managers, performing administrative tasks—payroll, pay rate calculation, benefits, training, recruiting, and performance evaluations—more than typical farm labor.

Right around the same time dairy farms were getting larger, the United States, Canada, and Mexico signed the North American Free Trade Agreement, tearing down barriers to commerce between the three nations. Free trade sounds good when you say it fast, but NAFTA has had some deleterious effects on the Mexican economy and way of life. For one, NAFTA required Mexico to eliminate its support program for small farmers, but it allowed the U.S. to maintain its own subsidies. The double standard has caused scores of small Mexican farms to go out of business and 2 million Mexican farm jobs to disappear. Actually, they didn't disappear, they just shifted north. Another NAFTA provision that ended up pushing people from Mexico was the required privatization of formerly state run organizations, such as the electric utilities. By the time this process had run its course, the private electric companies were selling most of the electricity abroad, leaving millions in Mexico—where the electricity was being produced—without access to power. Plenty of these people, many of whom were from Chiapas, not surprisingly decided to leave for a place where they could partake in twentieth-century technology.

For the farm workers that remained in Mexico, life got even tougher than it had been before NAFTA. The unions were destroyed, which resulted in flexible labor laws and massive layoffs. NAFTA also forced Mexico to overturn Article 27 of its constitution, a law added in 1917, after the Mexican Revolution, that granted communities communal ownership of the land. With Article 27 gone, much of Mexico's farmland was up for sale and turned into private property, further fracturing communities and ceding power to rich oligarchies that could afford large land purchases. These factors might as well have deported Mexico's citizens, because they made it nearly impossible to live there. Thus, ever since NAFTA was passed in 1994, the number of Mexicans migrating to the United States each year has increased substantially.

The U.S. dairy industry ended up pulling a fair number of those migrants into its ranks. Some of the first immigrant dairy workers in New York were actually Guatemalans who had finished picking onions in Oswego County and wanted to stay on in the state. So they went to the local state employment office and asked about more agricultural work. The state worker called up some dairy farmers a few counties away and one of them said, "Send them down." Latin Americans live in close social networks, and that county is now filled with Guatemalan dairy workers. The trend has spread throughout the country. Today, according to a 2009 survey by Cornell University, there are about 2,600 immigrant dairy workers in New York, and they work on farms of all sizes, not just big ones.[8] A 2007 study by the Wisconsin field office for the National Agricultural Statistical Service reported that there were more than 4,000 Hispanic dairy workers in that state.[9] Vermont, according to estimates by its Agency for Agriculture, Food and Markets, has about 2,000 immigrant dairy workers. And across the Western states, the majority of the 50,000 dairy workers are Hispanic, most of them undocumented, monolingual Spanish speakers.[10]

The poor prospects for livable wages in Mexico and Central America have certainly pushed millions of workers into the United States. But as Zoe Lofgren (d-ca), the ranking member of the House Judiciary Subcommittee on Immigration, Citizenship, Refugees, Border Security, and International Law, said on the *Colbert Report* in 2010, we have two signs at our borders: "No Trespassing" and "Help Wanted."[11] So, as much as Hispanic workers are pushed by poverty, they are welcomed with open arms into our fields and barns. Why is that? Most people you ask will acknowledge the truth: Americans just don't want to be farm workers. In 2010, the United Farm Workers put this idea to the test with its "Take Our Jobs, Please" campaign. In response to critics who claimed that immigrant workers took jobs from U.S. citizens, the ufw invited unemployed Americans to apply for jobs as farm workers and promised to help connect them with farm owners looking to hire. The campaign lasted a few months, and the ufw received thousands of inquiries (some of which were hate mail). All told, about a dozen U.S. citizens followed through with the process and began working in agriculture.

Ever since dairies have searched off the farm for workers, they've had trouble finding good labor. The hours of a milker are long and physically demanding; turnover rates are high. "A lot of farmers struggle to find people who are reliable and will stay for two or three or four years," says Tom Maloney from the Cornell University Extension Service. "In the mid-90s, people said to me, 'I don't know if I want to get any bigger, because I don't want to be in a situation where I've got 500 cows to milk and have several people quit at the same time.'" But once the market opened up for Mexican workers, farmers grabbed on to them. Maloney surveyed dairy farmers in 1999 about hiring Mexicans. At that time, there were no more than thirty farmers who had done so. "I was trying to decide in my own mind, Was it going to work? Was it going to catch on? Because of the language barrier and the cultural barrier," Maloney says. "It seems silly for me to say that now, because it caught on like wildfire." Indeed, from California to Vermont, many dairy farms just couldn't function without Hispanic labor.

Mike Haynes, a dairy farmer in northern Vermont, certainly couldn't get by without his crew of five Mexican milkers. Haynes founded his farm in 1986 with 40 cows. By 1997 his restless personality—and the realities of the industry—had caused him to expand to 1,800 acres and 1,900 cattle, 830 of which are milked three times per day. He hired his first immigrant laborers fifteen years ago, through a recruiting service that promised to handle all the paperwork and guaranteed the workers would be legal. Six months after the two milkers began working, the local customs agents showed up to review their documents. The workers turned out to be illegal, and ever since Haynes has done his own recruiting and verification. Haynes turned to immigrant labor for the same reasons most farmers do: no one else wants to do the work. He would place an ad in the local paper and get people who were on furlough from jail, or on house arrest and without a driver's license. "My past has taught me that these people are not going to stick around," he says. "They're here to take care of their immediate needs, but as soon as three weeks are up they're out of here."

After his bad experience with the first two immigrant milkers, Haynes hired two more on his own. They turned out to be worthless for other reasons. They didn't follow directions and had a poor work ethic, something you don't hear too often about Mexicans. "There's good and bad in each culture. You need to go through eight of them to find a good one," he says. But since then Haynes has found five good workers, and he holds on to them. They've been on his farm for years now, and when they want to visit Mexico they find their own temporary replacements from their community, and sometimes even train them.

Mike Marsh, the chief executive officer at Western United Dairymen (WUD), says that his member-farmers have similar trouble finding U.S. workers. Since he joined WUD thirteen years ago he's talked with farmers extensively on this issue, because it's so critical to the success of the farms. In all these conversations, he tells, "only one dairy producer has indicated that someone showed up at his dairy who was not Latino and looking for work." When asked why that was the case, Marsh acknowledges that the job is hard, usually has early or late hours, is dirty and manure-filled, and involves working with animals, which many people don't like. "Plus, it's a rural life," he says. "Probably not for city slickers."

True enough. But there are other reasons why you don't see Americans lining up for work on dairy farms, and many of them have to do with something called agricultural exceptionalism. This is not the farming cousin of so-called American exceptionalism, that certain *je ne sais quoi* that the United States is said to possess because of the way the country was founded. Agricultural exceptionalism is the somewhat misleading euphemism for a general lack of labor laws that apply to agricultural workers.

To understand this phenomenon, cast your mind back to the nineteenth and early twentieth centuries in American cities. Many were filled with factories and mills where men, women, and children toiled in unsafe, unsanitary, and oppressive conditions. The Triangle Shirtwaist Factory fire in 1911, which resulted in the deaths of 146 garment workers, most of whom were Jewish and Italian immigrant women, was considered the worst disaster in New York City history until the World Trade Center was destroyed ninety years later. It wasn't just that the workers had been packed into tight quarters; it was soon discovered that the bosses had locked the workers inside, so as to prevent the women from leaving their sewing machines. At that time, industrial workers and farm workers could expect similar treatment: backbreaking work, hazardous conditions, and low pay.

But the Triangle Shirtwaist disaster and many others led to the passage of progressive federal legislation in the 1930s that revolutionized the industrial workplace, while the American Farm Bureau and groups representing commodities growers lobbied hard to have agricultural workers exempted from these improvements. The labor reforms ushered in the forty-hour workweek and overtime pay; workers compensation laws; occupational safety and health rules coupled with a workers' compensation insurance system that gave employers lower premiums when employees had fewer accidents; federal and state minimum wage acts; and the National Labor Relations act, which gave industrial workers the right to collective bargaining.

Unfortunately, nearly every labor standard implemented at the federal and state level before 1960 excluded farm workers. This created a harsh dual world for workers. Factory pay, buoyed by minimum wage laws and union negotiations, floated higher and higher; farm worker wages, in a world of increased mechanization, sank to levels bordering on indentured servitude. A few states—the progressive ones, such as New York, New Jersey, and Michigan—passed basic laws that protected workers from unsafe transportation and overcrowded vehicles, and required employer-provided housing to have electricity and plumbing—but they were the exception, you could say.

That this unjust situation has been allowed to continue is a testament to the branding effort put forth by the agribusiness lobby. As it portrays farms as small, family operations struggling to make a living—and farm workers as free spirits who like to feel the sun on their backs and not be tied down to a desk job—it has succeeded in making the case that farms deserve to be exempt from labor laws, even though if you ask most citizens what they think of it, they'd probably disagree.

If you were a family member of one of the handful of U.S. dairy workers who died in 2009, you'd most certainly be upset that the Occupational Safety and Health Administration doesn't issue detailed regulations for most agricultural jobs. And you'd be more upset when you learned that this is the case even though the labor statistical category for dairy farming puts it at the top of a list of the five deadliest occupations, with a fatality rate that's more than double that of the runner up, the mining sector.[12] How do these workers die? Mostly in violent, bone-crushing ways. And farms, while sometimes punished with a fine from the state department in charge of workplace safety (many of which lack the manpower to enforce the regulations that do exist), seem to get off pretty easily. These examples come from a 2009 investigative report by Rebecca Clarren for *High Country News*:[13]

> Luis Alberto Enriq, 16, died on April 26, 2009, from internal injuries after a bull struck him and rammed him into a steel post. Penalty to dairy farm: None.
>
> Duarte Flores, 24, died on September 20, 2007, when, while clearing debris from a vacant lot, Flores drove a tractor into an irrigation canal. The tractor rolled, crushing Flores underneath. Penalty to dairy farm: $4,925.
>
> Chad Thompson, 30, died on March 6, 2008, when a fifty-foot-tall pile of silage collapsed on top of his truck. Thompson, inside the cab, was struck in the head and died instantly. Penalty to dairy farm: $1,700.
>
> Manuel Quintanilla, 64, died on December 27, 2007, after he fell off a tractor and it ran over him, crushing his head. Penalty to dairy farm: $1,800.
>
> Luis Gutierrez, 26, and Luis Armondo Gutierrez, Jr., 8, died on March 4, 2006, when they drowned in a ten-foot-deep manure pit. The pit was heavily contaminated and looked like solid ground. Both father and son were wearing large dairy boots that would have made swimming difficult. The pond had steep walls, and there were no witnesses. Luis Jr. didn't usually accompany his father to work. Penalty to dairy farm: $150.

But even if you survive the work on a dairy farm, you might not get paid for your trouble. Blanca Banuelos is an attorney at California Rural Legal Assistance (CRLA), whose mission is to secure economic justice and human rights for California's rural poor. CRLA is funded mostly by the Legal Services Corporation, an independent 501(c)(3) overseen by the federal government. It's the largest provider of civil legal aid for the poor in the United States. Banuelos started at

CRLA in 2004, and back then they were working mainly in behalf of nondairy farm workers. But that changed soon after Banuelos arrived. "We ended up realizing that, like other farm workers, dairy workers are very exploited," she says. "And I think, because they're so isolated, people don't know. You look at the way the dairy industry portrays itself to the public—the Happy Cow commercials—and that's not the reality."

The reality is that most dairy workers in California are paid an average of around $2,000 per month, work twelve to fourteen hours per day with little or no break, and often have to buy their own safety equipment. California is one of the very few states that has an overtime law for agricultural workers. But overtime pay doesn't kick in at forty hours; you need to work more than sixty hours per week on a California farm before that happens. Most dairy workers begin their jobs expecting to work ten hours per day, six days per week. Many times, however, the boss asks for more hours but doesn't pay the required overtime wages. "So you have workers working twelve-hour days and getting paid just a salary," Banuelos says. "So they're getting paid zero for those two hours of overtime."

That's where Banuelos comes in. She files lawsuits against dairy farms for back pay, and has won some big settlements. In 2005, for example, CRLA secured a $300,000 settlement from a Fresno dairy for unpaid back wages. In 2008, CRLA settled a case in Stanislaus County for $225,000, which was distributed among five workers who were often expected to work twenty-hour days. None of the settlement goes to pay CRLA's legal fees, so it all goes to the claimants. It's worth noting that, because it is funded by the Legal Services Corporation, CRLA can assist only legal, documented workers. But the wage and labor laws apply to all workers, legal or not. And it's against the law for a judge to inquire about the immigration status of workers filing for back pay.

One of CRLA's clients is Jose Pocotillo. On a sunny morning in a small farming town outside Fresno, Pocotillo, thirty-three, has his long frame draped over the engine of minivan that's got about as many miles on it as twenty trips around the earth (that is, 497,180).

He lives in a small, rusty trailer with his wife and two children, and is happy to call himself a former dairy worker. Pocotillo immigrated to the United States in 1999 from Sinaloa, Mexico, where he had worked as a trucker. He came here looking for a better life, "because it doesn't exist back there." His brother came first and got work on a dairy farm, and then got Jose a job there, too. He'd had some cows back in Mexico, so the animals weren't a problem for him. The milking machine was something new, but he learned quickly. His most recent dairy job paid $9.35 per hour, and Pocotillo was supposed to get a check every other week for $1,100. He thought he'd be working ten-hour days, but the usual day lasted twelve to thirteen. He worked from 6:00 a.m. to 7:30 p.m., straight. If he went to the bathroom or took a break, the dairy owner would yell at him, he says. When asked why he put up with this, he says, "We had to work. What can you do?"

In a usual shift, Pocotillo would milk 1,300 cows in a milking parlor designed to handle maybe 600. "We would eat and work at the same time," he explains. "The cows were wild. They didn't want to come into the milking area. And the foreman didn't want us to eat. So by 3:00 or 4:00 in the afternoon we were shaking from hunger. I worked ten days like that. And the one day I took a rest day, the farmer called me at 6:00 p.m. and told me I was fired. I asked, 'What about the ten days I worked?' He said, 'I already paid them to you. You can't do anything to me anyway, because I'm paying you with a personal check.'"

"That's why he called us," says the translator, a community organizer with CRLA. "He's getting ready to file for overtime."

If he could file for other expenses—such as the boots and gloves he'd have to buy for himself every few months, and that the dairy is supposed to provide—he would.

Pocotillo now works on a Caterpillar and doesn't miss his stints in the dairy barns. "I know the machinery and don't get hurt," he says.

Juan Hernandez is another CRLA client, and a former dairy worker in the San Joaquin Valley. Short and stoutly built, Hernandez, forty-four, wears a baseball cap bearing the name of his adopted home: U.S.A. As he talks about his dairy days, he alternates between Spanish and English. He's worked on numerous dairy farms since he emigrated from Veracruz, Mexico, to the United States in the early 1980s. He moved here figuring he'd work for a year, make some money, and move back. After all, he had finished high school in Mexico (where there's poor access to public education) and wanted to attend college. His plan was to work on a dairy farm to earn the money for school. When he arrived in the U.S., he began taking English classes at a local high school, and that's where he met a guy who tipped him off to the possibility of working on a dairy farm.

His first dairy job was on what he calls a "small" farm: one with seven to eight hundred cows. His schedule back then was 5:00 a.m. to 4:00 p.m., for which he'd receive $500 every two weeks. He stayed there for a number of years, and then moved to a bigger dairy for the remainder of his dairy career. When he left, in 2009, he was working split shifts for $950 every two weeks. A split shift is a long day made longer by a tantalizing break in the middle. His first shift of the day was from 7:00 a.m. to 2:00 p.m. He was offered no lunch break during that time, so he would try to sneak in a meal while milking cows. Then he went home to rest and came back to the farm at 7:00 p.m., where he'd do another shift until 2:00 a.m. That's fourteen hours of work in one "work day." When he took the job, Hernandez was told that he would work sixty hours per week. But the hours crept up quickly, especially during the winter, and Hernandez wasn't getting paid for the extra three or four hours every day. Aside from the long hours and trying to eat while frantically milking 1,200 cows, Hernandez was often kicked in the hands and chest by the animals, had to buy his own boots and safety glasses, and still suffers from a nail fungus he got while regularly handling chemicals without gloves. He lived in an old house on the dairy and had to fix leaky roofs, broken doors, and dripping faucets himself, or it wouldn't get done.

But on a pleasant day in the spring of 2011, the privations of dairy work are far from Hernandez's mind. He and his wife have two young children, and they just bought a new home in a small community next to a large paper factory where Hernandez works as a machine operator. He makes a livable wage and has health benefits. There's green grass on the front lawn, and the backyard has a shady veranda and a tall pine fence. As he hangs new curtains in the front window, his three-year-old son watches "Thomas the Tank Engine" on TV. Tortillas are heating in the kitchen. "I couldn't afford to buy a house when I worked at the dairy," he says, shaking his head, and adds that his friends on dairies are amazed that he's been able to get a good job and a place of his own. His wife sums up her feelings on her family's situation: "Gracias a Dios."

Hernandez's story isn't typical—except for the part about working fourteen-hour days without being paid overtime. Yet Mike Marsh at Western United Dairymen begs to differ. He says that every year one or two labor cases are filed against dairy farmers, but harsh treatment and unfair pay are not the norm for the industry. And he says most dairy farmers do the right thing: "Our message to our producers is clear: you have got to follow the law. If you are not providing rest breaks or lunch periods, or are working folks overtime without pay or not providing proper equipment, you're breaking the law and that is not OK. If any incidents like that come to our attention, we tell the dairy farmer that they need to get this fixed."

WUD does make an effort to assist farmers in following labor laws, by providing time clocks and a plethora of forms and legal resources on its website. And, for the most part, Marsh thinks that dairy farmers are doing a good job. In his view, he hears few stories of employee abuse because farm owners themselves were once immigrants, so they have a measure of empathy. "Many of our farmers are very close with their employees," he says, "even on some of the bigger operations we've got here in the state. I think part of that may be because the dairy farmers in California come from an immigrant background themselves. I would guess that 95 percent of the dairy farmers in the state are either Portuguese, Dutch, Irish, Italian, Swedish, or Swiss immigrants. Maybe that's why there's such a bond between dairy farm owners and their workers."

To the countless dairy workers putting in grueling days in dangerous conditions for below minimum wage, in violation of numerous labor laws, Marsh's description of the supposed rapport must seem puzzling. In fact, it sounds a little like J. Steven Wilkins's description of slavery in his biography of Robert E. Lee: "Slavery, as it operated in the pervasively Christian society which was the old South," he wrote with surprising conviction, "was not an adversarial relationship founded upon racial animosity. In fact, it bred on the whole, not contempt, but, over time, mutual respect. This produced a mutual esteem of the sort that always results when men give themselves to a common cause."[14] As a description of slavery in the antebellum South this stands in marked contrast to the narratives of the slaves themselves.

Normally, if workers' rights are regularly abridged, and if labor laws are flouted, a union will step in and negotiate in behalf of its members for better treatment and pay. But the lack of labor unions is yet another example of agricultural exceptionalism. The National Labor Relations Act, signed by President Franklin Delano Roosevelt in 1935, specifically exempted agricultural employees from its grasp, and most states have failed to pass their own version of the law that remedies the omission. California is one exception. In 1975 it passed the Agricultural Labor Relations Act, mostly as a result of protests, strikes, and organizing by Cesar Chavez and the United Farm Workers. There, the UFW has won innumerable victories for farm workers: things like sanitary bathrooms in the fields, shade on hot days, and bilingual warnings about pesticides and their possible health effects. Dairy farm workers, however, have been largely left out of these improvements, something that Ephraim Camacho finds both sad and somewhat inevitable.

Camacho, sixty, is a community organizer in CRLA's Fresno office. The office is on the third floor of a commercial building in the old part of the city, where art deco architecture and narrow, shady streets prevail in contrast to the rest of Fresno, which is dominated by vast sprawling grids lined with shopping centers. Around the corner from the office is a community of homeless people living in makeshift tents, with piles of firewood strewn about, hard against the embankment of Highway 99. The shantytown is hidden away like a dirty secret of this otherwise prosperous and sanitized California city.

On the wall in the clean, quiet waiting room are a few big-framed photographs that convey quickly what this place is all about: one is a black and white portrait of Cesar Chavez, beaming on a bright day, his thick black hair swept neatly back in combed rows; another is a color photo of a farm worker in a grape vineyard, wearing white cotton gloves and taking shelter from the sun with a baseball hat and various strategically placed bandanas. They almost talk to each other across the small space. Camacho, who has spiky salt-and-pepper hair, was born in Texas to farm worker parents and is one of eleven kids. His family eventually moved to Delano, California, and that's where Camacho first started working in the fields. When he was ready for a way out of that hard life, he took organizing classes put on by the UFW. Shortly after that, about twenty-eight years ago, he joined CRLA. Though he has an office job now, he doesn't spend much time behind a desk. Instead, he's out in the field talking to farm workers and helping them find adequate housing or stand up for their rights against the farm labor contractors who round up workers in the morning and drive them to the fields, and who won't hesitate to fleece them every chance they get. He's helped thousands of workers get better pay and working conditions, but the dairy workers are a notoriously difficult demographic.

Camacho explains that people learn about Cesar Chavez, the UFW, and the California Agricultural Labor Relations Act, and think that all farm workers are part of a union and thus well protected. But that's not true. Farm workers don't automatically become part of a union when they start working in the fields. The process is complicated. As a farm worker, you can join a union only if your employer has signed a union contract. But in order for that to happen, the workers must first collect enough signature cards to show that there's a critical mass of employees who are willing to join. If that happens, then the Agricultural Labor Relations Board (ALRB) facilitates elections, in which the workers vote to have a union such as the UFW represent them. But in between the collection of signature cards and the election, an opposing force gathers strength: the employer, who in all likelihood doesn't want a union telling him how to deal with his employees, hires "labor consultants," whose job is to convince the workers that joining a union is not in their best interests. "If they are successful," Camacho says, "the workers get scared and don't vote for the union. Sometimes employers will promise to raise wages and improve conditions if the workers don't join the union, and then they break those promises."

It's been difficult for dairy workers to organize because they live isolated from other workers and rarely leave the farms to meet people in their same situation. Plus, many of them live on the farm where they work, and that raises the stakes: if they lose their job, they will also lose their housing. Lastly, the so-called labor consultants don't always play nice; intimidation is not unheard of.

The most horrific example of this is the story of Rene Lopez, who worked at the Sikkema Dairy near Fresno.[15] Lopez, who came to the United States from Nuevo Leon, was bilingual and graduated from Carruthers High School in Fresno County. This made him a natural leader on the dairy, since none of his coworkers had the same amount of education or spoke good English. When he respectfully told Ralph Sikkema, the owner, that getting paid less than minimum wage for a sixty-hour work week was not to his liking, and requested a fair increase, Sikkema responded harshly and threatened to fire some of the workers and make the rest do all the work for the same pay. Not sure what to do, Lopez and others at the dairy asked for help from the UFW. Roberto Escutia, of the UFW's Horticulture Division, advised them to file for union representation. At the same time they petitioned for an ALRB election, the dairy workers on the farm decided to strike. Their justification for this move was that Sikkema had struck the first blow, by threatening to fire them.

In addition to milkers and farm hands, Sikkema also employed guards on the farm, and they often carried guns and clubs. Whenever the guards saw the workers speaking with UFW representatives, they would brandish these weapons and sometimes fire the guns into the air. The UFW filed for an injunction to prohibit the guards from carrying weapons, and while the court action was still pending, Lopez gathered enough support from the workers to hold an election.

On the day of the election, shortly after Lopez had cast his vote for the UFW, two of Sikkema's hired thugs—Dietmar Ahsmann, Sikkema's brother-in-law, and Donato Estrada, a Mexican connected to the drug trade—drove up to Lopez and his colleagues and motioned them to come toward the car. Lopez led the workers as they walked, and when he was within three feet of the car, Estrada shot him in the head, killing him. The date was September 21, 1983. Lopez was nineteen.

Estrada was sentenced to seven years in prison for the crime but, oddly, Ahsmann was acquitted, and Sikkema was never charged for his role in the murder. Though this tragedy is sinking further and further into the depths of history, it still serves as a reminder to dairy workers that if you speak up, you might get cut down.

But there is hopeful news, too. In 2007, the UFW secured its first contract in Oregon, for workers at Three Mile Canyons Farm, one of the largest dairies in the United States. Workers had been documenting and complaining about unfair labor practices, sexual harassment, intimidation, and abuse at Three Mile Canyon for years. Perhaps because of their uncommon willingness to vocalize these complaints, and perhaps because it is a huge farm with 250 workers, the Three Mile Canyon employees were able to coalesce for their own protection. Now, for the first time, according to UFW president Arturo Rodriguez, these farm workers in Oregon will have family medical benefits, a pension plan, regular wage increases, and better working conditions.

On most dairy farms, however, the workers live secluded lives and rarely join the nearby community. This makes laborers feel alone and vulnerable, but it's not necessarily great for farm owners, either.

While it does give the unscrupulous owners leverage over their workers, the more noble among them are counterparts in a state of mutual dependence. Workers need their bosses for everything from housing to groceries to medical care, and owners need their workers to keep the milk flowing.

In a 2009 survey of immigrant dairy workers in Wisconsin, the laborers expressed a "pervasive sense of surveillance and fear of apprehension within immigrant communities. . . . Many noted that rumors run rampant in immigrant communities about workplace raids and other immigration enforcement activity, creating a palpable sense of fear and a need to keep a low profile in public in order to reduce the risk of running into law enforcement."[16] This makes mundane things like food shopping difficult, but it is also a huge brake on the drive to learn English and contribute to the communities in which they live.

This precarious situation is made all the worse when on-farm housing is subpar. Without a grasp of English, or an understanding of building codes and zoning enforcement, how are these workers supposed to advocate for humane living conditions? For Anna and Jeffe Valdez, a couple living on a dairy farm in the San Joaquin Valley, the poor condition of their housing is something they've learned to live with but have never quite gotten used to.

On a beautiful spring day in 2011, with a sky deep blue and devoid of clouds, the small brown bungalow where the Valdezes live can be seen against an expanse of lush alfalfa. Across the street and about three hundred yards away is the nearest shade structure and mud wallow, where a herd of Holsteins gather. A lone palm tree stands guard in the scrub-grass of the backyard, while a small dog patrols the front. The giant sky and flat terrain are the opposite of claustrophobic, making these already vulnerable people seem all the more exposed and alone.

The Valdezes have been on this farm for fifteen years and in the United States since 1972, but they don't speak English. Anna stands on the porch of the house and leaves the front door open to let the dry air permeate the walls, since the roof leaks and has spawned mold in the sheetrock and attic crawlspace. Because the wiring is so old, they haven't been able to put insulation in the attic, so the house is cold in the winter. When they use the shower, water leaks out onto the floor. Behind the house is a slim garage with weathered clapboard siding and a roof patched here and there with tar paper. Everything points to deferred maintenance, to the bargain one makes to put food on the table instead of freshening up the paint or repairing nagging defects. "The owners want the workers to work a lot, and we asked them to make repairs, but they don't want to," Anna says. "The more you bother them about it, the less they will do."

Anna goes inside, where a TV plays a Spanish soap opera, and folds laundry and explains that she and her husband moved to the United States from Zacatecas, Mexico, first living in Arizona and then California. A teacher rented them a house near this dairy, and when Jeffe needed a job he asked the dairy's owner if he was looking for help. He hired Jeffe as a milker. The farm has nine thousand cows spread out over three separate locations. During the winter, he'll work ten-hour days, but when things get busier in the summer, a fourteen-hour shift is the norm. This type of work was fine when Jeffe was younger, but now he's sixty-three and his body is beginning to protest. He recently stopped milking cows because the cows' hide irritated his hands and gave him a nasty rash. The owner of the dairy refused to get Jeffe medical treatment, so they had to seek it out and pay for it on their own. He has a bad knee now, too, and has again asked the owner for permission to go to the doctor—he has no health insurance, so has relied on his boss to pay for his work-related illnesses—but has had trouble getting any kind of answer. Anna sometimes asks the owner's wife for help, but that doesn't get very far, either. The farmer tells his wife not to meddle with the workers.

When asked if the owner has been fair with them in their business dealings, Anna says, "I don't think so. It would be great if Jeffe had a lunch break, or if the owner gave us the meat he promised. Instead, at the end of the year, they gave us a check for $200 for the meat." To explain: instead of paying Jeffe a regular paycheck, they're paying him with housing and food. But the housing is unsanitary and dangerous, and the food never comes (except if you count the $200). When you add up the value of these benefits and factor in the amount on his paystub and that he works eleven to fourteen hours per day, six days per week, Jeffe's pay works out to about $6 per hour.

What's keeping them here, in this soggy, broken-down house, making less than minimum wage? "Where are we going to go?" asks Anna. "We're going to struggle even more if we go somewhere else." As Jeffe nears retirement, they'll have to make another choice: stay in the United States or go back to Mexico. Jeffe sometimes talks of returning to Zacatecas. Anna gives him a dose of reality: "What are you going to do over there?"

On the Haynes farm in northern Vermont, the immigrant workers are similarly vulnerable. All five of them live a few hundred feet from the milking parlor, in a five-bedroom cape-style house that looks weather-beaten but not horrible. This proximity isn't just for the sake of convenience. The workers, who have been in the United States for years, don't have driver's licenses and pretty much refuse to leave the grounds of the farm. Haynes buys the groceries they need. If the microwave is broken, he drives to the nearest city and picks up a new one. "When they need something," Haynes says, "I'm responding quickly, because I want to keep them happy." Despite the odd behavior of not leaving the footprint of the farm, and their unwillingness to obtain driver's licenses, Haynes assumes they're in the United States legally. After all, they do have valid identification. And maybe they don't want to spend the money on obtaining a license and a vehicle. But Haynes is no fool. He can satisfy his need for documentation, and on that level believe that his workers have a right to be in the country. In his heart of hearts, however, he knows that his workers are probably illegal aliens. For the time being, it's been fine to look the other way.

But how long can such an arrangement go on? Haynes certainly hopes something changes soon. He's tired of sneaking around and talking to other farmers about their immigrant workers in hushed tones, as though he has something to hide. And the milkers might seem sadly duct-taped to the farm, "but if anyone's shackled, I am," says Haynes. He's their lifeline and has to be on call around the clock.

One solution, some economists say, is to raise farm wages enough so that Americans would want to do farm work. According to Philip Martin, a labor economist at the University of California, Davis, if farm wages rose 40 percent, each household would spend about $15 more per year on groceries. Doesn't seem like much, right? "However," he has written, "for a typical seasonal farm worker, a 40 percent wage increase could raise earnings from $10,000 for one thousand hours of work to $14,000—lifting the wage above the federal poverty line."[17] That's great for workers, but there are more variables in the equation. The first one is cultural. Farmers have raised wages for decades and tried all manner of recruitment methods, but something in the American DNA seems incompatible with the prospect of hard labor, in the unforgiving elements, at odd hours. Then there's the stark economic consequences of raising wages. As Mike Haynes points out, the U.S. dairy industry is not an island—it is connected closely with the global milk market. So American dairy farmers need to operate with prices that make them competitive with farmers in other countries, where labor and the costs of doing business are less expensive, or where more generous subsidies exist. To understand his point, just look back to 2009. In the beginning of that year, the United States exported about 8 to 9 percent of its milk. When the dairy crisis reduced that number to 4 or 5 percent, milk prices plummeted by 35 percent. In the harsh volatility of the global dairy market, a 1 percent change in exports can cause a 10 percent change in milk price. We can raise farm wages and pass that cost on to the American consumer, but then international buyers would go elsewhere and we would lose a significant portion of the export market. It's a bona fide lose-lose: more expensive food for American shoppers, eviscerated markets for dairy farmers.

An even worse idea is to force employers to run immigration checks on job applicants with the Department of Homeland Security. In a process dubbed "E-Verify," this G.O.P.-sponsored bill intends to be a catalyst for increased wages by removing illegal workers. One thing is certain: it has seriously irked farmers.[18] And, since they traditionally vote along Republican lines, the bill has strained political relations between the two groups. Currently, employers ask to see a social security card and a photo ID from each applicant, but they don't bother to check the validity of those documents. Why? For one, there are antidiscrimination laws that discourage questioning an applicant's ethnic background. Plus, farmers like Mike Haynes know that Latino job seekers are most likely illegal, but the employers have little choice in the matter, since no one else comes forward to do the work. Georgia passed an E-Verify law recently and it was a disaster. Farmers ended up being short 11,000 workers, which the governor tried to replace with unemployed parolees.[19] The parolees, in turn, quit within hours, fed up with the working conditions. The law has had no measurable impact on wages, either. "The worst of all possible worlds," says Mike Marsh at the Western United Dairymen, "is mandatory E-Verify. It's like throwing dairy farmers under the bus."

The most promising solution to the conundrum of the dairy industry's reliance on illegal labor is federal immigration reform. Reform from what? Mainly from the H2-A agricultural visa program. It's deficient in many ways, but most acutely for dairy farmers in that it applies only to seasonal workers, such as the migrant apple pickers that swarm Washington State during the harvest and then go home when the trees are bare. But, obviously, cows need to be milked all year long, so dairy farmers can't benefit from this program.

Vermont senator Patrick Leahy has sponsored an amendment to the law: S.358, the "H2-A Improvement Act." It attempts a simple fix by adding sheepherders, goat herders, and dairy workers to the list of "temporary agricultural workers" that H2-A originally blessed with legal status. Senator Leahy sponsored the bill in September of 2010, and in a year's time it has gone nowhere. It's unlikely to pass because it does too little to remedy the problem. "H2-A is broken and we don't think there's any way it can ever be fixed," Marsh asserts. He and his cohorts from all the Western states wrote a "thanks, but no thanks" letter to Leahy, imploring him to think of something else. Dairy farmers' main beef with the H2-A program, even as it would be amended, is that it's too cumbersome. It requires employers to file multiple applications with state and federal labor offices, and they must predict sometimes years in advance how many workers they will need. Furthermore, the law requires employers to show that they put in a good faith effort to recruit American workers before applying for visas for immigrant labor, which adds yet another layer of administrative burden.

Not surprisingly, a good piece of immigration reform legislation has been kicking around the halls of Congress since 2000, but has been repeatedly scuttled. In a feat of acronymic creativity, this proposed bill was called AgJOBS: the Agricultural Job Opportunities, Benefits and Security Act. In essence, it should have appealed to politicians on both sides of the aisle—and farmers, since it provided undocumented farm workers a way to attain temporary legal status: legal status is tied to proving a history of working in agriculture and a clean record. These workers, it is assumed, are already here and providing a crucial service to farmers, so why not create a process to make them official? The bill has been included as part of the comprehensive immigration reform legislation in 2011, sponsored by U.S. senators Robert Menendez (D-NJ), Harry Reid (D-NV), Patrick Leahy (D-VT), Dick Durbin (D-IL), Chuck Schumer (D-NY), John Kerry (D-MA), and Kirsten Gillibrand (D-NY), but it remains to be seen how much the rest of Congress cares about this issue at the moment. In a Gallup poll from July of 2011, 31 percent of Americans polled said that the economy was the number one problem facing the nation. Immigration reform was a long way down the list, next to education and just beneath war, at 4 percent.[20] For dairy farmers, however, immigration is near the top of the heap of concerns. And understandably so. "This is critical to us," says Marsh. "We need workers who are year round and legal."

THE ANIMALS

DUELING NARRATIVES

If you're like most Americans, there's a space in your brain reserved for the image of a dairy farm. You might not realize it, but there's a battle raging for control of that space. In one corner is the animal rights movement, which wants you to picture pain and cruelty when you think of a dairy farm. In the other corner is the marketing arm of the dairy industry. It's not a fair fight, because the dairy industry merely has to maintain the status quo of your mental picture—that of a red barn and a green field and a bunch of cows treated like members of the family. The animal rights people have to be aggressive. You might even say they need to be offensive to get their message out.

It's hard to imagine an organization named Mercy for Animals (MFA) as being offensive. Aside from perhaps being a great name for a sarcastic punk band, the words connote softness, gentility, and goodwill. True, the name is a sort of declaration or commandment, but if you have to ask for mercy, it's pretty obvious which side of the power structure you're on, and that tempers the commandment into something more like a plea. In keeping with its name, the organization's mission is to prevent cruelty to farmed animals and to "promote compassionate food choices"—otherwise known as vegetarianism and veganism. It does this, mostly, through consumer education, television and print advertising campaigns, research, and grassroots activism. MFA even puts out a magazine—*Compassionate Living*—twice a year, sprinkled with the fruit of its activism and expert commentary designed to make anything but a non-farmed-animal lifestyle seem less and less morally tenable.

MFA's founder and executive director is Nathan Runkle. Raised on a farm in rural Ohio, Runkle was spurred into this line of work in the wake of a local farmed-animal abuse case in which a piglet was slammed head first into a concrete floor during a high school agriculture project. At a mere thirty years old he's sort of the wunderkind of the animal rights movement, having started the organization while in his late teens and grown it into a potent national force with offices in Chicago, New York, Ohio, and Texas. Like People for the Ethical Treatment of Animals (PETA), MFA has leveraged the power of celebrities toward its cause, using the likes of Bob Barker, Alec Baldwin, and James Cromwell in media materials and voice-overs in documentaries such as *Farm to Fridge: The Truth behind Meat Production* and *Fowl Play,* an expose of conditions on chicken farms.

These exposes are a part of MFA's most daring and effective strategy: using undercover investigations on farms to show the world how farmed animals actually live. Over the years, MFA has done more than a dozen of these investigations, on everything from fish slaughter facilities to egg hatcheries, pig farms, and turkey slaughterhouses. And, of course, MFA has done its share of snooping around on dairy farms, too. Its modus operandi is to have an investigator apply for a job on the farm and then wear a hidden video camera to work. Once the investigator has the damning evidence, he quits and applies elsewhere.

Fortunately for MFA, and unfortunately for the animals, the investigations of dairy farms in the past few years have been particularly productive. The first one came out in 2009, when an investigator secured a job at the seven-thousand-cow Willet Dairy, the largest farm of its kind in New York. In a nine-and-a-half-minute video, available on MFA's website if you've got the stomach for it, the investigator documents a litany of behavior that, to the untrained eye, smacks of neglect, abuse, and cruelty. There are cows with bloody open wounds, prolapsed uteruses, pus-filled infections, and swollen joints. Workers are seen beating cows and using electric prods to get them moving. Newborn calves are dragged along the ground away from their mothers. In a segment that's especially hard to watch, calves are "dehorned" with a hot cautery device—basically, it burns the horn buds off—without any anesthetic. As you'd expect, these calves writhe in pain and bellow plaintively. Also hard to watch is a worker "tail docking" a calf, which involves cutting the tail off with a tool that looks like a bolt-cutter. The general conditions of the farm are no better, with overcrowded milk sheds and cows lying around on wet, manure-coated concrete floors. Dr. Holly Cheever, a New York–based veterinarian that MFA uses frequently to comment on the conditions it documents, said, "[It] is my professional opinion that the environment that this dairy provides as well as its cattle-handling techniques are improper, unhygienic, dangerous, and inhumane."

MFA scored again in 2010 when its investigator got a job at the two-hundred-cow Conklin Dairy Farm in Plain City, Ohio. Instead of what you might call the "structural" neglect and abuse that was documented at Willet Dairy, this time MFA found a bona fide sadist who acted out his demented urges on cows. The man's name was Billy Joe Gregg, Jr., and over the course of four weeks he was videoed stabbing cows with pitchforks, body-slamming calves to the ground, beating restrained cows in the face with a crowbar, twisting cows' tails until they snapped, punching cows' udders, and bragging about the whole thing. While he was doing these things, Gregg was in training to be a police officer. Luckily for the public of Plain City, MFA delivered its footage of Gregg to the local authorities, and Gregg was prosecuted. He pled guilty to six misdemeanor counts of animal cruelty and was sentenced to eight months in prison, ordered to pay a $1,000 fine, and is barred from contact with animals for three years.

The final movement in MFA's dairy triptych came in March of 2011, with the investigation of the E6 Calf Ranch in Texas. These ranches, which are becoming more common as dairy farms get bigger and outsource the services not directly connected to milk production, specialize in raising dairy calves from the time they're weaned until they are ready to return to the dairy farm and enter the herd. E6 has a herd of about 10,000 dairy calves, and the video shows that they're confined in cramped hutches caked with manure and urine, barely able to stretch their legs or turn around. But if their waking moments are miserable, it's nothing compared with the ordeal that injured or sick calves suffer before they die. Instead of providing veterinary care to these calves, or humanely euthanizing them, the workers at E6 were documented bludgeoning the animals on the head with hammers and pickaxes, sometimes needing five or six blows to finish the gruesome job. Workers were seen kicking "downed" calves in the head, standing on their necks, dragging them by their ears, and throwing live, conscious calves onto piles of the dead. When Temple Grandin, an animal welfare advisor to the USDA, saw the footage, she remarked, "It is obvious that both the management and the employees have no regard for animal welfare."

The standard response to investigations like these is, "There are always a few bad apples in the barrel." Runkle, of course, sees it a different way. "Shockingly," he said, "all three dairy facilities where we've done investigations have been selected completely at random," he said, "which leads us to believe that many of these abuses and conditions are standard or at least widespread within the industry."

But that's just one version of the story, and a very pointed one at that. There are plenty of advocates for the other side. One is Karen Jordan, a large animal veterinarian who testified in 2007 before the Subcommittee on Livestock, Dairy and Poultry of the Committee on Agriculture at the House of Representatives. Jordan was there on behalf of the National Milk Producers Federation (NMPF), the lobbying organization for thirty-one dairy cooperatives representing 40,000 dairy producers, to persuade the legislators not to put any farmed-animal protections in the 2008 Farm Bill. Her justification for this position is the classic industry message about animal welfare on dairy farms: "Simply put," she said, "what is good for our cows is good for our businesses." The logic is fairly sound, at first blush: healthy cows produce more milk and are therefore more profitable than unhealthy cows. To improve cows' health, Jordan reported, the industry has done extensive research on animal well-being and cow comfort, research that has resulted in fans and sprinkler systems to keep cows cool in the summer, rubber mats to keep cows comfortable, and clean bedding to keep them from getting infections. "Through a combination of modern production technologies and experience gained across generations of dairying," she testified, "today's milk producers know how to maximize cow comfort and well-being in order to achieve the record levels of milk production that you are seeing today."

No one knows how to put flesh on the bones of that story better than the California Milk Advisory Board (CMAB), the "promotion instrumentality" for the California Department of Food and Agriculture. CMAB is responsible for the wildly popular Happy Cow advertising campaign. In case you haven't seen the ads, they tend to show pristinely clean Holsteins situated amid vast expanses of emerald pastures, underneath bright sun and azure skies. The Happy Cows aren't just contented, they're also smart, as evidenced by the witty banter they trade while grazing.

In one of the ads, titled "Who Is She?" a herd of cows is standing around grazing as a new cow approaches.

"Hey, here's the new girl," one of them says.

"*This* could be interesting," another replies.

They greet the new girl and ask how she's doing.

"Ooh, I love it here," she says in a distinct Wisconsin accent. "No snow on the grass."

"Huh?"

"Cause I hate the big snow-drifts, don't ya know?"

The others are silent and confused.

"Ok, then. See ya!" the Wisconsin cow says, and walks away.

"What's snow?" one of the California cows asks.

"I don't know," says another.

"She's been tipped one time too many."

Then a voice-over comes on with the standard tag line: "Great milk comes from happy cows. Happy cows come from California."

In "Alarm Clock," the ad opens with a rooster crowing as a rustic barn appears on screen. Inside, two Holsteins are lounging on a bed of luxuriant hay, having just woken up.

"So, what do you think, then? Get an early start on that alfalfa on the back 40?" one says.

"What's the hurry?" the other quips, annoyed to be awake. "Hit the snooze."

Presently, the offending rooster is kicked out of the barn and bounces off a washbasin. Cue the tag line.

These ads are funny and finely tuned—Hollywood at its best. And they were effective. According to internal CMAB documents obtained in a public records request, the board has spent more than $180 million on the campaign over the past nine years, and for that princely sum it has achieved a 74 percent awareness of California dairy products by consumers across the United States. Keeping with the farm theme, board CEO Stan Andre called the campaign the "golden goose."

These conflicting images of dairy farms leave consumers in a bit of a quandary. Which should they believe: the grotesque nightmare courtesy of MFA, or the sun-drenched Club Med pushed by CMAB?

THE LEGAL LANDSCAPE

As Paul Waldau wrote in *Animal Rights: What Everyone Needs to Know*, "There has been no time in recorded history when respect and concern for some nonhuman animals was not an element in the human story."[1] During the ancient religious ages in China, India, Israel, and Greece, the sages implored people to extend their concern to the entire world, not just to humans. At that time, respect for the sacred rights of all beings was part of standard religious teaching, as shown by numerous animal-friendly quotations throughout the Old and New Testaments, ancient Chinese texts, Indian and Buddhist scriptures, the words of Greek philosophers, and in the Qur'an.

Interestingly, the first animals given legal protection in modernity were farmed animals. One of the earliest examples of an anticruelty law comes from 1641, courtesy of the Massachusetts Puritans: "No man shall exercise any Tirrany or Crueltie towards any bruite Creature which are usually kept for man's use."[2] About two hundred years later, the British parliament passed Martin's Act, a law designed to prevent the cruel and improper treatment of "Horses, Mares, Geldings, Mules, Asses, Cows, Heifers, Steers, Oxen, Sheep and other Cattle."[3] The law's namesake was Richard Martin, nicknamed Humanity Dick, an Irish politician and leading founder of the Royal Society for the Prevention of Cruelty to Animals. An avid duelist—this was nineteenth-century England, after all—when asked why he so fervently defended animals he reportedly replied, "Sir, an ox cannot hold a pistol!" Thus, his law gave magistrates the power to fine or imprison any "person or persons who shall wantonly and cruelly beat, abuse, or ill-treat" the named animals.

These laws codified an unwritten contract between farmers and their animals: we take care of you, and you take care of us. There was a built-in enforcement mechanism in this agreement, for poorly treated animals were unlikely to do their jobs well. But as farming entered the era of technology, the rules began to change and the opportunities for cruelty without consequence expanded. Take, for example, the advent of the railroad. Before trains, it was pretty much impossible to haul cattle long distances to be slaughtered. The only way you could do it was with an old-fashioned cattle drive, and the cowboys were forced to go at the cattle's speed. But with railroad cars, the animals could be packed into tight quarters and rolled across the plains for days on end, and it didn't much matter how they felt when they got there—it was the end of their lives, too. This situation gave rise to the first federal law on animal welfare in the United States: the twenty-eight-hour law of 1877. The law, which is still in effect, provides that animals can't be transported across state lines for more than twenty-eight hours by rail without being given at least five hours of rest, watering, and feeding.[4]

The rights and plights of farmed animals would go largely unnoticed until 1964, when Ruth Harrison published *Animal Machines,* a groundbreaking expose of the conditions at factory poultry, veal, and cattle farms in the United Kingdom. Harrison gathered material for her book by simply traveling around the UK and documenting what she saw: castration, tail docking, dehorning, battery cages (high-density confinement systems), veal crates, and more. With a foreword by the newly influential Rachel Carson (author of *Silent Spring*), *Animal Machines* was published in seven languages and prompted the British government to investigate the conditions on farms and ask whether the parliament should establish animal welfare standards.

Should we protect animals? It's a question some of the world's most renowned philosophers have mulled. Immanuel Kant thought of animals as "man's instruments," and argued that they deserved protection only if it would help human beings in their relation to each other. "He who is cruel to animals," he wrote, "becomes hard also in his dealings with men."[5] Jeremy Bentham said, "The question is not, Can they reason? Nor, Can they talk? But, Can they suffer?"[6]

Another important question is: Are they property? Traditionally, the law has said yes. "Pecuniary" comes from the Latin word *pecu,* meaning cattle or flock. "Chattel" is a relative of the word "cattle." But if animals are, in fact, property, then protecting them pits their rights against the property rights of the humans who possess them. Out of this balancing act came two distinct philosophies on how to protect animals. There are the animal welfare advocates, such as the ASPCA, who rally for stronger laws preventing animal cruelty and requiring animals to be treated humanely. Then there are the animal rights people—for example, PETA—who believe that animals are not ours to "eat, wear, experiment on, or use for entertainment."

Peter Singer's *Animal Liberation* is considered the bible for animal rights activists. Published in 1975, the book argues against what Singer, the Ira W. DeCamp Professor of Bioethics at Princeton University, coined "speciesism," or discrimination based on a being's species. The most powerful and controversial idea in the book is that all beings capable of suffering deserve "equal consideration," and that treating animals less humanely than humans, simply because they are not humans, is just as wrong as discrimination based on skin color. The only way out of the whole fraught situation, Singer asserts, is to adopt a vegan or vegetarian diet, something all animal rights activists ultimately are working toward.

The position of the animal rights camp is, admittedly, quite radical. Only 7.3 million Americans are vegetarians, and just 1 million are vegans, according to a 2008 study by *Vegetarian Times*. For omnivores, much thought has been devoted (mostly in Europe) to how to use animal products yet not be complicit in acts of cruelty or abuse. Not long after *Animal Liberation* came out, the English parliament appointed the Brambell Committee to study the policy possibilities for improved animal welfare. The Brambell report then spurred the creation of the Farmed Animal Welfare Council in 1979, which established a template for humane treatment across Europe, in the form of the "Five Freedoms." These are the freedom from hunger and thirst; discomfort; injury, pain, or disease; fear or distress; and the freedom to express normal behavior.

In the wake of this Magna Carta of animal welfare, other European nations have added animal friendly laws to their books. In 1991, Switzerland banned battery cages for chickens; the method of choice is now the aviary, with nest boxes and perches. In 2002, Germany became the first European nation to guarantee animal rights in its constitution, simply by adding the words "and animals" to a clause that requires the states to respect and protect the dignity of human beings. Sweden passed a law requiring cattle to be grazed if they're over six months old. Then the EU implemented a trade regulation banning battery cages and veal crates among its members by 2012. The Treaty of Rome, the founding document of the European Economic Community, was recently amended to require EU legislation and its members to "pay full regard to the welfare requirements of animals in the formulation and implementation of the community's policies on agriculture, research and transport."[7]

It would be an understatement to say that the farmed animal welfare laws in the United States are less robust. And that's much to the frustration of Matthew Liebman, a young staff attorney at the Animal Legal Defense Fund. ALDF, which is based in San Francisco, was founded in 1979, the same year that the Farm Animal Welfare Council created the Five Freedoms, and it's mission is to protect animals and advance their interests through the legal system. That means it sues people to stop animal abuse and expand the boundaries of animal law, and helps others in the legal and legislative arenas do what they can to give animals a stronger position in a human-centered world.

Liebman is from Texas, which is probably one of the least likely ecosystems to produce fervent vegans, but he started on his animal rights path as a sophomore in high school, when he acquired a pet parrot. The pet store owner told Liebman he could feed the parrot anything he himself could eat. One day, Liebman was eating chicken and was about to feed some to his parrot. But before he did, a rogue thought struck him: "I realized how weird that felt, almost cannibalistic, to feed chicken to a little parrot," he recalls. "I had the epiphany that if he was too close to the chicken for him to eat it, then why would I be willing to eat the chicken and not eat him? That moment made me go vegetarian. As I learned more about factory farming, I gave up eggs and dairy as well." In college, Liebman read *Animal*

Liberation and considered how to make the biggest impact for the animal rights movement. Instead of getting a Ph.D. in philosophy, Liebman opted for Stanford Law School with the singular intent of studying animal law. Indeed, Liebman seems to be part of a larger trend toward legal concern for animals: in the last decade, animal law has become a distinct field, and today more than 130 U.S. law schools offer courses on the subject.

Animal law in the United States is actually fairly simple. The thing is, life is complex, so simple laws tend either to mask gaping holes in protection from wrongdoing, or are so broad that they proscribe an activity absolutely. Perhaps you can guess which one describes the animal welfare laws. As Liebman explains, aside from the twenty-eight-hour law, which is rarely enforced, and the Humane Methods of Slaughter Act, which applies solely to slaughterhouses, the only federal law that governs the treatment of animals is the Animal Welfare Act. Enforced by the Animal and Plant Health Inspection Service, a subagency of the USDA, the AWA sets minimum standard for the care and treatment of animals bred for commercial sale, used in research, transported commercially, or exhibited to the public. In short: puppy mills, science labs, and zoos. Notably missing from this list are farms, which account for 99 percent of animal cruelty cases in this country, and have over 9 billion animals under their control. That makes the AWA somewhat tantamount to an antidiscrimination law that applies only to Native Americans.

At the state level, protection for farmed animals gets a little better, but not much. Generally, most states have criminal anticruelty laws that apply to all animals, but they're worded very broadly and don't have affirmative requirements, such as exercise, space, light, clean living conditions, and ventilation. When they do spell these things out, the laws don't provide enough detail to be effective. To make matters worse, thirty-seven of the fifty states have "common farming" exemptions from their anticruelty laws. "This means that even if a practice is unnecessary or unjustifiable, in terms of the suffering it causes to an animal," Liebman explains, "if it's common within the industry, it's exempted from coverage by the state animal cruelty law." As a comparison, wrote David J. Wolfson and Mariann Sullivan in *Animal Rights: Current Debates and New Directions*, "imagine a law that provided chemical corporations have not polluted (and, consequently, not violated criminal law) so long as they released pollutants in amounts 'accepted' or viewed as 'customary' by the chemical industry. In effect, state legislators have granted agribusiness a license to treat animals as it wishes."[8]

Another reason anticruelty laws are rarely used is that, unlike regulatory laws, they are criminal in nature. This raises a host of barriers to enforcement. First, there's a higher burden of proof—"beyond a reasonable doubt," instead of a "preponderance of the evidence." Then there's the so-called rule of lenity, which states that ambiguous criminal laws must be construed in favor of the defendant. Given the vague, broad nature of anticruelty laws, this rule is especially crippling. Finally, there's the tricky issue of evidence. In a regulated field, the agency in charge has the power to inspect facilities for compliance with regulations. But in the world of criminal law, investigators need a warrant to enter a farm and see how the animals are treated. Since these anticruelty laws are enforced by local police and prosecutors, who are often busy with other cases, the effort is rarely made to get a warrant from a judge and bring down the full force of the law on the offending party. In the rare cases when they do, it's more often to protect dogs, cats, and horses, not farmed animals. "Seeing it as a criminal issue instead of a regulatory issue adds a lot of burden," Liebman says, "and the result is that farmed animals get virtually no protection under state cruelty laws."

HORROR STORY OR HYPERBOLE?

Do dairy animals need stronger legal protections? Predictably, Liebman and other animal rights activists think so, and they have quite a harmonious bill of complaints against the dairy farming system. Liebman likes to organize the claims into three categories: cruelty inherent to the nature of the dairy industry, no matter the size of the farm; cruelty associated with the different production methods; and gratuitous violence against animals, as in Conklin Dairy case.

Yet Liebman is not a veterinarian. Neither are most animal rights activists. In order to put their claims in context, it helps to have the insights of a person who is both passionate about animals and works with them enough to know how they're treated and what they deserve. In this case, the role of "independent auditor" will be played by Joe Klopfenstein, a large animal veterinarian based in Vergennes, Vermont, a dairy stronghold in the Champlain Valley south of Burlington. Klopfenstein grew up in Indiana and had his first inkling of a career path while working at a zoo as a young man. He thought he wanted to be a zoo veterinarian until he went to work on a farm and became intrigued by the dairy industry. He likes cows and he likes people, so he seems to be in the perfect job. "Those relationships with the farmer are really important to me," he says, "and that's what drives me."

In 2010, Klopfenstein was named the Bovine Practitioner of the Year by the American Association of Bovine Practitioners. Ninety-five percent of his clients are dairy farmers, and they have herds that range in size from sixty to seven hundred cows. When asked how he thinks most dairy farmers treat their cows, he says it's like a bell curve, "but the majority of farmers I work with are farmers because they really love their animals. They treat them well, but that's different for each person. From my perspective, someone who is more objective, among the dairy farmers who are left after the last fifteen to twenty years, when we've weeded out a lot, the level of animal care and animal welfare has improved significantly. There's certainly a ways to go, and there are still some issues out there we need to address, but in general, people treat their animals with respect and kindness."

Many of the animal rights activists' claims are founded upon the belief that cows are conscious beings with brains more intelligent and complex than we've traditionally given them credit for. They point to studies showing that calves exhibit increased heart rates and more animated behavior when they learn new things, evidence that cows love an intellectual challenge. In an issue of *Compassionate Living*, Mercy for Animals featured an anecdote by the veterinarian Holly Cheever, who said she saw a cow who secretly gave birth to twins and brought only one calf back to the barn, leaving the other hidden in the woods to raise as her own. "Imagine what this cow was capable of," Cheever said. "Not only did she possess memory—the memory of losing all of her previous calves after bringing them to the barn—but she could also formulate and execute a plan."[9]

Klopfenstein is a little more circumspect. "Obviously, they have a consciousness and they feel pain, fear, happiness, and comfort," he says, "but I really think that's the limit of how they perceive things." On the spectrum of sentience, with humans on top and insects on the bottom, Klopfenstein puts cows and other herd animals beneath dogs and cats and above fish. "It's a basic level of intelligence," he offers.

Under the category of "cruelties inherent to dairy farming," a popular complaint is that severing the bond between the mother cow and her calf causes severe psychological trauma to mothers, which is evidenced by the cows' bellowing for their young in those hours just after the calf is removed. This removal is done, in case it's not obvious, because the cow's milk needs to go to the milk tank, instead of her calf, which will be fed colostrum immediately after birth and then a controlled amount of milk. "Regardless of how humane the conditions," Liebman says, "virtually every dairy cow will have her babies taken away from her almost every year." Is that cruel? It depends.

"I don't know if there's enough psyche there to have psychological trauma," Klopfenstien opines. He thinks the maternal instinct is strong, and that a mother cow wants to know where her baby is, but he's not confident that the calf is asking, "Where's my mom?"

As for the bellowing, which is a common occurrence, Klopfenstein says, "Those behaviors within a few hours are gone." Plus, there are some good reasons to remove the calf, aside from the need to harvest the cow's milk. In a confinement system, for example, there's some danger to the calf if it's left among the larger animals. And there's an increased risk of disease to the calf, whose immune system is just getting going. Overall, Klopfenstein doesn't buy this line of reasoning.

Another complaint is a twofold argument that all dairy farms feed other systems of animal cruelty and death—namely the veal and beef industries. Barring the use of sexed semen, half of the calves born on a dairy farm will be sent away to die. Some will go to veal ranches, where, before being slaughtered, they are stored in small crates and fed an iron-deficient diet to keep their flesh a light color. Other male calves will go to plants that turn their stomach linings into rennet for cheese making and their bodies into protein paste for animal feed. Of course, even if the dairy industry disappeared, it's likely the practices of eating veal or feeding animals the protein from other animals wouldn't disappear, so dairy farms are only complicit in cruelty to calves (if you feel that way) as a supplier of the raw material.

As for the dairy industry's connection to the beef industry, well, it's strong: dairy farms turn over (in other words, sell off) about 30 percent of their herd every year, and most of those animals become beef. Another way to say a 30 percent turnover is that a cow's average life on a dairy farm is about three years. Animal rights advocates are quick to remind us that a cow's natural lifespan is twenty years or more. Thus, exterminating large numbers of cows well before the end of their natural lives, they argue, is a form of cruelty.

"I think there's some degree of validity to that," Klopfenstein says. At the same time, he explains that the premature death is not wanton or malicious, but a business decision: cows produce less milk as they get older, and younger ones are always coming up the ranks. It's like baseball, he says. You've got the minor leagues, which consist of young heifers about to have their first calves, and the major leagues, with the money-making cows that produce milk. They're all on the same farm and must be fed, and a barn can only accommodate so many animals, so choices must be made. "A lot of times," Klopfenstein says, "a young player is a better value, because they're just as talented, or more talented, and you're paying them less money." In dairy terms, what Klopfenstein means is that the genetics are improving so quickly in cows that younger generations are more efficient and more profitable than their forebears.

Yet that's not the entire story. Production concerns are just one reason cows leave farms so soon, and it's the reason the industry tends to give when confronted with this sort of inquiry. Another reason cows leave farms after three years is that they're too lame to do their job. Lameness, says Klopfenstein, is the number one animal welfare issue on dairy farms. The research bears that out. A study published in 2011 in the *Journal of Animal Science* looked at the physical condition of dairy and beef cattle at auction houses through out the western United States in 2008. The study reviewed nine thousand dairy cows (95 percent were Holsteins) during 125 sales and found that 45 percent of them were lame.[10] In comparison, just 15 percent of the beef cattle were identified as lame. "Ouch," Klopfenstein wrote in an email after he reviewed the study. "That's certainly hard to justify." One possible cause of this statistic is that, according to a 2007 USDA study of animal management on 2,194 dairy farms, roughly half of the farms keep their cows on hard, sometimes slippery concrete flooring. Pasture was the predominant floor surface for only 5 percent of the animals.[11]

Klopfenstein also explained that dairy cows might be in worse shape than beef cattle at auction because dairy farmers tend to hold on to their sick animals longer, trying to get them better. "If I can put any kind of shine on this discouraging data," he wrote, "I would say that slaughter data doesn't represent the quality of life for the majority of the animals, but it is pretty damning for how we treat animals at the end of their productive lives. We in the dairy industry can do better."

The second category of animal cruelty on dairy farms, according to Liebman, is the kind that increases in proportion to the factory-ness of a dairy farm. The strongest association people have with factory dairy farms is that of a feedlot and no pasture, of cows crammed into barns and never seeing a blade of grass. In this kind of environment, the animal rights argument goes, cows can't express their natural behavior, and frustrating the genetic urge is a form of cruelty. It's true that cows evolved to graze on pasture, but it's another thing entirely to say that modern cows are the genetic equivalent of the ancient ones. In fact, we know humans have changed the genetics of cows quite drastically over the years. Put simply, "natural behavior" is gone. What we're left with is animals made in the image we've sketched.

"I guess the best way to look at it is to understand that domesticated animals are no longer deer—they have been developed to be productive in association with people," Klopfenstein explains. "A good analogy would be your pet dog. 'Normal' behavior would be scavenging carrion out on the street, yet none of us would allow or want that to happen. Cows obviously developed as grazers and we've developed feeding systems to recognize that fact."

The most important components of their natural behavior, Klopfenstein adds, are opportunities for socializing with other cows; free access to water and feed; and to be comfortable and not compete with other cows for a place to lie down. Ignoring the environmental concerns with confinement systems, cows can do all those things in a barn or in a field. "At this point in their association with us cows need to be trained to graze," Klopfenstein says. "You can't just let them out the gate and assume they will revert to their primordial state if they are used to being fed in confinement."

Another animal welfare claim leveled upon CAFOs and "factory" dairy farms is that they engage in routine mutilations of cows in ways that subject the animals to more pain than is necessary. By "mutilation" animal rights activists mean dehorning and tail docking. Dehorning is actually less common than "disbudding," which is done when calves are less than four weeks old, before their horns have had a chance to fuse to the skull, but both are done for safety reasons; so cows don't gore farmers or each other. The undercover videos by MFA show the dehorning process at its worst—being done to older calves and without any anesthetic. Figuring out the standard practice on most dairy farms, and gauging its cruelty, is a little tricky, however. The American Veterinary Medicine Association recommends the use of anesthesia if the dehorning is done when calves are more than four weeks old. Yet the aforementioned 2007 USDA found that the vast majority of farms dehorn or disbud, but only 17.7 percent of the procedures were done using an anesthetic. The unknown, at this point, is how old the calves were in the study. If they were less than four weeks old, the lack of anesthesia isn't necessarily a problem. Klopfenstein, for his part, says he works hard in his practice to disbud instead of dehorn, and to do the procedures in ways that result in the least pain possible for the calves. His regular process is to use a local anesthetic and a sedative, followed by a hot iron that burns the ring of skin where the horn would grow. "If you look at their behavior, you would think nothing is happening," he says. "After they wake up, they're drinking milk from a bottle."

While dehorning has a useful purpose, tail docking doesn't. It used to be thought that tail docking reduced the spread of disease by preventing cows from slinging their manure-and-urine-soaked tails around. A lot of Klopfenstein's clients still engage in docking, but "it's really, really hard to defend," he says. "As a vet, I like to make recommendations based on science and evidence; there's no evidence that it keeps cows cleaner." California has gone so far as to ban the practice, but it still happens on plenty of dairy farms in other states.

As for the gratuitous violence witnessed at Conklin Dairy, it's hard to get a sense of how prevalent that sort of behavior is. Granted, Klopfenstein is just one veterinarian among thousands who work on dairy farms, but it's his guess that "there's not as much of this going on as some of these organizations [MFA, PETA, and so forth] would have you believe." Clearly, it does happen, but it's likely just a few lone actors with mental illness of some kind, not the average dairy farmer.

The blanket response from the dairy industry to any accusations of mistreatment of cows is that farmers want to keep their cows healthy so they can be more productive and, therefore, more profitable. Liebman and the animal rights crowd don't buy that. "If you pump the animals with enough hormones, they'll continue to produce, even if they're in conditions that don't meet their basic needs," he says. "If you industrialize it enough, you can disregard welfare while still having yields that are economical." For an analogue, just witness the poultry industry. Chickens on industrial poultry farms are not "healthy" in the conventional sense of the word—they can barely stand up, because their breasts are so big—but the result is lots and lots of white meat. On dairy farms, says Klopfenstein, a similar scenario is possible. "There are things you can do to cows to make them more productive that are not healthy," he notes. When farmers routinely get rid of one-third of their herd every year, clearly there isn't a concern about longevity; the priority is productivity. It's become part of the art and science of dairy farming to keep cows just healthy enough to serve their three years, while producing the maximum amount of milk. After all, dairy farming is a business. Klopfenstein acknowledges this fact, but throws one more nod to the dairy farmers who have survived bout after bout of price fluctuations and crashes. "The ones that are in it now are in it because they're good business people," he says, "and they understand their animals and the value of their health."

So what's a guy like Liebman to do when he's an animal rights lawyer and animals have almost no rights? Well, at the very least, he can plow a furrow in California, one of the thirteen states without a farmed-animal exemption. A few years ago, Liebman and ALDF sued the owners of the 10,000-animal Mendes Calf Ranch on the grounds that the calves were confined in isolation for up to sixty days at a time in crates not much bigger than the animals themselves. ALDF alleged that this sort of management was a violation of California Penal Code section 597t, which states that it's a misdemeanor to confine an animal without "adequate exercise area." Unfortunately for ALDF, the court dismissed the action for lack of "standing," a legal technicality that requires the plaintiff to have a defined interest in the outcome of the case.

"But even the losses can be wins," Liebman says. "This is a struggle that's going to succeed or fail on public awareness. Even losses can educate people. Legally speaking, we'll keep looking for ways to use litigation and legislation to improve the plight of animals on dairies, but I think it's going to be an uphill battle. The law just isn't hospitable to these kinds of claims."

PETA VS.
THE HAPPY COWS

Since 2002, PETA has tried to protect dairy cows in a slightly different way: not by suing farmers for their abuse of the animals, but by suing the state's marketing office for false advertising.

PETA's first arrow was slung in a California district court, alleging that the Happy Cow campaign violated fair competition laws, since they created a misleading impression of how cows are kept and treated. In the same year, PETA filed another complaint, this time to the Federal Trade Commission, with basically the same underlying claim: that the advertisements were false and calculated to mislead. Unlike a district court, the FTC has the discretion to hear complaints or ignore them. In this case, the FTC chose to do nothing. The court, meanwhile, dismissed the action, without even addressing the merits of the claim, by ruling that the California Milk Advisory Board, which makes the ads, is a state agency and thus not subject to competition laws. The trial judge's decision was upheld on appeal. "The interesting thing about it," says PETA litigation counsel Martina Bernstein, "is that California agencies are incredibly involved in advertising." There are multi-million-dollar campaigns, for example, for raisins, grapes, and avocados. To this day, it strikes her as unjust that such a large player in the world of marketing can operate unregulated.

But it wasn't a total loss for PETA. The appellate court judge gave them a big hint: sue CMAB under the California Marketing Act, he said, and you won't get hung up on the whole sovereign immunity issue. So that's what they did in June of 2011, claiming that CMAB's newer campaign, "Family Farms," a more documentarian work, misrepresents how cows are treated.

The idea behind the ads, according to Western United Dairymen executive director Mike Marsh (CMAB declined to comment), is to have consumers get to know the dairy farmers behind the milk. The loudest message that comes through is that California dairy farms are 99 percent family owned, a deliberate attempt to dispel the notion that farms in California are owned by some unthinking, unfeeling corporation. Of course, most dairy farms in California *are* owned by corporations; it's just that families usually own the entity.

In one commercial about a fourth-generation Tulare County farmer, the farmer gets a little choked up on screen, thinking about growing up on the farm and how important it is to him. "This was a lifelong dream, really, for me and my family," he tells the camera. Then the tag line: "Meet the families behind real California Dairy at Realcaliforniamilk.com." In another, the sun peaks over a mountain in Sebastopol as the farmer on screen begins speaking. "I grew up right here," he says. "Really, that's about all we ever did is just work and play here." Images of a mud-splattered hay wagon and a crisp blue sky appear. Poignant piano music plays in the background.

In addition, the campaign includes six mini-documentaries designed to show just how much farmers care about their cows. One farmer particularly enjoys raising calves, and he explains what he does from the moment they're born: give them colostrum right away; get them dried off and cleaned up; perhaps put them under a heat lamp in the winter, or shade in the summer; then into individual hutches; then into the "playpen" where they can walk around with other calves. At the end of the piece, the farmer says that these cows are his life, and that's why he treats them so well.

Strategically, to tee-up it's latest lawsuit, PETA made a public records request, asking CMAB for any documents that would support its claims about the health, welfare, and standard of care for cows. The board produced a handful of documents and claimed trade-secret protection for some six thousand additional documents. PETA then used its lawsuit to force CMAB to turn over the six thousand documents. In PETA's analysis, those documents show that CMAB knew the Happy Cow ads were misleading, but took the risk anyway.

As the marketing entity for a commodity, CMAB has a challenging job. A commodity, by definition, is a uniform product that should be the same if it comes from Vermont, Wisconsin, Idaho, or California. The Happy Cow ads were an attempt to differentiate California products in the minds of consumers, so that when they had a choice about the provenance of their milk, they would think about the Happy Cows and choose a product from California. It would have been blatantly illegal to claim that California milk is superior to other milk, because that's just false. So CMAB sought to create a cast of whimsical dairy cows that would stick in the mind of consumers. And if people made the leap that California's cows, because they were "happy," made better milk, then so be it.

Of course, the advertisements worked fabulously for a while. That is, until PETA came up with its counter-campaign: Unhappy Cows. The television spot is narrated by actor James Cromwell and asserts that the California "dairy industry is allowed to lie to the public about how their cows are treated." In truth, Cromwell says, cows never see a blade of grass, are forced to produce unnatural amounts of milk, suffer painful udder infections, and are abused and neglected in various ways. "Decide for yourself if California's cows are happy," he concludes.

PETA's ads were such a direct attack on the Happy Cow campaign that CMAB undertook a study in January of 2010 to find out how much damage, if any, they were doing to the dairy industry. In the executive summary of the report, compiled by a media consulting firm, the impact is clear:

> Opinions about the dairy industry and dairy farmers are significantly damaged by the Anti-Dairy campaigns.

> The campaigns dramatically undermine perceptions that the industry is responsibly raising cows.

> Make a majority of dairy purchasers feel dairy farmers do not treat their cows well, care about their cows, or even that they are respectable and hardworking.

> Consumers exposed to the Anti-Dairy campaigns indicate a very significant decline in future dairy product purchases.

In response to this report, board CEO Stan Andre addressed the California Dairy Industry Animal Welfare Task Force with a strong message: "An entire industry is being decimated before our very eyes. . . . There are impending threats to our industry regarding animal treatment concerns and . . . we need a strategy for dealing with them."

What to do? The Happy Cow campaign was the central focus of CMAB's promotions, something California dairy farmers have invested hundred of millions of dollars in over the course of eight years. "Our industry needs to debunk the prevailing myth that California dairy farms are 'factory farms,'" Andre said. In May of that year, the board made the solemn decision to pull the plug on the Happy Cow campaign and take the promotion in a different direction: Family Farms. They immediately allocated $17 million to develop the new campaign, dipping into their cash reserves to pay for the project.

Predictably, the Family Farms campaign didn't appease PETA. "It's as misleading as the Happy Cows campaign," PETA lawyer Martina

Bernstein asserts. "These dairy families and their supposed care of cows are just a big myth, and I would say that finding a farmer who loves his cows and takes care of them is as unlikely as finding a cow who's dancing and singing in the meadow." Furthermore, she adds, the Happy Cows were brought to the public with a wink and nod; this time, it's a "blatant lie."

How is PETA so sure that the Family Farm message is a lie? They're relying on numerous studies, but most prominently the 2011 study in the *Journal of Animal Science* showing the decrepit condition of dairy cows at the auctions, and the 2007 USDA study of animal management on dairy farms. The former is certainly more damning than the latter, because it shows that, contrary to what the industry might say, cows are being removed from farms not just for productivity reasons but also because they're too lame to be milked. If there's any smoking gun in all of this, the prevalence of lameness is it. As of this writing, the PETA lawsuit is in the discovery phase and hoping to secure an injunction from the court, requiring CMAB to stop making false claims to consumers about animal welfare.

For Mike Marsh at Western United Dairy, PETA's litigation "really is not about animal welfare at all. . . . It's about PETA's agenda to force folks into a vegan lifestyle." As CMAB has said in defense of the Happy Cow campaign, the ads were intended as a fun, whimsical way to get people thinking about California dairy products, not a statement of fact. Marsh calls the ads "about as realistic as the Aflac duck." In essence, he says, the PETA campaign is being doggedly literal, a conceit that only thinly veils its ultimate goal of removing animal products from consumers' diets.

So where does all of this leave the American consumer who wants dairy products yet cares about animal welfare? The hard line, courtesy of Liebman, is that dairy is a "really tough industry to reform," so the strategy is to educate consumers about the alternatives to dairy, such as soy and almond milk. For Liebman, there is no win-win. Runkle also contends that veganism is the surest way to avoid an ethical dilemma, but he seems a bit more pragmatic. There are gradients of cruelty on dairy farms, and if you're careful you can choose the path of least suffering: cows that live in open pastures and live longer, more natural lives. "That being said," Runkle explains, "get to know your farmer is my main piece of advice for anyone who wants to continue to consume dairy."

MONOPOLY

MONEY

On a sunny day in mid-September 2009, during the depths of the dairy crisis of that year, hundreds of dairy farmers streamed into the city gymnasium in St. Albans, Vermont, to see a show. They came, young and old, weathered and ruddy, and sat down in folding chairs lined up on the polyurethaned floor, underneath basketball backboards stowed into the ceiling and fluorescent lights that cast a jaundiced glow over the big room. At the front, two long tables with microphones faced each other, and an easel with a line graph was propped up facing the audience. The people had come down from their farms that day because Patrick Leahy, the Democratic senator from Vermont, who chairs the Senate Judiciary Committee, had organized a field hearing titled "Crisis on the Farm: The State of Competition and Prospects for Sustainability in the Northeast Dairy Industry." The guest of honor was Christine Varney, the assistant attorney general for the Antitrust Division of the Department of Justice, who was supposed to sit, listen, and sound concerned. The farmers, being both naturally skeptical of politicians yet willing to give the veteran senator the benefit of the doubt, showed up even though they suspected this was a well-orchestrated PR stunt. Of course, they also hoped to be proven wrong.

Leahy, in his gravelly voice, addressed the crowd: "There has been a breakdown in competition. Vermont dairy farmers are not getting their fair share of the retail price of milk, but it seems that some of the corporate processors rake in profits even as they raise prices to the consumers. This is way out of whack."

Then came Vermont's other senator, Bernie Sanders, an earnest guy from Brooklyn who has no trouble speaking his mind and who was months earlier the first one to push Christine Varney to launch an antitrust investigation of Dean Foods. With his shock of white hair and his New York accent, he's a politically pugilistic Norman Mailer type, who crafts his oratory in one-two punches, priming the listener for a damning left hook. He opened with a striking fact: one company, the milk processor Dean Foods, controls at least 70 percent of the milk market in the triangle between Michigan, Florida and New England. He advanced with more numbers: in the last year, milk prices to farmers had dropped from $19 per hundredweight to just $11. Then he came in with the knockout blow: "Meanwhile, Dean Foods reported $76.2 million in profits for the first quarter of 2009, up 147 percent from the first quarter of 2008. Is there anybody in this room who doesn't see a connection between those facts?" Nobody raised a hand.

The real question on everyone's mind was whether small and medium-size dairy farms, the entities that mostly keep the eastern United States supplied with fresh milk, could survive in an environment so dominated by one corporation. Varney wondered that too, but she was more curious about whether Dean Foods' market share was a violation of the nation's antitrust laws. Varney, a petite woman with dark, shoulder-length hair, had been appointed to her position after a career in both the private and public sectors. She'd worked in the antitrust practice group of a big law firm in Washington, DC, had been a commissioner at the Federal Trade Commission, and had served as an assistant to the president and secretary to the cabinet during the Clinton administration. When she took her post in the Antitrust Division, she promised to prosecute anticompetitive practices more rigorously, implying that after a period of lax enforcement under the Bush administration a new sheriff was in town. Not lacking an instinct for political theater, one of her first acts in office was to shred a set of guidelines developed by the Justice Department under President George W. Bush that made it much more difficult for the agency to challenge monopolistic corporate behavior.

She knew all of that meant little to the people before her in St. Albans, so she mentioned a different part of her background when introducing herself. "As I think you know, I care deeply about this issue," she said. "My family in Ireland are dairy farmers. I am probably the only assistant attorney general in modern times who actually knows how to milk a cow and has done it many times." She explained that she was concerned about the consolidation of the dairy industry for two main reasons. Foremost was the possibility of a monopsony, a condition where a single buyer wields power over many smaller sellers, thereby reducing or eliminating competition for those inputs. When one company processes a large majority of the milk, for instance, it can dictate to a certain degree how much it will pay for that milk, and the dairy farmers have few alternatives. The other thing she worried about was the increased vertical integration in the dairy industry, a situation where the manufacturer of the product participates in the other parts of the supply chain, such as processing and distribution. Vertical integration can be good for companies because it affords them a guaranteed flow of quality inputs and reduces transaction costs along the path to the consumer. But vertically integrated businesses, especially in the agriculture industry, are notoriously opaque, which can make it easier for such firms to engage in anticompetitive activities. "I am a firm believer," Varney offered, "in what Justice Brandeis said in another context: 'Sunlight is said to be the best of disinfectants; electric light the most efficient policeman.'"

Sanders liked the sound of that, and before turning the hearing over to Leahy and the agricultural economists and dairy farmers who would testify, he reminded Varney that the Justice Department had investigated the consolidated state of the dairy processing industry in 2006 and recommended prosecuting Dean Foods under the Sherman Antitrust Act, but no action was taken.

"Are you prepared to take action?" he asked Varney.

"I can give you every assurance, Senator, that any investigation that I undertake that leads us to believe there is evidence sufficient to prosecute will be prosecuted," Varney replied. "There is no doubt that we will prosecute that kind of activity should we find it."

==

If Varney ever indeed was to take action, it would be against a force almost singlehandedly built by Gregg Engles, the chairman and CEO of Dean Foods. As Sanders told the crowd in St. Albans with seething reproach, over the past five years Engles had personally gained $116 million in compensation while dairy farmers all over the country were losing everything. Engles was not just the leader of a company that represented greedy, ruthless cunning, the Darth Vader to the dairy farmers' Luke Skywalker: the national consolidation of dairy processors was something he'd been scheming since the early 1990s.

Engles was born in Durant, Oklahoma, in 1957 and raised in Denver. His father was one of four physicians among his five siblings, and his mother was a schoolteacher. After high school he went east to Dartmouth College and then to Yale Law School, after which he clerked for Anthony Kennedy. At the time, Kennedy was a judge on the Ninth Circuit Court of Appeals, but he would later be appointed to the U.S. Supreme Court. Engles, however, never practiced law. His first job after the clerkship was in the office of a Dallas investor, where he hatched the idea to sell time-shares in corporate jets. It was the mid-1980s, however, long before such ventures became popular, so it never took off. His next investment idea was real estate, but again his timing was wrong. Just a few years after he and a business partner put some money into Texas real estate, the market tanked. An entrepreneur at heart, Engles was not deterred. In fact, he seemed emboldened. With the same business partner from the real estate investments, Engles borrowed almost all of the $26 million purchase price of a packaged-ice company in Texas—Reddy Ice, the original business that launched the 7-11 stores. The third time was a charm. Soon Reddy Ice was making enough money to allow Engles to go out and buy other small, regional ice companies. In a few years, Reddy was the largest packaged-ice company in the United States. Engles appeared to have found his niche: mergers and acquisitions.

With the ice business humming along, Engles was on the prowl for another opportunity. A mentor who worked in the dairy industry suggested that the milk business would probably be amenable to the same serial acquisition and consolidation that had worked for the ice industry. Indeed, there were similarities between ice and dairy: each needed refrigerated transportation logistics and had been controlled by local companies for years. In addition, the supermarket industry was going through its own waves of consolidation, and as those buyers became bigger, they would desire to do business with larger producers. In a land where behemoths stride, the small get stepped on. Engles looked at the industry and sensed the chance to make loads of money while not only sharpening his deal-making skills but also bringing an old-fashioned localized industry into the modern era.

By 1993, Engles and his partners had amassed startup capital and a long-range business plan. That year, they bought Suiza Dairy, a processor in San Juan, Puerto Rico. The following year, they purchased another processor, Velda Farms, and in 1995 they merged the ice business with the fledgling dairy operation to form Suiza Foods Corporation. One year later, they went public and obtained more capital for further acquisitions. Another year went by—now it's 1997—and Suiza Foods has sales of $1 billion. Engles wildcatted antiquated industries and in milk had found a gusher.

Between Suiza's initial public offering in 1996 and 2000, it purchased more than forty dairy processors all over the United States and Puerto Rico, turning it into the largest dairy processor and distributor in the country. Even WalMart took notice of Suiza's rise, naming it dairy supplier of the year in 2000 because of its on-time delivery track record and innovative marketing programs.

But Suiza wasn't just buying up processing plants and taking them all under its wing. There was something more to it than that. All along, Suiza's business model had been to strategically purchase plants just to close them down, which had the effect of funneling all the raw milk in a region into fewer and fewer buyers. Consolidation was killing competition.

=====

While Engles was busy rearranging the face of the dairy processing business, the production side of the industry was undergoing its own sort of transformation. Yes, the farms were growing in size and decreasing in number, but another—probably underappreciated—shift was also taking place: the consolidation of the dairy cooperatives. In essence a cooperative is the embodiment of the idea that there's strength in numbers: when people band together, whether it's in groups to hunt prey on the savanna or as consumers to buy in bulk, the whole is greater than the sum of its parts. Looked at one way, cooperatives operate with the same logic as the corporation that seeks to consolidate an industry, because power in business transactions is a form of capital. Therefore, as the consolidation of the supermarkets prepared the soil for the consolidation of the processors, the consolidation of the dairy processors encouraged the consolidation of the dairy cooperatives. They're all buyers and sellers wrangling for strategic advantage. No one wants to be little in a world of giants, so the little try to get big.

The first dairy cooperatives in the United States sprang up in 1810, but they became more widespread and diverse with the advent of the interstate railroads. Railroads had the transformational effect of increasing geographical markets from the radius of a few towns to swaths of land that encompassed numerous states. In such an environment, farmers perished or profited by their ability to get their produce to the markets, and that meant they had to deal with the railroad companies. But the railroads were far from a straightforward and efficient system. For example, there might be a few (and thus competitive) long-distance carriers but just one (and thus noncompetitive) local carrier; or "rate wars" would send the price of transportation up one week and down another. Smaller shippers, of course, lost out to bigger shippers in both price and convenience. Individual farmers, long accustomed to making their own arrangements for distribution, found themselves beholden to the whims of the railroad companies and their sundry machinations. That changed, to a degree, in 1867, when Oliver Hudson Kelley led farmers to organize the National Grange of the Patrons of Husbandry. The word "grange" comes from the Latin word *granum*, meaning a grain house or a farm. Kelley was successful in encouraging farmers to form networks of marketing cooperatives that would increase their bargaining power against the railroads and coordinate to set fair and sustainable prices for their products. In just eight years from its founding, the Grange had 800,000 members and served as a catalyst for other cooperatives to sprout up across the U.S. By 1890 there were about a thousand farmer cooperatives, most of them devoted to marketing and selling dairy products.

Into this arms race for business advantage soon came a new weapon: the large corporation. For most of the nineteenth century, businesses were small and owned by one or a few people as sole proprietorships or partnerships. The owners usually managed all or most of the affairs of the business, which produced a single product for local markets. Think of the blacksmith or the owner of a general store. These vocations still existed in 1870, but they were now part of an ecosystem that included such concerns as Standard Oil and Carnegie Steel. "Big Business," as the term was coined, had a few hallmarks: ownership separate from management, operations that required huge amounts of capital, and products and services sold on national or international scales. The railroad corporations were a prime example of the complexity of big business. They pioneered modern management structures that included separate divisions for finance, operations, accounting, legal, and marketing, and made use of the securities markets to grow their businesses and amass power.

The only problem with this path of evolution, from a business standpoint, is that the system couldn't foresee the latent drawback to geographical expansion. When companies moved into regional and national markets, they ended up expanding their zones of competition. This led to excess capacity in numerous areas, where supply was greater than demand. And industrial corporations, invested heavily in machinery and equipment, couldn't just transfer their assets into some other sector. They were forced to play the hand they had dealt themselves. Prices dropped, profits disappeared, and out of the sheer necessity of survival evolved yet another organization: the business trust.

The brainchild of John D. Rockefeller, then the head of the Petroleum Refiners Association, the business trust is an adaptation of the much older and more general trust instrument, in which assets are poured into an entity managed by a trustee for the benefit of the beneficiaries. The trick of the business trust was that the assets weren't just money, real estate, or chattels but entire groups of corporations in a single industry. The control of these corporations was transferred via irrevocable deeds to boards of trustees charged with managing the businesses on behalf of the shareholders of the corporations. Trusts had the effect of calming nervous markets, but they accomplished this by way of ceding complete control of whole industries—sugar, whiskey, lead, and petroleum, for example—to a few men. Thus empowered, they could tinker with supply to keep prices high, horizontally integrate to lower their own costs, and vertically integrate to own all the levels in a supply chain. In other words, these trusts could act unchecked in their own best interests and hold consumers hostage to their greed. Though the trust would eventually lose favor to the "holding company," the public still associated big business run by rich white men in smoke-filled rooms with trusts, and the government's response to anticompetitive behavior would incorporate the moniker into its marquee.

The Sherman Anti-Trust Act, passed in 1890, was initially created at the behest of businessmen who believed that they had been unfairly harmed by the power of industry cartels, holding companies, and the other various species of competition-killing conglomerates. Yet the act wasn't created to protect businesses so much as to ensure that consumer prices stayed reasonable. Over time, this goal was to be prosecuted by taking action to prevent monopolies from forming, or diluting those already in existence.

More than 120 years after the law was signed by President Benjamin Harrison, the Sherman Act is largely unchanged and constitutes the core of the federal government's toolkit against anticompetitive behavior. It's a fairly simple law, too. Section one of the original text began: "Every contract, combination in the form of trust or otherwise, or conspiracy, in restraint of trade or commerce among the several States, or with foreign nations, is declared to be illegal." Section two then targets monopolies: "Every person who shall monopolize, or attempt to monopolize, or combine or conspire with any other person or persons, to monopolize any part of the trade or commerce among the several States, or with foreign nations, shall be deemed guilty of a felony. . . ."

Naturally, the small business community praised the Sherman Act. But one rather important corner of the community wasn't so happy: farmers. By the stroke of a pen, the act had basically rendered farmer cooperatives illegal. Some tension in the system had to be released, and the dairy industry was the pressure point. In 1916, dairy marketing organizations felt they were being singled out for antitrust enforcement, so they formed the National Cooperative Milk Producer's Association to merge their interests and protect themselves. Then they joined with the National Grange, the National Farmers Union, and other farm organizations to lobby for a farm-specific exemption to the Sherman Act. "We therefore urge upon Congress," they declared, "the necessity of such an amendment to the antitrust laws as will clearly permit farmers' organizations to make collective sales of the farm, ranch, and dairy products produced by their members. Such organizations, with liberty of action, can insist that the agencies engaged in processing and distribution sell such products at prices as low as may be consistent with the cost of production and distribution."

The fruit of their labor arrived in 1922 in the form of the Capper-Volstead Act, which allowed producers of agricultural products to "act together" to process, handle, and market their goods, and make contracts with each other toward those ends. The big "however" in Capper-Volstead is that these associations must be operated for the mutual benefit of the farmer-members. Theoretically, this provision, along with the limitation of the exemption to "producers" of agricultural goods, would protect cooperatives from being co-opted by business concerns—such as processors and marketers—that, in effect, feed off of the producers' activity, and ensure that these associations wouldn't divert money from farmers to the executives of the cooperatives.

Capper-Volstead was a watershed law for farmer cooperatives. Most important, it restored the rule of "strength in numbers" to farmers. Now they could, without fear of prosecution under the Sherman Act, work together to strengthen their economic position, weather tough times, and deal more equally with processors and distributors. It also allowed them to raise capital to build expensive processing facilities and coordinate to get their products to market. Whether they processed their own products or dealt with independent processors, Capper-Volstead protected some of the most vulnerable actors in the economy from market gyrations and big businesses trying to squeeze every last penny between the farmer and the consumer.

It's worth noting here that the dairy industry has never been as uniformly wholesome as the product it brings to market. Shady deals happened all the time. An alleged conspiracy between processors, milk truckers, a farmer cooperative, and municipal officials in the Chicago area gave the U.S. Supreme Court its first chance to interpret Capper-Volstead. The big question was: how much leeway do associations organized under Capper-Volstead have when it comes to anticompetitive behavior? The case was *United States v. Borden*, decided in 1939, and the relevant facts are fairly straightforward: the conspirators colluded to fix prices for farmers and distributors, prevent individual distributors from serving Chicago, and, more generally, to control the supply of fluid milk brought into Chicago from Illinois, Michigan, Indiana, and Wisconsin. The Court was rather clear in its appraisal:

> In this instance, the conspiracy charged is not that of merely forming a collective association of producers to market their products, but a conspiracy, or conspiracies, with major distributors and their allied groups, with labor officials, municipal officials, and others, in order to maintain artificial and noncompetitive prices to be paid to all producers for all fluid milk produced in Illinois and neighboring States and marketed in the Chicago area.... Such a combined attempt of all the defendants, producers, distributors and their allies to control the market finds no justification in §1 of the Capper-Volstead Act.[1]

In other words, Capper-Volstead allows producers to cooperate to market their products, but it doesn't grant them immunity from antitrust liability when they collude with nonproducers, such as processors and distributors. The case has not been overruled.

Now that dairy cooperatives had a sense of the boundaries of Capper-Volstead, they continued to amass bargaining power the only way they could: by joining ranks. The 1950s and 1960s were not good times for dairy farmers. Their incomes were low, and off-farm jobs were abundant and better paying. Partially for these reasons, the number of dairy farms in the United States dropped 61 percent between 1955 and 1965. That, coupled with the technological changes of the Green Revolution that boosted milk production and quickened processing times, resulted in weaker cooperatives and stiffer competition between once isolated areas.

The overwhelming urge was to link farmers in cooperatives not just locally but across wide chunks of the country. Picture little magnetic spheres rolling toward each other, forming massive nodes of influence. Associated Milk Producers, Inc., formed in 1967, attracted 111 smaller cooperatives from Kansas, Texas, Oklahoma, and Arkansas, and by 1971 its 31,000 dairy farmers supplied 75 percent of the milk to the markets of Chicago, Dallas, Houston, Indianapolis, Madison, Memphis, Oklahoma City, and San Antonio. Mid-America Dairymen, formed in 1968, drew together cooperatives from Iowa, Kansas, Missouri, Nebraska, and Minnesota, and by 1971 represented 23,000 dairy farmers. Then there was Dairymen, Inc. Also formed in 1968, it was composed of twenty-four cooperatives from the Southeastern and Central states, and by 1971 had 9,800 members. Put them all together and in the four years between 1967 and 1971, about 170 local cooperatives had merged into three organizations representing 64,000 farmers.

It didn't take long for the Department of Justice to get suspicious. In the mid-1970s, it filed antitrust actions against the three cooperatives for violations of Sections 1 and 2 of the Sherman Act. The DOJ claimed that the co-ops had monopolized the raw milk markets by requiring processors to contract for a set quantity of milk, under pains of penalty, and entering into membership agreements that unreasonably restricted the rights of members to withdraw if a more competitive offer came along. The judges in all three cases—in the federal district courts in Texas, Kentucky, and Missouri—agreed, and enjoined the cooperatives from entering into or enforcing agreements for a term longer than one year. The DOJ struck again in 1977, this time solely against Mid-America Dairymen, and won a consent decree that restrained the cooperative from coercing dairy farmers to join the organization or not leave; playing fast and loose with the milk marketing order regulations; or entering into milk sales agreements of a term longer than one year.

So it was in 1998 that Mid-America Dairymen, still bound by the consent decree from 1977, joined with three other cooperatives to form Dairy Farmers of America (DFA), becoming the largest dairy co-op in the country. It remains so today.

===

Gregg Engles and the Suiza management must have looked upon the consolidation of the cooperatives with a mixture of fright and cautious optimism. On the one hand, a massive cooperative like DFA could potentially vertically integrate and cut Suiza right out of the equation. But on the other hand, if Suiza could make DFA's operations simple and predictable, perhaps they could work together and both make money. And that's what happened. DFA bought 33.8 percent of Suiza and was now big enough to enter into a "full supply" agreement with the processor, guaranteeing that only DFA's milk would be processed at Suiza's facilities. Now the nation's largest cooperative was tightly allied with the nation's second largest processor and distributor. At least Dean Foods was still out there as competition for Suiza.

Until it wasn't. In December of 2001, Engles arranged Suiza's acquisition of Dean Foods in a $2.5 billion deal. Dean Foods was founded in northwestern Illinois in 1925 as an evaporated milk processor and, like Suiza, had grown into a national concern by acquiring processing plants over a period of years. By 2000, Dean was Suiza's only match, pound for pound, on the national market. When they merged, they accounted for 30 percent of the nation's milk money. Engles became CEO of Dean Foods in 2002 and was the proud leader of a company that claimed more than fifty brands of dairy products, including Silk soy milk, Horizon organic dairy and juices, and International Delight coffee creamers. It also licensed brands such as Land-O-Lakes, Hershey's, and Folgers for its milkshakes, creamers, and coffee drinks. In the popular press at the time, Engles was being compared to Herb Kelleher of Southwest Airlines and, believe it or not, Sam Walton. He was praised for forcing efficiency and economy of scale on an industry that, like a colt, had been stubborn in the breaking.

To its credit, the Department of Justice wasn't completely asleep at the switch when this historic merger took place. In fact, after months of negotiation with the companies, it established some conditions to the deal that would tend to preserve competition. The conditions were twofold: first, the full-supply agreement between DFA and Suiza had to be modified to allow Suiza to buy milk from sources other than DFA; second, the newly merged Dean and Suiza had to divest eleven plants to a third company that would compete with them.

Both conditions were largely thwarted. Not only did Dean maintain full supply agreements with DFA, it had the nerve to get around the 1977 consent decree (the part prohibiting contracts that lasted longer than a year) by signing a series of twenty successive one-year agreements and promising to pay DFA $47 million if it breached any of them. To dodge the divestiture requirement, Dean and DFA got even more creative. Dean sold the plants to National Dairy Holdings (NDH), a newly formed partnership created by DFA and two former Dean executives. How did NDH get the money to buy these plants? DFA loaned it more than $400 million. Whom did DFA install as the CEO of NDH? A gentleman by the name of Allen Meyer, accused by the DOJ of colluding with DFA to eliminate competition while appearing as an independent competitor. Specifically, the DOJ has alleged that DFA and Meyer have "a long history of friendly and mutually profitable financial dealings," and that Meyer "has a substantial incentive to keep DFA happy so that he can continue to receive profitable business opportunities." In 2004, with Meyer doing such a great job at NDH, DFA bought out the other two partners in the business and left Meyer as its sole investment partner in NDH. The upshot: Dean and DFA are so closely intertwined that they might as well be one. Strangely, the DOJ sat on its hands and watched it happen.

One might be inclined to cut the DOJ some slack. Perhaps it was too much of a leap to assume that an inbreeding of Dean and DFA would have disastrous consequences on competition for farmers' milk. But, in fact, they had a precedent to refer to: the Stop & Shop case. Stop & Shop is one of the largest supermarket chains in New England, and before February of 2000 it processed its own fluid Grade A milk at its plant in Readville, Massachusetts. That plant was supplied in full by the milk produced by Vermont dairy farmers who were members of the St. Albans Cooperative Creamery. By the same token, St. Albans, founded in 1919 and the largest co-op in Vermont, sent most of its milk to the Readville plant, so it's safe to say they had a symbiotic relationship.

That relationship started to crumble in early 2000, when Suiza paid Stop & Shop $50 million to shut down its plant, sell the assets to Suiza, and agree to sell fluid milk products bottled solely by Suiza for the next fifteen years. But DFA was the exclusive supplier to Suiza, which left St. Albans in a tricky spot: who would now buy their milk? The attorneys general of Connecticut, Massachusetts, New Hampshire, and Rhode Island were aware of this impending deal and worried that it would hurt competition in the Northeast. So they got Suiza to agree to buy 30 million gallons of milk from non-DFA farmers in New England for five years; not restrict Stop & Shop from selling competitors' milk; and not buy the Readville processing plant assets from Stop & Shop. On paper, it seemed fair: a win for the good guys. In practice, the agreement was completely ignored. Almost before the ink was dry on the agreement, Stop & Shop shut down the plant and sold the assets to Suiza, increasing Suiza's market share to about 80 or 90 percent in Boston and Rhode Island, and 65 percent in New England.

St. Albans Creamery was left flapping in the wind. Under the terms of the agreement, Suiza had to buy milk from St. Albans members for five years, and then they could be cut free. Soon it became clear to the leaders at St. Albans that they had little choice but to join DFA. After all, if their milk could be processed only by plants that buy milk solely from DFA farmers, St. Albans farmers wouldn't be able to sell their product unless they joined. Which is what they did in 2003. In a defeated tone, St. Albans issue the following statement to its members in February of that year:

> Over the last several years processing plants in the Northeast
> have been closed or acquired by major processors. St. Albans
> Cooperative Creamery, Inc. experienced a significant change in
> its Class I account in 2000 with Stop & Shop's decision to close
> their bottling facility. . . . After careful and full analysis, the St.
> Albans Cooperative Board of Directors has agree to an annual
> membership and marketing agreement with DFA.

As if to preserve a shred of dignity as the victim of a hostile takeover, St. Albans added: "This is not a merger of these two organizations. This is an annual marketing and membership agreement that will assure St. Albans Cooperative access to markets in the Northeast and allow St. Albans to be competitive in its returns to its dairy farmers."

Dean and DFA have used this strategy all over the Eastern seaboard, from Maine to Florida. When you get far enough away from the tangled mess of subsidiary corporations and back-room deals, the whole thing comes into clearer focus. Dean uses its muscle to buy up processors, and because of a cozy relationship with DFA executives it agrees to buy milk only from DFA farms. Suddenly, any farmer outside the DFA cabal is forced to make a choice: go out of business or join DFA.

Yet there's one more wrinkle that's important to note, just for its sheer jaw dropping gall. DFA didn't just contract to be the full supplier for Dean, it also used its financial resources—made on the backs of dairy farmers—to go out and buy its own processing plants. You might think this is a benign business decision—diversify!—until you realize that under the USDA rules, cooperatives are not obligated to return to members profits made on nonfarming businesses. In some nefarious plot line that could only have been dreamed up by the protesters in the Occupy Wall Street movement, the guys in the silk suits running the cooperative's business dealings take the dairy farmers' money, turn it into more money, and then never let the farmers share in the profits. But they didn't have to dream it up, because reality will suffice. The details of these transactions are often convoluted, but the gist is the same: money comes out of DFA, goes into a subsidiary to buy plants, and then the profits get distributed to cronies through stock transfers, ownership rights, or just plain cash.

In 2001, for example, DFA and Robert Allen jointly acquired the Southern Belle processor for $18.7 million. DFA supplied $18 million, and Allen contributed $1 million. Despite this capital investment disparity, DFA granted Allen 100 percent control of the management of the entity, 100 percent of the voting shares, and 50 percent of the profits, while guaranteeing Allen's $1 million up front investment.[2]

Another example is the formation of NDH to buy the eleven divested plants from Suiza. Three individuals contributed $5 million toward that purchase, while DFA financed the rest. But three years later, DFA purchased ownership stakes from two of those investors for a total of $41 million. It's highly unlikely that their investment more than quadrupled in value in such a short amount of time.

Also in 2001, the CEO of DFA arranged for an unauthorized transfer of $1 million to DFA board chairman Herman Brubaker, through the DFA affiliate NDH. The transaction was concealed from DFA's board of directors. Seven years later, DFA was auditing NDH's books and saw the mysterious transfer. The new CEO of DFA, Rick Smith, informed members of the "unfortunate" unauthorized transfer and appointed a committee to investigate. No charges were filed and the money mysteriously reappeared, plus interest.

The graft continued in the Southern half of the country in 2002. That was when DFA and various coconspirators formed the Southern Marketing Agency to market all of DFA's milk sold in the Southeast. Aside from accomplishing its intended purpose, executives from DFA, Dean Foods, and other independent businesses, who were of a piece with SMA, began using the entity as a way to funnel money to themselves.

The first way this became obvious was through SMA's marketing expenses, which were unreasonably high. How to explain? One reason was that SMA contracted with a guy by the name of James

Baird, the owner of Bullseye, a Texas-based milk trucking company, to be its sole transporter. Baird, it turned out, made a habit of hauling unnecessarily large quantities of milk from the Southwest to the Southeast, and used extraordinarily long routes in the Southeast, all to pad his trucking expenses and maximize his takeaway. SMA tolerated this because Baird was SMA.[3]

One might wonder why anyone was trucking milk across the desert from New Mexico to, say, South Carolina. To a rational person, that seems like a waste of resources. If there was a shortage of milk in the Southeast, why not make up the difference from the Midwest?: because some of the owners of SMA were also heavily invested in freshly built megadairies in New Mexico, and they were faced with a surplus of milk in their home region. A surplus meant a lower price, less profit, so they formed yet another marketing agency (Greater Southwest Agency, Inc.) to market their New Mexico milk where the supply was a little tighter—the Southeast. The only way this made any economic sense was because SMA agreed to buy as much Southwestern milk as the dairies wanted to sell, and it covered GSA's cost of transporting the milk two thousand miles east. This, of course, made the New Mexico farmers and cooperative executives quite happy. But it also had the effect of flooding the Southeastern region with milk, thereby lowering the price to farmers there. And—get this—SMA includes those exorbitant transportation expenses as overhead in its operation, a line-item expense that's paid for with a deduction from Southeastern farmers' milk check. This resulted in a double deduction on Southeastern farmers: lower milk prices, and more subtractions from whatever measly sum they might have gotten in the first place.[4]

· That, largely, has been the effect on every dairy farmer on the East Coast who is affiliated with DFA and, by association, Dean Foods. But the same is not true for consumers: they've been paying an increasing amount for a gallon of whole milk for the last fifteen years. If farmers have been getting less for their milk, and customers have been paying more, it can mean only one thing: processors have been taking home the difference. The numbers bear that out. For example, from May 2004 until November 2006, the raw fluid Grade A skim milk price paid to dairy farmers in New England dropped from $1.29 per gallon to $0.96, while the processors' margin increased from $0.64 to $0.78.

What's also telling is that milk prices paid to farmers in the Northeast have been lower than those paid in the Midwest. That is the opposite of how it should be, because milk production costs are higher in the Northeast: it costs more to transport, and much of it remains as higher-priced fluid milk while Midwestern milk is predominantly sold at the Class III rate to make cheese and other dairy products. "So why are [milk] prices lower in the Northeast than the Midwest?" asks Ronald Cotterill, a professor of agricultural economics at the University of Connecticut. "The answer is that . . . Northeast raw milk markets, relatively speaking, are dominated by the milk channel firms at the expense of the region's dairy farmers. Monopsony power in the Northeast dairy market is a major force."

=====

It is wise to remember that DFA, being a cooperative organized under the auspices of the Capper-Volstead Act, must operate for the mutual benefit of its members. So why have DFA's dairy farmers tolerated the selfish and feckless behavior of the people in charge of the cooperatives? Why would they let their money be funneled away from their member-owned cooperative into the hands of a few corporate executives and their buddies? Peter Carstensen, a professor of law at the University of Wisconsin-Madison who specializes in antitrust law, gives a few plausible reasons. First, he says, "They've got farmers in a very tight vice. It's not like they can take their cows and walk away." An even more disturbing reason is that, endowed with this market power, the cooperatives have chosen not to be transparent and inclusive, but opaque and clandestine. This is one pitfall of the separation of ownership and control that happens when organizations get very large. "In theory," Carstensen says, "the dairy farmers own the company. In reality, they've got this dispersed network of local and regional boards culminating in some kind of board of directors." And these dispersed boards, exercising their selfish regional interests, feed into an organization that handles a lot of money yet isn't regulated like a traditional public corporation. "They're not required to use the generally accepted accounting principles," Carstensen says. "They're not required to file the kind of reports that a public corporation of the same size would have to file."

Along those lines, cooperatives are theoretically overseen by the USDA, but that agency exercises no real power over the entities, either because of lack of will or lack of resources. Cooperatives are putatively subject to the laws of the states in which they operate, but that net is full of holes, too. DFA, for instance, is organized under the laws of Kansas, which has perhaps a handful of cases interpreting the statutes that authorize its existence. "If you're a lawyer looking at this," Carstensen opines, "there's enormous uncertainty. There's nobody policing, nobody adopting rules, no accountability in the way that the corporate management behaves." It's tempting to pin this problem on the larger trend of consolidation, because back when co-ops were composed of fifty farmers, they could manage their own affairs without government regulations. Today, DFA has close to 10,000 members and tentacles spreading out into related but nonfarming business, and such an animal is too complex and powerful to be spared a leash. Yet no one has been willing to change the legislative framework of Capper-Volstead to create more oversight for co-ops. You don't blame the present for being different from the past; you simply do the hard work that justice requires.

As a former staff attorney in the Antitrust Division of the Department of Justice, Carstensen is especially troubled by the DOJ's failure to crack down on Dean Foods and DFA. He tried for years to get the DOJ to investigate the milk markets, which they did in 2006, but it was basically a fool's errand because nothing ever came of it. "That frustrates me to no end," he says. Don't get him started on the monkey business where Dean Foods divested eleven plants to a company it had a significant interest in. There are conspiracy theorists out there, he says, who think the DOJ was corrupt and that maybe they were the end recipient of the $1 million that disappeared in 2002. It's more likely that the Bush administration exerted political pressure on the DOJ to look the other way. "It's one of the things that remains a real mystery to me," Carstensen admits. "I've had conversations with midlevel staff attorneys at the Antitrust Division and they say, 'Well, gee, I'm just not going to talk to you about that.'"

John Bunting, an industry observer who writes a blog widely read by dairy insiders, offers a broader explanation. "The day Reagan took office, he reduced antitrust enforcement resources at the DOJ to one-eighth of what they'd been the day before," he says. "They must have been demoralized." Prior to that, government antitrust attorneys were known to be a vicious lot, fighting tooth and nail for the public good. They were World War II veterans who had gone to school on the GI Bill and had a strong sense of justice. But when they were basically told to slow-walk their investigations, they looked forward to retiring and taking their pensions, which were based on the top three years of earnings. "You're not going to get to your top three years by rocking the boat," Bunting says. "Plain and simple." Things didn't get any better for the Antitrust Division under the George W. Bush administration.

After advocates of competition in the dairy industry got nowhere with the DOJ, they went another route and influenced class action lawyers to sue DFA and Dean Foods. The first of those cases, which covered the Southeast, was filed in 2008. The second, with a class in the Northeast, was filed the following year. Together they represented not just DFA farmer members but also any dairy farmer in the relevant geographic area whose milk price had been reduced as a result of collusion and anticompetitive behavior by Dean and DFA. It worked out to more than 15,000 dairy farmers, with damages estimated in the hundreds of millions of dollars. They both alleged violations of sections 1 and 2 of the Sherman Act, laying out in lurid detail the systematic and coercive march to market domination.

Given the scope and scale of the lawsuits, they didn't take long to wrap up. Dean Foods settled the Northeast case in early 2011 for $30 million, and the Southeast settlement came shortly after that, for a whopping $140 million. Each farmer in the Northeast class was expected to receive close to $3,000 out of the settlement, right around Christmas of 2011. It wasn't enough to turn the tide at a struggling farm, but a nice bonus nonetheless. Dean Foods has denied any wrongdoing in the Northeast.

About the Southeast case Engles said, "We continue to be confident that we have operated lawfully and fairly at all times. Settling this case allows us to focus on the business challenges we face, and to continue to take costs out of our operation while avoiding the expense, uncertainty and distraction of a protracted litigation and the likelihood of a protracted appeals process."[5] DFA, on the other hand, has not agreed to settle in either case, and it's unclear at this writing how it will be affected by the lawsuits.

Dean Foods today, while still a powerful force in the dairy industry, is not the flush corporation that Bernie Sanders castigated at the St. Albans field hearing in 2009. After the Dean and Suiza merger back in 2001, the company's stock price rose from about $20 per share to almost $50 in 2007. At the end of 2011, Dean Foods was trading at $9 and change, and it had incurred substantial debt—to the tune of $3.5 billion—to keep itself operating. The class action settlements won't help Dean's situation, but they also won't be a major setback. What's more of a problem for Dean is the continued consolidation of the supermarket industry, and WalMart's increasing power not only to dictate prices but also to influence consumer trends. One of those trends is the shift to "private label" milk products, branded under and an in-house name and sold at a lower price than comparable name brand goods. It remains to be seen if Dean Foods can still make a profit on milk under these conditions. It might end up that WalMart processes its own milk, or even buys the processing assets from Dean.

But before that possible eventuality, Dean seems to have been chastened a bit by the class action lawsuits. The evidence of that comes in the form of "Dean Direct," its new way of buying milk directly from dairy farmers on the open market and paying the going rate, plus premiums. Whether Dean can really afford this strategy in the long term is another open question.

=

Christine Varney sat politely through the entire field hearing in St. Albans and attended others on the same issue in different parts of the country. But despite the class action settlements, and the evidence those cases have turned up, her department hasn't taken any official action. In fact, it's not even Varney's department anymore: she left in 2011 to return to private practice. The law is clearly on the side of dairy farmers; it's just that litigation is costly, time consuming, and, at the level of the DOJ, politically fraught.

A better solution, though equally fraught, is stronger regulation of cooperatives by the government. In a blue-sky way, Carstensen outlines his vision: the USDA establishes an office of cooperative regulation headed by a panel of three people appointed by the president, writes rules, and has the independent authority and gumption to exercise its powers.

To the free market libertarians who scoff at such an idea, John Bunting has a few words: "The invisible hand does not milk cows."

GRASS-FED, FREE-RANGE, STREAMLINE BABY

It's easy to see the beginning of things, and harder
to see the ends. —*Joan Didion, "Goodbye to All That"*

Nobody knows when the last small dairy farm will milk its last
cow; when the kinetics of consolidation and ruthless efficiency
will defeat the inertia of tradition and community; when the wor-
ship of the Cheap will finally overtake our allegiance to the Good.
Given the rate of farm loss in states like Vermont, New York, and
Connecticut, perhaps the species of dairy farm that most adults
today grew up with will be extinct in fifty years. That ending could
be out there, in the hazy future, and it's not so drastically different
as to be unfathomable. For much of the Northeast, there would be
no such thing as local milk. It will be made somewhere out West
on a CAFO, turned into powder, trucked, and reconstituted. The
good agricultural soil will go to seed or be paved over. Communities once defined by farms will be dotted with Toll Brothers tract
housing instead of cows.

But the beginning of a better future may already be at hand. It is in
this glass of chocolate milk that tastes like liquid ice cream. The man
who poured the glass, setting it on the table the way a poker player
lays down a royal flush, is Dr. Sam Simon. Tall of stature, with a slight

stoop and a hitch in his walk, he has a youthful face that is a smooth canvas painted with bushy eyebrows and classy, rimless spectacles. Put him in a dark suit and he would be at home in a white-shoe law firm in Manhattan; in a white coat, he'd fit in on the rounds at Mass General. When he brings out his husky New York accent, a voice that belies his relatively lithe appearance, all pretense melts away. "Now, *that's* some fuckin' chocolate milk, isn't it?"

It is indeed. The secret to this creamy, bracing beverage is really no secret at all. It's emblazoned right on the plastic carton whence it came: Hudson Valley *Fresh*. But the milk isn't just fresh—no more than thirty-six hours from teat to supermarket—it's also 4 percent milk-fat (regular whole milk is 3.2), contains premium cocoa, and is probably the highest quality milk you can buy, bar none. The real secret is how Sam has made this product—and its brethren: regular milk, sour cream, and yogurt—more than just an oddity you might stumble across in some general store in the sticks. How he sells 4 million pounds of it per year and guarantees his dairy farmers a living wage. How he has thumbed his nose at an entrenched, benighted food system that doesn't create value so much as transfer it from the many to the few. Has this Jewish doctor from Poughkeepsie solved the Rubik's Cube that is the dairy industry?

=====

Sam Simon, sixty-six, grew up on a small dairy farm in New York. You might say he's a third-generation farmer. His grandfather, Albert, was a cattle broker in Germany and had contracts to provide the German government with horses and grain, which he would buy and sell at the Russian border. Although, as a Jew, Albert could not own property in Germany, he figured he was close enough to the establishment that his ethnicity was not a liability. "Bullshit," Sam says. "They threw his ass in jail one day, and the light went on in his brain." Albert sent his sons to the United States: first Sam's uncle, who was a butcher and got a job with Hebrew National, and then Sam's father, Kurt. By 1937 the whole family had escaped the Third

Reich. Knowing cattle, they bought a farm in Middletown, where Kurt did most of the work raising cattle and milking cows. When Sam reached grade school age, Kurt was happy to have the extra set of hands on the farm. From the earliest he could remember, Sam idolized doctors and vets, but he was forced to farm. "I had to work," he recalls. "I did whatever my father said. Either that or get a fork up your ass. Take your choice. It was real simple with him." While Sam's friends were venturing to the Bronx to see the Yankees, Sam was stuck at the farm, milking cows.

He had almost escaped his little version of Green Acres in 1969, when he went to Missouri for medical school. But Sam's father died that year, at the age of fifty-three, leaving his wife, who was just forty-two, and his daughters, aged sixteen and nine, to fend for themselves. Kurt had had no life insurance policy; the farm *was* his life insurance policy. Sam, all of a sudden, had to support his family while training to be a doctor. In those days, dairy farming was still a viable way to make a living, so he handed the day-to-day operation over to the herdsman his father had hired two years before. He talked to the herdsman every day from Missouri and flew back to New York once a month to check in. He'd arrive at LaGuardia on a Friday night and be in the barn by four the next morning to give the herdsman a two-day break, the guy's only time off during the entire month. On Sunday night, he would return to Missouri and gross anatomy. During the summers, he moved back to the farm to handle the crops, fill the barn with hay and the silos with corn and grain. The pattern continued for nine years: four in medical school and five in residencies.

In 1982, when Sam sold the dairy operation, farmers were getting more for their milk (adjusted for inflation) than they would be in 2009. He didn't get out because dairying was going sour but because he had a bustling practice as an orthopedic surgeon in Poughkeepsie. When he moved there in the late 1970s—Middletown wasn't taking more doctors—he became the first orthopedist in the area to do total knee, shoulder, and hand surgery. He also operated on scoliosis at Columbia University's Helen Hayes Hospital and worked on traumatic spine injuries. Over a period of two decades, he built his practice into one of the busiest in the Hudson Valley, with 30,000 patients. He performed surgery five days per week.

In 1995, a patient of his was sitting in the waiting room looking at a photo of Sam's old Middletown farm. It looked a lot like the patient's nearby farm where, once upon a time, registered Holsteins had grazed. The patient was now the sole surviving sibling from the farm family and he was trying to unload the property. He asked if Sam was interested. It turned out he was. Although Sam was barely fifty years old, he was thinking about retiring and getting back into dairy farming. "I wanted to do it one more time," Sam recalls, "my way, where I could be immersed in it." They visited the farm on a sunny day in February, negotiated a purchase price, and closed the deal by May 1. The land hadn't been cropped in years, so Sam spent the next three seasons bringing it back into production. He had finally found his hobby. "Some people like to play golf and tennis, but that's not me," he explains. "I'd rather work with cows, pick rock, work with hay." He retired in 1998, at the age of fifty-two, and when he sold his practice the new doctor had to hire two more doctors and a physician's assistant just to keep up.

The restless energy that Sam had poured into his 30,000 patients transferred seamlessly into reviving Plankenhorn Farm, which sits on 150 acres of high rolling land in the town of Pleasant Valley, seven miles northeast of Poughkeepsie. It needed a lot of work. Gravity had run roughshod over the place. Barn roofs were caved in and the old stone walls had sunk into the ground. He fixed those things and then gutted and renovated the old farmhouse.

Given a nearly blank slate and a generous savings account, Sam had the luxury of designing the farm the way he wanted. The barns dated to the 1800s and 1930, but instead of transforming them into a modern free-stall facility, where cows can roam around and lie down where they want, Sam stayed with the older, tie-stall configuration that was already there. He not only stuck with old over new, he went backward in efficiency, making each stall bigger, which meant there was room for forty-four cows instead of sixty-two. They would be tied in their stalls with a loose chain and rest on state-of-the-art waterproof mattresses filled with tire bits—"comfort beds." It was an early indication that Sam wasn't going to follow the herd into the land of More Is Better, but create something he believed in, something both classic and meticulous.

Why is a tie-stall better than a free-stall? In Sam's opinion, it's a visibility and cleanliness thing. Cows in a tie-stall are always in the same place; in a free-stall, they're like subatomic particles wandering around. "You can't see the cow in her totality easily in a free-stall," he says. "Here, I can see everything I want to see on a cow in a split second." The free-stall creates another problem: access to a clean bed. In general, with a free-stall, farmers can cram more cows into the space than is optimal, and there are only a limited number of beds. At any given time, 25 to 30 percent are eating, and it's impossible to know which cows want to lie down. "So she's either standing in shit or lying in shit, lying in the alleyways. I don't want to see that," he says. Sam ran his dairy less like a farm than a hospital. When people walked into his milk house, they often remarked that it looked like an operating room, with gleaming stainless steel appliances and not a spec of dirt on the floor.

He bred purebred Holsteins, but not in the usual way. He outbred for genetic diversity, valuing body conformation—health, strength, and longevity—over production. "I don't give a fuck about production!" he declares. That's because he knew that if he fed and cared for his animals properly, they would produce just fine. Which they did. His mature cows gave 35,000 pounds of milk per year and had a lifespan of eight years or more. To him, it made more sense to have a cow that gives an average of 30,000 pounds per year for six years than an industrialized cow that gives 40,000 pounds for three years. It seems like simple math, but it's really more like a philosophy, a respect for the animal and an unwavering commitment to quality.

Sam's cows didn't leave the farm because of lameness or disease—he didn't ever have one case of laminitis, an infection of the hoof—but because cows, like humans, lose their fertility after a while. Cows that can't get pregnant also can't make milk. Every day he brushed each cow from head to tail. He fed his calves milk and whole wheat bread for ninety days, and never lost one. Almost everything he fed his animals was grown right on the farm—hay, corn, alfalfa, and oats. The rest, high-protein grain for the milkers, came from a farm in Germantown, just up Route 9G on the banks of the Hudson River.

From the moment he started making milk on Plankenhorn Farm in 1999, he received quality premiums from Agrimark, the cooperative that makes Cabot Cheese. These premiums recognize the low raw bacteria and somatic cell levels in farmers' milk. The raw bacteria count is a measure of the cleanliness of the environment. The somatic cell count, a measure of the white cells in the cow, is an indication of the cow's health. By both standards, Sam's farm was outstanding. The industry standard for raw bacteria count is 50,000 cells per milliliter; Sam's numbers were consistently below 5,000—ten times lower. The industry calls a somatic cell count of less than 200,000 cells per milliliter "premium"; Sam's milk always ran between 49,000 and 129,000.

If you want to get a feel for the regulation of milk in this country, look at the *maximum* somatic cell count that milk can have before it's ineligible for pasteurization and sale: 750,000. "Pus is one million!" Sam says, getting worked up, as he often does. "So if a farm has a pooled somatic cell count of 600,000 or more there must be many animals with an individual count of more than a million. You're drinking a lot of pasteurized pus." In the EU, by contrast, milk processors won't even pasteurize milk that comes into the plant with more than 400,000 cells/ml. "That would disqualify most U.S. dairy farms right off the bat," Sam says.

One of the benefits of a low somatic cell count, aside from just purer milk, is that it results in a higher amount of omega-3s, the beneficial fatty acids that protect against cardiovascular disease, autoimmune disorders, diabetes, arthritis, and arrhythmia. The highest levels of omega-3s can be found in fish oil from anchovies and sardines, something the American diet does not usually provide. People try to take omega-3 supplements, but its fishy aftertaste is hard to tolerate. Milk, however, is in almost every American refrigerator, and as long as it's high quality, it can be a significant source of omega-3. Lower quality milk has less omega-3s because the cow is using her omega-3 stores to fight off her infection. Healthy cows have an excess and naturally give it off in their milk. Bonus, indeed.

Another important thing happens to milk when the somatic cell count goes up: the enzymes that break down the protein (protease) and fat (lipase) also go up. That results in a shorter shelf life and a product gutted of nutritional value. This presented a problem for the industrializing dairy business. The milk coming from CAFO dairies is not only higher in somatic cell count—thus shortening the shelf life—but it usually travels a long way before it gets to the kitchen table, thereby necessitating a *longer* shelf life. The industry got around this by using a processing method known as ultra-high temperature (UHT) pasteurization. Conventionally pasteurized milk is heated to 164 degrees Fahrenheit for twenty seconds. When you start with a clean product, that's all the heat you need to create a baseline level of bacteria that's safe for everyone. The UHT method, however, cooks the milk at 280 degrees for a few seconds, which kills not only bacteria but also the lipase and protease. When you break down those enzymes, milk can have a two-month shelf life. At that point, however, it's not much more than, well, "I don't know what it is," Sam says. "Something white, I guess."

To make up for the tendency of a high somatic cell count to strip milk of omega-3s, and the simultaneous awakening of the public to omega-3's importance, milk processors have started adding omega-3s to the milk after it's pasteurized. Sam is skeptical of this ploy. He calls it "marketing bullshit." "Okay, so you started with shit milk and then ultra-pasteurized it, and then you're going to add omega-3s to make people better? Please. It's like vitamins A and D: fat soluble.

You may absorb 10 percent of the supplement and the rest goes out your stool. It's not the same."

By nearly any measure that matters to consumers, Sam was farming the right way. His cows lived long and produced well. Their milk was clean and nutritious. All of the farm's inputs came from within a forty-mile radius, most of them from the very ground on which his cows grazed, making Plankenhorn environmentally sustainable. But by the one measure that matters most to the farmer, the bottom line, Sam was doing something wrong. Yes, he was getting a 30-cent premium on every hundredweight of milk he made, but the extra work it took to produce such a high-quality product cost him more like $3 per hundredweight. He and a few other farms in the area were also getting premium milk awards from Agrimark, which usually came in the form of a $250 check at the end of the year. The check was nice, but really nothing more than a token. *Big deal*, he recalls thinking. *I need a $25,000 check.* Sam could withstand the imbalance between the cost of production and the compensation he received because he had a financial cushion padded with years of a doctor's salary. He wondered how the other dairy farmers, not similarly endowed in the asset department, were surviving. "They were paying us $15 but it cost us $18. I said, 'That's an insult.'" He knew something had to change. Would he sacrifice his ideals and farm like much of the rest of the industry, or could the system improve?

=====

What Sam was running into was the bane of most dairy farmers: the commodity trap. If all milk is the same, why should consumers buy one brand over another? Why should farmers take the time to make really good milk? California, later on, would try to escape this trap with its Happy Cow campaign. But before that, the industry came up with another idea: organic milk. The organic food movement, sprung from the natural food movement of the 1960s, had been gaining steam as a counterpoint to the industrialization of the food system—the pesticides, the slave labor, the environmental degradation. Organic food, presumably, could be a neatly packaged antidote to all that injustice, a social movement of the stomach. Until the early 1990s, organic food advocates didn't have the dairy industry on their radar; largely, they didn't see anything in the dairy system to fight against. That changed in 1993, when the Food and Drug Administration approved the use of recombinant bovine growth hormone to increase cows' milk production. rBGH, as it's known, was invented by Monsanto and marketed under the brand name Posilac. Almost immediately, people started making claims that milk from cows injected with Posilac presented a higher risk for breast, colon, and prostate cancer. The scientific evidence, however, wasn't there. The FDA claimed, rightly so, that milk from cows given rBGH was identical to that from cows not given rBGH. Then came Robert Cohen in 1997 with his book: *Milk: The Deadly Poison*, and suddenly the growth hormone was a touchstone for food purists, and a golden opportunity for organic milk.

Unlike the rest of the organic foods, which were gaining market share slowly and steadily, organic milk hit the market like, ironically, a product on steroids. In 1998, financial analysts were estimating a 50 to 80 percent sales growth annually, with total sales for that year of about $60 million. Organic products as a whole, by way of comparison, were growing at something more like 20 percent per year. Why the difference? In 1997, Katherine DiMatteo, the executive director of the Organic Trade Association, had a plausible answer: "People who don't buy any other organic products are purchasing organic milk." The marketing executives in the dairy industry, long accustomed to battling the commoditization of milk, had themselves a live one, and they capitalized on it. By creating a product that met a government standard of no pesticides, it made the public feel secure that it was getting something pure and wholesome, not Franken-milk. To go with this hard standard, the industry played to the soft side of the consumer's desires, emphasizing that the organic milk came from small family farms with happy cows in harmony with nature.

Melanie DuPuis, a professor of sociology at the University of

California at Santa Cruz, and the author of *Milk: Nature's Perfect Food*, wrote a paper in 2000 ("Not in My Body: rBGH and the Rise of Organic Milk")[1] that parses out the popularity of organic milk from the larger organic market. Organic food production, from the perspective of many sociologists that studied the system before she did, is just another "Post-Fordist" form of capitalism, where big corporations become more flexible and can move from mass production of single products to a portfolio of products able to meet new consumption demands. "The fracturing of consumption has created various market niches that include a demand for a form of food defined as 'organic,'" she explained. To provide this product on a mass scale, however, means that producers need to make use of industrial farming methods, thus reverting back to some of the practices that organic food advocates originally railed against. "The consumer, in this framework, is either a victim of false consciousness or is part of an elite class of people who eat particular organic products as a way of displaying their cultural capital," DuPuis wrote.

Organic milk fell right in line with this pattern, starting out as a product from independent farms and cooperatives such as Horizon Organic, Alta Dena, and Organic Valley. All of those businesses ended up being bought by Dean Foods, which saw how the cache of organic standards could add brand power and profit margin to its commoditized business. Through a savvy co-opting of organic standards as a seal of quality, Dean Foods and others were able to divert consumer attention away from the criteria that have a true bearing upon the quality of a product: the process by which it is made. As DuPuis points out in her paper, the issue of mastitis on dairy farms provides a nice example of the dissonance. On factory dairy farms, where cows are crowded into barns, pushed to produce milk, and lack access to open space, the infection of cows' udders is more frequent than on smaller farms. Since organic farms can't give their cows antibiotics when they get mastitis, they are faced with a choice: either put the cow in a healthful environment where the disease is less likely (such as on Sam's farm) or pack them into industrial barns, milk them until they get an infection, and then just "retire" them to the slaughterhouse. Many have chosen the latter. Consumers that buy organic milk just because it's organic, therefore, are either fooled into believing that organic equals high quality, or they don't truly care about how their organic milk is produced as long as it makes them look good in the checkout line. Could such a system really add value to the consumer, and stability to the milk market?

Sam Simon didn't think so. He knew that despite their claims of purity and sustainability, despite the high prices organic farmers were getting for their milk, organic dairies weren't the lily white knight, the savior of the small farmer. All he had to do was look at their somatic cell counts, which were regularly in the range of 400,000 to 600,000. Which is why, most of the time, you'll see organic milk is UHT pasteurized. "Go to some organic farms! They're a bunch of shit holes!" Sam says. When he thought about a better way of dairy farming, organic wasn't it.

He did agree with one thing the organic milk makers were doing: branding. He just wanted his brand to mean something. So he started with quality. Dairy farmers have a general sense of how their colleagues operate, and Sam knew that there were other farmers in the Hudson Valley whose milk was as good as his. Then the thought came to him: *We need to put this premium milk under its own label, not commingled with anybody else's milk. That's the challenge.*

Which raises an important point: chances are, you don't know where your milk comes from. Sure, you might know that it came from New England or the West Coast, or you might even be able to narrow it down to Vermont or New York or California, but that's as close as you'll get. You won't know which farm actually made your milk. This is because milk is pooled from farms in the same cooperatives and sometimes multiple cooperatives, usually spanning states. The milk trucks go from farm to farm and fill up their tanks, then they drive to the plant and unload the milk into a bigger tank. Good milk, "shit milk," it all gets mixed together and pasteurized—or ultra-pasteurized—and bottled. That means there's little incentive, besides the paltry quality bonuses and premium awards, to make an excellent product. Under this system, consumers are deprived of the power to choose the maker of their milk. And the farmer is deprived of the financial recognition for creating a premium good. Sam knew what he had to do: create a niche product that's transparent, where customers don't have to guess, and where farmers are held accountable to stringent quality standards. "Transparency means I know every cow and what she's doing, and anybody can find the same information," he says.

So in 2003, Sam and three other farmers swam against the stream. All around them, farmers were making big investments aimed at transforming their operations into organic farms. This entailed making significant changes to meet the standards of the USDA's National Organic Program. The pasture and cropland providing the cows' feed must be managed organically for a minimum of thirty-six months, and the cows must be fed a 100 percent organic diet and receive organic health care for twelve months before the farm is certified. This also means a change in the business model. Organic feed costs more than conventional. And cows can't be given antibiotics, so the herd's productivity may suffer. The payback was supposed to come in the form of much higher milk prices.

Sam and his three colleagues did something much simpler: they bought two bulk milk tanks with a total capacity of 5,200 gallons and installed them at Ronnybrook Farm, an independent milk producer in Ancramdale, New York, that processes and packages its own milk in glass bottles. Sam's plan was to use the tanks to hold only the milk from his new venture, Hudson Valley Fresh (HVF), a small nonprofit cooperative composed of only the highest quality dairy farms in the region. Ronnybrook would process Ronnybrook milk and put it into glass bottles, then flush the lines and process HVF milk and put it into plastic containers (Sam did market research and found that plastic sells better than glass and has no quality or taste drawbacks). For this, Ronnybrook would get a processing fee.

There was more to it than this, however. One of the major costs of bringing milk to market is in trucking it from the farm to the plant, and then from the plant to the supermarket. This job is usually done by the cooperative on the early side of the transaction, and the distributor later on. In Sam's case, he had to convince Agrimark to continue trucking his milk, and to buy any amount that the HVF farmers could not sell under their own label. This was a fairly easy sell. These farms were making really good milk, and Agrimark didn't want to lose them; doing so would only hurt Agrimark. So, for a fee of $4 per hundredweight ($2 after one million pounds), Agrimark agreed to truck HVF milk to the Ronnybrook plant and take the excess to its own plants in Vermont. The farmers would still get a monthly milk check from Agrimark, but they would get an additional check from the sale of HVF products.

This was working well enough, and the products were exceptional enough, that Sam soon had other farmers asking if they could join HVF. That is when Sam would show them how serious he was about the quality of the milk he needed for HVF. He required new applicant farms to be monitored for a year to see if they were hitting the right somatic cell and raw bacteria counts. "If a farmer has been meeting the standards for a year," he says, "you don't have to educate him how to do it. If he's been doing it for a week or two, it's bullshit. Those don't count." In addition, every herd had to be registered and inspected by the Dairy Herd Improvement Association (DHIA), which, for a fee, comes to a farm every month and inspects the cows and tests the milk for quality, cleanliness, and composition (such as protein and solids). This information is put on the national registry, where anybody can find it, thus fulfilling Sam's transparency imperative. Once an aspiring HVF member clears those hurdles, he has to pony up $3,000 to invest in the cooperative and agree to do tastings and product demonstrations, what Sam refers to as "hand-to-hand combat." In exchange, HVF would endeavor to provide each of its farmer members with $22 for every hundredweight of milk branded and sold under its name. With the federal milk prices known to dip into the low teens, that was quite a breathtaking promise.

HVF stayed with Ronnybrook for almost two years. In that time, it picked up five more dairies and had to find a bigger plant. The demand for the product was good, and they had more than Ronnybrook could process. Sam had another processor in mind: Boice Brothers Dairy, in Kingston. Founded in 1914, Boice Brothers is the longest-running independent processor in New York, and still family owned. Walk through the front door at the plant astride the railroad tracks, with a miniature cow above the stoop, and you will probably bump into Richard Boice, eighty-seven, or his son, Richard, Jr. They and thirty-two employees run the plant, an independent dinosaur in a land of processors owned by multinational public corporations.

Sam had been eyeing Boice Brothers for some time and knew that they were in rough financial shape, being undercut by larger plants. Their fortunes had shifted in a two-step process. First, all five prisons in the Hudson Valley stopped making their own milk—the cost of production was getting too high—and had contracted with Boice. Then Sam came along with a sweetheart of a deal: he would bring them enough milk to be their exclusive dairy, and Boice Brothers would realize a greater profit margin from the branded milk. In addition to the prisons, Boice was already providing milk to public schools and nursing homes. Now all of them would get the high-quality milk made by HVF farmers, but under the Boice Brothers brand name. Later, Sam secured more education contracts, but with a different sort of clientele: private schools such as Rye Country Day, Dutchess Day, and the Hackley School; and colleges such as Bard, Vassar, Marist, the Culinary Institute of America, and New York University. Which gave prisoners and some of the most privileged kids in America something in common: they all drank the best milk you can buy. In Boice Brothers, HVF had its own plant, processing only HVF milk—no commingling. In HVF, Boice Brothers had a premium product and was soon back in the black. In both, customers had a local supply chain they could trust, a carbon footprint they could feel good about, and the ingredients for one heck of a milkshake.

When Sam struck the deal with Boice Brothers, HVF had eight

farms all within a forty-mile radius. One of them was Walt's Dairy, owned by Bill and Rosalie Kiernan. The farm had been founded in 1927 by Rosalie's grandparents in Shelton, Connecticut, about ten miles from the Long Island Sound. It was a simple thirteen-cow farm that produced, bottled, and sold its own raw milk, delivering to customers on a milk route. In the early 1950s, the farm joined a cooperative, the Connecticut Milk Producers, and expanded the herd to thirty-five. Rosalie grew up on the farm, but Bill did not. His father had been a maintenance electrician and a merchant marine. But from a young age, Bill had taken a special interest in farming. He worked at a dairy farm in the afternoons during middle and high school, but then, after college, went to work at the Remington Arms factory in Bridgeport. When Bill married Rosalie, he married her farm too. In 1972 Remington was closing the plant and offered Bill a job at the new location, in Arkansas. They didn't want to make the move, so they decided to work on the farm full time. The suburbs were encroaching, however, and in 1985 they pulled up stakes and bought a farm in Copake, New York, a small town northeast of Poughkeepsie, near the Taconic Mountains. In actuality, suburban sprawl wasn't the only reason for the move. "We were a kind of sea-going beach people," Bill says about his family. "Now we're land lovers. When people asked us why we moved up here from Connecticut, I said, 'Well, there's no rocks in the soil.'" Their farm today spans about eight hundred acres (some of it is rented), which they use to grow their own corn, soybeans, grass, hay, and alfalfa. They milk about 160 registered Holsteins that live in a tie-stall barn with mattresses and straw bedding.

They connected with HVF in the third year of its existence. "We were starting to get those big fluctuations in milk prices, where we'd have these big peaks and valleys," Bill recalls. "We thought this was a good way to try to insulate ourselves from that." Aside from a steady living wage, the Kiernans were also excited about getting into the retail side of dairying. Rosalie's parents had started the farm that way, selling directly to consumers, and something about that appealed to the Kiernans. With HVF, they could have a branded product to stand behind at tastings, to show the world what good dairy farming really means.

Bill called up Sam and said he wanted to join the co-op. The first question Sam asked was: "How's your quality?" Bill sent him the DHIA reports for the previous two years. Upon reviewing them, Sam said, "You're just the kind of people we're looking for." The Kiernans have long focused on running a clean operation, and they have received numerous quality awards from Agrimark. "We've always drunk our own milk and fed it to our kids," Bill says. "Like I told my wife, if we can't put good milk on the table, then we shouldn't be making it at all. That was always our philosophy."

With the best tasting milk on the market, and the story of farms like Walt's Dairy, Sam and the other HVF farmers engaged in "hand-to-hand combat" in the Hudson Valley and the New York metro area and won accounts at all sorts of outlets. Because the product was something more than just commodity milk slapped with a special label, and because people don't tend to pay attention to the milk they buy, it was crucial for HVF to make store owners and managers their biggest fans. Then *they* could do hand-to-hand combat with customers on a daily basis and unleash the word-of-mouth campaigns that would surely follow. "You need somebody in the store to help people understand that this is not the same as other milk," Sam says.

One of their earliest and most vocal advocates was Eli Zabar, the son of the founders of Zabar's market, and the owner of Eli's Manhattan, a premium grocery store on the Upper East Side. Eli grew up in a family that worshipped high-quality food, scoured the earth to find it, and then proudly delivered it to customers in their store on Broadway. Eli does the same thing today, but on the other side of the island. He's also been a big supporter of local agriculture, maintaining about a half-acre of greenhouses in Manhattan and running the Amagansett Farmer's Market, on the eastern end of Long Island, in the summer. When Sam walked into his store and gave Eli a taste of HVF milk, Eli immediately knew he was on to something special. "It had this very smooth, rich flavor, and I thought it was better than everything else we carried," Eli recalls. Then he heard Sam's story, his mission to provide punctilious dairy farmers with a living wage in a way that conserves land and is good for the environment. "I thought it was noble and admirable," Eli said. "It all worked into my philosophy when he showed up." And Eli has the bully pulpit to communicate that philosophy. He calls it "encouraging" his customers. "We encourage them in a lot of different ways. One way is by eliminating what they think they want. It's a very direct and results-oriented method," he says. For example, if he carried a few different brands of milk and then found one that made the rest seem shoddy, he would just stop carrying the shoddy ones. And he would stand behind this bold move by offering customers their money back if they don't like the milk. So far, no one has asked for a refund. The only push-back he's received is from people who buy only organic food. It's extremely hard, he says, to convince die-hard organic food fans that any nonorganic product is as healthful for them as organic food. So Eli still, grudgingly, carries organic milk. "Unfortunately, I don't really have any outstanding examples of organic milk," he admits. "None of them are as good as Sam's milk, by a lot."

Across the street from the Amagansett Farmer's Market, where HVF is the best-selling milk by far, is Jack's Coffee, a specialty coffee shop that stir-brews its coffee for a smooth, blended taste. The owner, Jack Mazzola, started the business with a shop in the West Village, where New York Magazine said you could find the best cup of coffee in Manhattan. Mazzola, like Eli, was an early adopter of HVF milk. Mazzola liked it not just because of its localvore street-cred, but because the milk, with its high level of omega-3s, foams up like no other, providing the ideal component for lattes and cappuccinos. Dean and Deluca and a number of other premium coffee shops have since followed suit.

The bread and butter of HVF's sales don't come from places like Eli's and Jack's, however, but from supermarkets such as Shop-Rite, Stop & Shop, Whole Foods, and Hannafords. These stores make it possible for HVF to sell 4 million pounds of milk per year, and reap $2 million in sales. In most of these outlets, the price of a half-gallon of HVF milk is about a dollar less than its organic competitors, and usually about 50 cents more than commodity milk and private label brands.

Organic milk has turned out not to be the smart investment that many farmers had hoped. In fact, it ended up being more like the real estate bubble that burst in 2008. Between 2000 and 2005, the number of certified organic milk cows increased an average of 25 percent per year, to more than 86,000 in 2005. The number of organic farms increased threefold, to 1,600, between 2002 and 2007. Ken Preston, a dairy farmer in Randolph Center, Vermont, was a believer. He switched to organic in 2005 and saw his income rise by 20 percent. But then the price of organic feed shot up, the recession hit, and organic milk was one of the first things strapped families could do without. Organic Valley, a nationwide cooperative, saw its sales growth stop dead in it tracks, from about a 20 percent speed limit six months before. Preston's co-op cut him loose in 2009; in the space of a month, he found himself with truckloads of expensive organic milk that no one wanted to buy. "I probably wouldn't have gone organic if I'd known it would end this way," he told the *New York Times*.[2]

What made the scenario worse was that these dairy farmers had taken out loans and put hundreds of thousands of dollars into their organic operations. When the market tanked, credit was harder to come by, and there was no demand for organic herds. Farmers had to kill cows to avoid the expense of feeding them. At a meeting of the Maine Organic Milk Producers in April of 2009, the farmers wondered if they could add value to their milk by marketing it as "local." The problem was that a lot of Maine's milk is processed out of state. Is Maine milk trucked to New York and back to Maine local? Probably not.

Sam Simon didn't like to see dairy farmers anywhere struggling, but he was happy that the members of HVF weathered the 2009 dairy crisis without much damage. Because the price differential between commodity milk and HVF milk wasn't that big, people for the most part weren't reverting to less expensive milk when their budgets shrank. As a result, HVF farmers were still receiving $22 per hundredweight on a nice portion of the milk they produced. In a time when the standard milk price was around $11 per hundredweight, that extra cash was very helpful. "Any dollar at that time helped out enormously," Bill Kiernan says.

For Bill, the difference between his financial position and his neighbor's was especially heart breaking. Walt's Dairy shares a border with Hi-Low Farm, where owner Dean Pierson killed himself and fifty-one of his milking cows in January of 2010. Bill and Pierson weren't friends, but they helped each other out as neighbors often do. When Bill saw Pierson's barn on fire, for example, he and his son ran over and removed all the valuable equipment from the workshop it was attached to (nobody was home at the Pierson place). On the morning Pierson killed himself, it was Bill's son who found his body, and Bill who dug the grave for the cows. That fateful morning, Pierson's mother had one more thing to worry about: the $30,000 in cash she had recently lent her son so he could pay some farm bills. They later found the money in the glove compartment of Pierson's truck. Perhaps he couldn't bring himself to actually use the loan.

=====

Dairy farming is the biggest sector of New York's agricultural economy, generating $2.4 billion in sales every year. And yet, the future is not secure. In Dutchess County, where many of HVF's farms exist, there are now only 26 dairy farms; in the 1970s, there were 275. It's no wonder this is the case, when you realize that for every dollar a consumer spends on milk, less than 15 cents goes to the farmer in a conventional co-op.

In this unlikely environment, HVF has been a resounding success for farmers. It has returned $40,000 to each farmer on their initial $3,000 investment in the co-op—just for doing basically nothing more than they'd always done: making high-quality milk. Instead of reaping 15 cents from the consumer's dollar, HVF farmers get 40 cents.

And HVF has been a boon to the community. It is estimated that each milk cow adds $15,000 to the local economy each year. At that rate, HVF's 1,200 cows annually contribute $18 million in economic activity to the Hudson Valley. The eight farms comprise five thousand acres of open space—land that might otherwise be commercially developed. "If you keep the steward of the land on the land," Sam says, "you don't need the Dutchess Land Conservancy or Scenic Hudson to buy it. The farmers will take care of the land; they just want a living wage. They don't want to drive Land Rovers. They just want to be able to get a John Deere or a baler when they need it. But if you don't get enough revenue from your milk, you can't get the machinery to grow your own feed."

For all this, HVF is not in the promised land yet. In fact, it has a long way to go. Right now, it's able to give farmers $22 per hundred-weight on about 30 percent of the milk they make. "I want it to get big enough so that the farmers can sell 75 percent of their milk under the Hudson Valley Fresh label. That would be ideal," Sam says. "Then I would guarantee them a living wage in perpetuity." At that size, it would be big enough to be self-sustaining, but not outgrow its ethos. Bill Kiernan has seen the danger of big cooperatives and he knows the story. "The bigger you get, the more professional management you need, and that starts eating into the profits," he explains. "You start building up a bunch of people who may not have the passion you have for the business, and they require a pretty big wage to keep them on the payroll."

Sam is more succinct: "The goal is to give back to farmers, not line the pockets of some guys in silk suits."

But it's not easy. Others have tried to bottle and market their own milk, and failed. The big stumbling block is the capital outlay for a processing plant, which costs a minimum of $2.5 million. Back in 2004, Sam took a road trip with some farmers to see seven farms that had built plants to bottle their own milk. They got grants from nonprofits or various government agencies. They took out loans. Within three years, all but one were belly up. They didn't have the cash flow to pay the daily costs of running the plants. The one that survived was in Richmond, Virginia, owned by three siblings who each handled different parts of the operation. They started in their region, sold the product under their family name, and slowly expanded outward. That's mainly what HVF has done: created volume and brand loyalty first, and then grown in concentric circles from Poughkeepsie.

When you break it down, there are six factors that have allowed HVF to get to where it is:

1. Nearby farmers producing premium milk. Only 25 percent of farms in the United States can meet HVF's standards for somatic cell and raw bacteria count.
2. Access to a milk plant that processes only HVF milk.
3. Agrimark's agreement to haul HVF milk.
4. Access to the New York Metro Area, which is chock full of educated people with some money.
5. A burgeoning local food movement.

Last but not least, you need some people who are willing to work for free, or close to it. Sam Simon, Bill Kiernan, and a few others in HVF put a lot of time into the organization. Sam himself sold his dairy herd in the fall of 2011—the auctioneer had never seen such a collection of perfect cows from one farm—and now works nearly full time keeping the cooperative moving forward. All the farmers in the co-op do three or four tastings per year. "That's part of the deal: if you're going to be a member, you've got to volunteer," Bill says. "Some people put in more time than is required, because they want to see it succeed. That's kind of where I am. That's the reason I do it. I want this to work.

"I see this as hope for the future," Bill continues. "It's one of the only lights at the end of the tunnel."

ACKNOWLEDGMENTS

I first uttered my idea for this book to my friend Tom Zoellner on a quiet evening on the Dartmouth quad. An author himself, he paid no mind to the fact that I'd never before written a book. Instead he talked me through it, gave me encouragement and technical advice, and, most important, believed in me. This book might not have been possible without Tom's help.

Another person who believed in me was my agent, Jennifer Griffin. Throughout the process she's been kind, straight-talking, and tenacious. I can't thank her enough.

I'm also grateful for the patience and fine counsel of my editor at UPNE, Stephen Hull. He's one more person who, perhaps against the odds, believed I could write this book.

Along the way, lots of friends, family, and colleagues have offered crucial support in numerous ways. These people have included Joe Olshan, Deidre Heekin, Joni Praded, Alan Weisman, John Seabrook, Bill McKibben, Garret Keizer, Barry Estabrook, Chad DeChow, Doug and Patty Reaves, Todd and Carole Stall, Jane Kardashian and Vatche Soghomonian, Paul and Sherry Doton, Elizabeth Reaves, Michael Zsoldos, Theo Padnos, Ephraim Camacho and the people at California Rural Legal Assistance, and Lupe Martinez, Brent Newell, and the people at the Center on Race, Poverty and the Environment.

I owe the largest debt of gratitude to my wife, Kate, for giving me the time and encouragement I needed to write this book. She's been a saint.

Finally, I'd like to thank my parents for, well, just about everything imaginable.

NOTES

one DOWN AND OUT ON THE FARM

1. James M. MacDonald et al., "Profits, Costs and the Changing Structure of Dairy Farming," USDA Economic Research Service, Report No. 47, 2007.

2. Clifford Geertz, "Religion as a Cultural System," in Geertz, *The Interpretation of Cultures* (New York: Basic Books, 1973), 99.

3. Andrew Delbanco, *The Real American Dream* (Cambridge: Harvard University Press, 1999), 2.

4. Elisabeth Kübler-Ross, *On Death and Dying* (New York: Touchstone, 1997).

5. Michael R. Rosmann, "The Agrarian Imperative," *Journal of Agromedicine* 15 (2010): 71–75.

6. Marilyn Shrapnel and Jim Davie, "The Influence of Personality in Determining Farmer Responsiveness to Risk," *Journal of Agricultural Education Ext.* 7 (2001): 167–78.

7. Joyce Willock et al., "Farmers' Attitudes, Objectives, Behaviors and Personality Traits: The Edinburgh Study of Decision Making on Farms," *Journal of Vocational Behavior* 54 (1998): 5–36.

8. Peter Applebome, "The Morning the Milking Was Finished," *New York Times*, February 4, 2010.

two THE FIRST DAIRY FARMERS

1. Hodder Westropp, *Prehistoric Phases* (London: Bell and Daldy, 1872), 4–5.

2. Ibid., 8–9.

3. Ibid., 9–10.

4. Anne Mendelson, *Milk: The Surprising Story of Milk through the Ages* (New York: Alfred A. Knopf, 2008), 5.

5. Matthias Schulz, "How Middle Eastern Milk Drinkers Conquered Europe," *Der Spiegel*, October 15, 2010, http://www.spiegel.de/international/zeitgeist/0,1518,723310,00.html.

6. Mendelson, *Milk*, 15.

three THE CONTROL OF AMERICAN MILK

1. Christopher McGrory Klyza and Stephen C. Trombulak, *The Story of Vermont: A Natural and Cultural History* (Hanover, NH: University of New England Press, 1999), 90.

2. Margaret G. Henderson, Ethel Dewey Speerschneider, and Helen L. Ferslev, *It Happened Here: Stories of Wisconsin* (Madison: State Historical Society of Wisconsin, 1955).

3. John C. Culver and John Hyde, *American Dreamer: A life of Henry A. Wallace* (New York: W. W. Norton and Company, 2000), 124.

4. Don P. Blayney, "The Changing Landscape of U.S. Milk Production," U.S. Department of Agriculture Statistical Research Bulletin No. 978, June 2002.

5. Raymond Hernandez, "Senator's Defection May Doom Milk Bill," *New York Times*, May 16, 2001, http://www.nytimes.com/2001/05/16/us/senator-s-defection-may-doom-milk-bill.html.

6. Sallie James, "Milking the Customers: The High Cost of U.S. Dairy Policies," Cato Institute Trade Briefing Paper No. 24, November 9, 2006.

7. Ibid.

six THE WORKERS

1. "The Economic Impacts of Immigration on U.S. Dairy Farms," June, 2009, http://www.nmpf.org/files/file/NMPF%2Immigration%20Survey%20Web.pdf.

2. Philip Martin, Michael Fix, and J. Edward Taylor, *The New Rural Poverty: Agriculture and Immigration in California* (Washington, DC: Urban Institute Press), 2006, 4.

3. Ibid.

4. Charles D. Thompson, Jr., and Melinda F. Wiggins, eds., *The Human Cost of Food: Farmworkers' Lives, Labor, and Advocacy* (Austin: University of Texas Press), 2002, 119.

5. Martin et al., *The New Rural Poverty*, 5.

6. Ibid.

7. Ibid., 35.

8. "Survey of New York Dairy Farm Employers," March 2011, http://dyson.cornell.edu/research/researchpdf/rb/2011/Cornell-Dyson-rb1101.pdf.

9. "2007 Dairy Producer Survey," July 2007, http://www.nass.usda.gov/Statistics_by_State/Wisconsin/Publications/Dairy/dairyproducer2007.pdf.

10. Rebecca Clarren, "The Dark Side of Dairies," *High Country News*, August 31, 2009. Accessed August 26, 2011, http://www.hcn.org/issues/41.15/the-dark-side-of-dairies/article_view?src=feat&b_start:int=0.

11. "Fallback Position — Migrant Worker," September 22, 2010, http://www.colbertnation.com/the-colbert-report-videos/359888/september-22-2010/fallback-position---migrant-worker---zoe-lofgren.

12. Cyril Tuohy, "Dairy under Watch among Top Five Deadliest Occupations," *Risk and Insurance*, April 18, 2011. Accessed August 26, 2011, http://www.riskandinsurance.com/printstory.jsp?storyId=533336159.

13. Rebecca Clarren, "The Dark Side of Dairies," *High Country News*, August 31, 2009.

14. J. Steven Wilkins, *Call of Duty: The Sterling Nobility of Robert E. Lee* (Nashville, TN: Cumberland House Publishing, 1997), 303.

15. Susan Ferriss and Ricardo Sandoval, *The Fight in the Fields: Cesar Chavez and the Farmworkers Movement* (Orlando, FL: Paradigm Productions, 1997), 231.

16. Jill Harrison, Sarah Lloyd, and Trish O'Kane, "Immigrant Dairy

Workers in Rural Wisconsin Communities," July 2009, Program on Agricultural Technology Studies, University of Wisconsin-Madison, http://www.pats.wisc.edu/pubs/102.

17. Philip Martin, "Calculating the Costs and Benefits," *New York Times*, August 18, 2011. Accessed August 26, 2011, http://www.nytimes.com/roomfordebate/2011/08/17/could-farms-survive-without-illegal-labor/the-costs-and-benefits-of-a-raise-for-field-workers.

18. Jessie McKinley and Julia Preston, "Farmers Oppose G.O.P. Bill on Immigration," *New York Times*, July 31, 2011. Accessed August 26, 2011, http://www.nytimes.com/2011/07/31/us/politics/31verify.html?scp=3&sq=immigrant%20labor&st=cse.

19. Lisa Garcia Bedolla, "Jobs That Americans Don't Want," *New York Times*, August 18, 2011. Accessed August 26, 2011, http://www.nytimes.com/roomfordebate/2011/08/17/could-farms-survive-without-illegal-labor/jobs-that-american-workers-dont-want.

20. "Americans Still Stuck on Economy as Top Problem," July 21, 2011, http://www.gallup.com/video/148616/Americans-Stuck-Economy-Top-Problem.aspx.

seven THE ANIMALS

1. Paul Waldau, *Animal Rights: What Everyone Needs to Know* (New York: Oxford University Press, 2011), 76.

2. Waldau, *Animal Rights*, 133.

3. "Martin's Act." In Encyclopædia Britannica (2011). Retrieved from http://www.britannica.com/EBchecked/topic/366965/Martins-Act.

4. 49 USC 80502.

5. Immanuel Kant, *Lectures on Ethics*, trans. Louis Infield (New York: Harper Torchbooks, 1963), 240.

6. See Jeremy Bentham, *The Principles of Morals and Legislation* [1781] (Amherst, NY: Prometheus, 1988), chap. 17, sect. 4, 310–11.

7. David J. Wolfson and Mariann Sullivan, "Foxes in the Hen House: Animals, Agribusiness and the Law: A Modern American Fable," in *Animal Rights: Current Debates and New Directions*, edited by Cass R. Sunstein and Martha Craven Nussbaum (New York: Oxford University Press, 2004), 223.

8. Wolfson and Sullivan, "Foxes in the Hen House," 215.

9. "Gentle Giants: The Intellectual and Emotional World of Cows," *Compassionate Living*, Fall/Winter 2010, 14.

10. J. K. Ahola et al., "Survey of Quality Defects in Market Beef and Dairy Cows and Bulls Sold through Livestock Auction Markets in the Western United States: I. Incidence Rates," *Journal of Animal Science* 89 (2011): 1474–83.

11. USDA. "Dairy 2007, Part I: Reference of Dairy Cattle Health and Management Practices in the United States, 2007," USDA-APHIS-VS, CEAH, 2007. Fort Collins, CO.

eight MONOPOLY MONEY

1. *United States v. Borden*, 308 U.S. 188, 205 (1939).

2. As alleged in the Class Action Complaint and Jury Demand in the case of *Allen et al. v. Dairy Farmers of America et al.,* filed in the U.S. District Court for the District of Vermont, October 8, 2009.

3. As alleged in the Consolidated Amended Complaint in the case of *Sweetwater Valley Farm, Inc. et al. v. Dean Foods et al.,* filed in the U.S. District Court for the Eastern District of Tennessee, June 8, 2008.

4. Ibid.

5. Susan Carey, "Dean Foods Reaches Settlement with Dairy Farmers," *Wall Street Journal*, July 13, 2011.

nine GRASS-FED,
FREE-RANGE, STREAMLINE BABY

1. E. Melanie DuPuis, "Not in My Body: rBGH and the Rise of Organic Milk," *Agriculture and Human Values* 17 (2000): 285–95.

2. Katie Zezima, "Organic Dairies Watch the Good Times Turn Bad," *New York Times*, May 28, 2009.

BIBLIOGRAPHY

Anderson, Virginia DeJohn. *Creatures of Empire: How Domestic Animals Transformed Early America*. Oxford: Oxford University Press, 2004.

Arax, Mark, and Rick Wartzman. *The King of California: J.G. Boswell and the Making of a Secret American Empire*. New York: Public Affairs Books, 2003.

Bakken, Henry H., and Marvin A. Scharrs. *The Economics of Cooperative Marketing*. New York: McGraw Hill, 1937.

Barker, Graeme. *The Agricultural Revolution in Prehistory: Why Did Foragers Become Farmers?* Oxford: Oxford University Press, 2006.

Chandler, Jr., Alfred D., and Bruce Mazlish, eds. *Leviathans: Multinational Corporations and the New Global History*. Cambridge, UK: Cambridge University Press, 2005.

Cobia, David W., ed. *Cooperatives in Agriculture*. Englewood Cliffs, NJ: Prentice-Hall, 1989.

Culver, John C., and John Hyde. *American Dreamer: A Life of Henry A. Wallace*. New York: W. W. Norton and Company, 2000.

Darwin, Charles. *The Origin of Species*. New York: Penguin, 2003.

Dawn, Karen. *Thanking the Monkey: Rethinking the Way We Treat Animals*. New York: Harper, 2008.

Delbanco, Andrew. *The Real American Dream: A Meditation on Hope*. Cambridge, MA: Harvard University Press, 2000.

DuPuis, E. Melanie. *Nature's Perfect Food: How Milk Became America's Drink*. New York: New York University Press, 2002.

Eissinger, Michael. *African Americans in the Rural San Joaquin Valley, California: Colonization Efforts and Townships*. Charleston, SC: Create Space, 2009.

Ferriss, Susan, and Ricardo Sandoval. *The Fight in the Fields: Cesar Chavez and the Farmworkers Movement*. Orlando, FL: Paradigm Productions, 1997.

Freidberg, Susanne. *Fresh: A Perishable History*. Cambridge, MA: Belknap Press, 2009.

Fussell, Betty. *Raising Steaks: The Life and Times of American Beef*. Orlando, FL: Houghton Mifflin Harcourt, 2008.

Gumpert, David E. *The Raw Milk Revolution: Behind America's Emerging Battle over Food Rights*. White River Junction, VT: Chelsea Green, 2009.

Harrison, Ruth. *Animal Machines: The New Factory Farming Industry*. New York: Ballantine Books, 1966.

Imhoff, Daniel, ed. *The CAFO Reader: The Tragedy of Industrial Animal Factories*. Berkeley, CA: Foundation for Deep Ecology, 2010.

Johnson, Paul A. *Making the Market: Victorian Origins of Corporate Capitalism*. Cambridge, UK: Cambridge University Press, 2010.

Katz, Sandor Ellix. *The Revolution Will Not Be Microwaved: Inside America's Underground Food Movement*. White River Junction, VT: Chelsea Green, 2006.

Kirby, David. *Animal Factory: The Looming Threat of Industrial Pig, Dairy, and Poultry Farms to Humans and the Environment*. New York: St. Martin's Press, 2010.

Klyza, Christopher McGrory, and Stephen Trombulak. *The Story of Vermont: A Natural and Cultural History*. Hanover, NH: University Press of New England, 1999.

Kramer, Mark. *Three Farms: Making Milk, Meat and Money from the American Soil*. Cambridge, MA: Harvard University Press, 1987.

Kübler-Ross, Elisabeth. *On Death and Dying: What the Dying Have to Teach Doctors, Nurses, Clergy and Their Own Families*. New York: Touchstone, 1969.

Lopez, Ann Aurelia. *The Farmworkers' Journey*. Berkeley: University of California Press, 2007.

Maroney, Jr., James H. *The Political Economy of Milk: Reinvigorating Vermont's Family Dairy Farms*. Leceister, UK: Gala Books, 2009.

Martin, Philip, Michael Fix, and J. Edward Taylor. *The New Rural Poverty: Agriculture and Immigration in California*. Washington, DC: Urban Institute, 2006.

Matthiessen, Peter. *Sal Si Puedes (Escape If You Can): Cesar Chavez and the New American Revolution*. Berkeley: University of California Press, 2000.

Mayhew, Anne. *Narrating the Rise of Big Business in the USA: How Economists Explain Standard Oil and Wal-Mart*. New York: Routledge, 2008.

McCay, Clive. *Notes on the History of Nutrition Research*. Bern: Hans Huber, 1973.

McKibben, Bill. *Deep Economy: The Wealth of Communities and the Durable Future*. New York: Times Books, 2007.

———. *Eaarth: Making a Life on a Tough New Planet*. New York: Times Books, 2010.

Melville, Herman. *Moby Dick or the Whale*. New York: Penguin, 1992.

Mendelson, Anne. *Milk: The Surprising Story of Milk through the Ages*. New York: Alfred A. Knopf, 2008.

Overton, Mark. *Agricultural Revolution in England: The Transformation of the Agrarian Economy 1500–1850*. Cambridge, UK: Cambridge University Press, 1996.

Perkins, John. *The Secret History of American Empire: Economic Hit Men, Jackals, and the Truth about Global Corruption*. New York: Dutton, 2007.

Pollan, Michael. *The Omnivore's Dilemma: A Natural History of Four Meals*. New York: Penguin, 2006.

Porter, Valerie. *Beautiful Cows*. London: Ivy Press, 2010.

Price, T. Douglas, ed. *Last Hunters, First Farmers: New Perspectives on the Prehistoric Transition to Agriculture*. Santa Fe, NM: School of American Research Press, 1996.

Radcliffe, Evelyn. *Out of Darkness: The Story of Allen Allensworth*. Menlo Park, NJ: Inkling Press, 1995.

Rimas, Andrew, and Evan D. G. Fraser. *Beef: The Untold Story of How Milk, Meat and Muscles Shaped the World*. New York: HarperCollins Publishers, 2008.

Rothenberg, Daniel. *With These Hands: The Hidden World of Migrant Farmworkers Today*. New York: Harcourt Brace and Company, 1998.

Royal, Alice. *Allensworth: The Freedom Colony*. Berkeley, CA: Heyday Books, 2008.

Russell, Nicholas. *Like Engend'ring Like: Heredity and Animal Breeding in Early Modern England*. Oxford: Oxford University Press, 2004.

Schlosser, Eric. *Fast Food Nation: The Dark Side of the All-American Meal*. New York: Houghton Mifflin Company, 2004.

Scully, Matthew. *Dominion: The Power of Man, the Suffering of Animals, and the Call to Mercy*. New York: St. Martin's Press, 2002.

Sharpes, Donald K. *Sacred Bull, Holy Cow: A Cultural Study of Civilization's Most Important Animal*. New York: Peter Lang, 2006.

Stephen, Lynn. *Transborder Lives: Indigenous Oaxacans in Mexico, California and Oregon*. Durham, NC: Duke University Press, 2007.

Sunstein, Cass R., and Martha C. Nussbaum, eds. *Animal Rights: Current Debates and New Directions*. New York: Oxford University Press, 2004.

Thompson, Jr., Charles D., and Melinda F. Wiggins, eds. *The Human Cost of Food: Farmworkers' Lives, Labor and Advocacy*. Austin: University of Texas Press, 2002.

Waldau, Paul. *Animal Rights: What Everyone Needs to Know*. New York: Oxford University Press, 2011.

Warwick, Everett James, and James Edward Legates. *Breeding and Improvement of Farm Animals*. New York: McGraw-Hill, 1979.

Wilkins, J. Steven. *Call of Duty: The Sterling Nobility of Robert E. Lee*. Nashville, TN: Cumberland House, 1997.

Woodford, Keith. *Devil in the Milk: Illness, Health and the Politics of A1 and A2 Milk*. White River Junction, VT: Chelsea Green, 2009.

INDEX

antibiotics, 13, 51

antitrust issue, 46–47, 185–90, 193, 195–97, 204–6, 207

artificial insemination (AI), 51, 76–78, 83–85, 88–90

aurochs, 78–79

Babcock, Stephen, 44–45

BACT (best available control technology), 126

behavior, cow, 12–13, 75–76, 175

Boice Brothers Dairy, 222

Boswell, J. G., 120, 121

bracero program, 134–35

branding of quality milk, 210–29

breeding: artificial insemination, 51, 76–78, 83–85, 88–90; cross-breeding program, 91–92; functional vs. aesthetic purposes, 89, 91, 213; genetic analysis, 85–87; health issues for inbred Holsteins, 89–91; historical developments, 79–83; Simon's outbreeding for diversity, 213

buffer zones to prevent farm runoff, 112–13

bull associations, 83

bulls, 78, 84

Bunting, John, 205, 207

business trust, 192

butter production in New England, 43

by-products in cow feed, 93–94

Cabot cooperative, 58, 63

CAFO (confined animal feeding operation), 105, 117–18, 125, 128–29, 175

California: animal rights vs. dairy industry marketing, 163–64, 177–82; environmental issues for dairy industry, 103, 106–8, 120–29; labor relations, 135, 143–51, 148; as megadairy center, 10, 104–5

calves, treatment of, 162, 172–73, 177–78

calving problems for Holsteins, 91

Capper-Volstead Act (1922), 83, 194–95, 204

Carstensen, Peter, 203–5, 207

Central Valley of California, 104–5, 106–8, 120–29

CEQA (California Environmental Quality Act) (1970), 122

Chavez, Cesar, 103–4, 135, 148

cheese production, 42, 43, 70–71, 75

Chicago Mercantile Exchange, 7, 53, 55

Class system for milk quality, 54

Clean Air Act, 108, 126, 128

Clean Water Act, 110

CMAB (California Milk Advisory Board), 163–64, 178–82

Cohen, Robert, 217

comfort, cow. See well-being and comfort

health issues: air pollution effects in California, 106–7; cow physiology and, 73–76; for inbred Holsteins, 89–91; mastitis in cows, 12, 218–19; nutrition, cow, 63, 92–95; psychological aspects of dairy farming, 19–27, 64–65, 101; quality of milk and, 12, 13, 92, 214–15, 219, 221; reports on dairy products, 5–6

heifers and artificial insemination vs. bulls, 78

heredity and cow breeding, 79–81, 87. *See also* breeding

Hispanic labor on dairy farms. *See* immigrant workers

historical perspective: breeding aspect, 79–83; Depression to 1990s, 46–56; eighteenth-to-nineteenth centuries, 39–43; fluid milk market value identification, 43–46; monopsony issue for dairy industry, 191–93; Northeast Dairy Compact, 56–59; origins of dairy farming, 29–37; subsidies' beginning, 59–61

A History of Domesticated Animals (Zeuner), 79

Holstein breed, 51, 82–83, 88–91

hotlines and helplines for farmers, 24, 25

housing, substandard, for farm workers, 152–53

Hudson Valley Fresh (HVF), 210–29

hybrid vigor, 91

illegal immigrant labor, 131–33, 135–36, 139, 140, 152, 154–55

immigrant workers, 131–41, 144–47, 152–57

Immigration Control and Reform Act (IRCA), 136

immigration reform issue, 133–34, 136, 156–57

Jevons Paradox, 72

J. G. Boswell Co., 120, 121, 123

karst formation, 118, 119–20

King of California, The (Arax and Wartzman), 121

Klopfenstein, Joe, 171–77

labor relations: agricultural exemption from labor laws, 141–43; dairy farm violations of labor laws, 143–48; immigrant labor, 131–41, 144–47, 152–57; robotic milkers and saving on labor costs, 101; unionization challenges, 148–51

omega-3 fatty acids in high-quality
milk, 215
operating costs, burden of, 5, 9–10,
49–50, 94, 105
organic milk, 216–19, 220, 226
ozone pollution, 106, 107, 127–28

pasture-based dairy operations:
cows' suitability for grass
feeding, 74; vs. factory farm
environment, 128–29, 174, 175;
hay cutting practices, 94–95;
nutritional quality of milk and,
92; organic milk, 216–19, 226;
shift to corn from, 51; Simon's
operation, 209–16, 219–29
People for the Ethical Treatment
of Animals (PETA), 160, 178–82
phosphorus pollution, 110, 117–20
physiology, cow, 73–76
Pierson, Dean, 26–27, 227
pipeline milkers, 97
PM (particulate matter) 2.5, 107
PM (particulate matter) 10, 106–7,
127–28
pollution from dairy farms. See
environmental issues
population increases and loss of
farms, 19
poultry industry and animal
welfare issue, 177
poverty and immigration, 136–37
price supports. See subsidies

pricing of milk: challenges of
finding uniformity for, 44;
contribution to 2008–2009
dairy decline, 5; cooperatives'
influence on, 46–47, 202–3;
current system, 53–56;
federal controls on, 46–47;
relationship to supply, 69;
retail, 15, 105–6, 120; subsidies,
46, 49–50, 52, 53, 59–61;
volatility of factors affecting,
59–60
processors. See milk processors
production and productivity:
analyzing, 87–88; breeding's
effect on, 78, 89; gamble of
increasing production, 9, 52;
Holstein's contribution,
82–83; increase in cows',
69–70, 73–74; vs. longevity
and animal treatment, 173–74,
177; origins of, 32–35, 82–83;
technology effects, 43–44,
95–101
property rights vs. animal rights,
166–67
psychological aspects of dairy
farming, 19–27, 64–65, 101

quality of life for dairy farmers,
technology's impact on, 101
quality of milk, 12, 13, 53, 54, 92,
214–15, 221

transporting milk, Simon's challenge for HVF, 221

turnover of cows to slaughter for beef, 173–74, 219

udder qualities and breeding, 86–87

ultra-high temperature (UHT) pasteurization, 215, 219

undocumented immigrant labor, 131–33, 135–36, 139, 140, 152, 154–55

Unhappy Cows campaign, 180–81

unions for dairy farm workers, 148–51

United Farm Workers, 135, 139, 148, 150–51

United States v. Borden, 195

USDA (U.S. Department of Agriculture), 18, 47, 72, 204

U.S. workers, difficulty of finding for farm work, 139–41, 155

Varney, Christine, 185–88, 207

veal and animal cruelty issue, 173

vegan or vegetarian diet as animal rights solution, 167, 182–83

Vermont: Circle Saw Farm, 1–10; as dairy capital of early United States, 42; dairy cow research, 73–74; immigrant labor in, 140, 154–55; loss of dairy business to Midwest, 46; Moo Acres, 77–78, 85–86; Mooreland Farm, 10–17; Rainville farm, 98–100; Ranney,

39–42, 43, 45, 48, 51–52, 61–67; water pollution contribution, 109–16

Vermont Migrant Farmworker Solidarity Project, 132–33

volatile organic compounds (VOCs), 107, 128

wages for farm workers, 143–47, 154, 155

Wallace, Henry, 47, 49

WalMart, 206

water pollution, 109–20

wealth, cow as symbol for, 36

well-being and comfort, cow: breeding priorities' effects on, 89; calm and quiet environment, 12–13, 75–76; comfort beds, 213; dairy industry's claims of attention to, 163; lameness problem, 174, 182; natural lifespan of cows, 173–74, 213; pasture-based operations, 128–29, 174, 175; Simon's dedication to, 213, 221

well contamination in Wisconsin, 118–19

Western United Dairymen (WUD), 127, 140–41, 147, 179, 182

Wisconsin, 42–43, 116–20

workers. *See* labor relations

World War II, 48–49

Zabar, Eli, 224–25

DATE DUE